Scotland after Britain

James Foley is a lecturer in politics at Glasgow Caledonian University. He is the author of Yes: *The Radical Guide to Scottish Independence* and the editor of *Contesting Cosmopolitan Europe*.

Ben Wray is a freelance journalist and researcher. He was formerly editor of digital media site *CommonSpace* and, prior to that, head of policy at the Common Weal think tank.

Neil Davidson (1957–2020) was a historian, socialist activist, and lecturer in Sociology at the University of Glasgow. Author of numerous books, Neil won the Isaac and Tamara Deutscher Memorial Prize for *Discovering the Scottish Revolution*.

Scotland after Britain

The Two Souls of Scottish Independence

James Foley and Ben Wray

with Neil Davidson

VERSO

London • New York

First published by Verso 2022
© James Foley, Ben Wray, Neil Davidson 2022

1 3 5 7 9 10 8 6 4 2

Verso
UK: 6 Meard Street, London W1F 0EG
US: 388 Atlantic Avenue, Brooklyn, NY 11217
versobooks.com

Verso is the imprint of New Left Books

ISBN-13: 978-1-78873-581-0
ISBN-13: 978-1-78873-583-4 (US EBK)
ISBN-13: 978-1-78873-582-7 (UK EBK)

British Library Cataloguing in Publication Data
A catalogue record for this book is available from the British Library

Library of Congress Cataloging-in-Publication Data

Names: Davidson, Neil, 1957–2020 author. | Foley,
James (Founding member of the
  Radical Independence Campaign), author. | Wray, Ben (Freelance
  journalist, writer and researcher), author.
Title: Scotland after Britain : the two souls of Scottish independence /
  Neil Davidson, James Foley and Ben Wray.
Description: London ; New York : Verso Books, 2022. | Includes
  bibliographical references.
Identifiers: LCCN 2022013711 (print) | LCCN 2022013712 (ebook) | ISBN
  9781788735810 (paperback) | ISBN 9781788735834 (ebk)
Subjects: LCSH: Scotland – Politics and government – 21st century. |
  Scotland – History – Autonomy and independence movements. | Home
  rule – Scotland. | Income distribution – Political aspects – Scotland.
Classification: LCC JN1228 .D38 2022 (print) | LCC JN1228 (ebook) | DDC
  320.9411 – dc23/eng/20220518
LC record available at https://lccn.loc.gov/2022013711
LC ebook record available at https://lccn.loc.gov/2022013712

Typeset in Minion Pro by Hewer Text UK Ltd, Edinburgh
Printed and bound by CPI Group (UK) Ltd, Croydon, CRO 4YY

Contents

Preface

Neil Davidson started this journey with us; tragically, he never got the chance to finish it. In the early stages of writing the book, Neil collapsed during a conference he was hosting on Trotsky's theory of uneven and combined development. Soon after, our worst fears were realised, as Neil was diagnosed with cancer. He died within the year, during the early phase of the pandemic.

The devastating irony was that this tragedy began during a conference that was the culmination of a life's project. Neil had sought to make Scotland a centre for scientific socialist theory and, conversely, to use those theories to cast a critical eye on Scotland's various left-wing pretensions. The conference, which brought to Glasgow such figures as Justin Rosenberg, Charlie Post and Robert Brenner, testified to Neil's growing reputation in the field of historical materialism. It was international in scope, but sufficiently embedded in the local to attract critical theorists from across the field of Scottish studies.

Neil contributed one full chapter to *Scotland after Britain*, Chapter 3, which we have retained largely as he intended. Via discussion and notes, he contributed directly or indirectly to other chapters. More broadly, his ideas and his spirit were an inspiration to us both. We learned a lot from Neil's teaching, but we learned equally from his example, as someone who never sold out or bought in to the mythologies of the Scottish establishment. There is thus something of Neil in every chapter here. Neil's ethic was defined by unsparing critique for both Scottish and Westminster ruling philosophies, especially when the status quo was framed as 'progressive'.

Equally, final editorial judgements are our own. We had some minor, nuanced differences of perspective with Neil, over issues such as the role of professional–managerial elites in capitalism, or the importance of the transnational dimension in politics. And naturally we insist that any errors or omissions here are ours and ours alone. But we also wish to respect how much of this book reflects Neil's ideas and contributions. It was Neil's wish that we should finish this book and, in doing so, we have sought to honour his critical spirit.

We have had to balance our respect for Neil's work with bringing coherence to a moving target that has been constantly changing shape. Above all, we had to address the shifting ideologies of the post-2014, post-Brexit Scottish governing class and their counterparts in London; and address the complicated, evolving role of 'leftism' in these debates. In all that, we have endeavoured to retain our original parameters: a respect for the moment of 2014, for the principle of independence and for the outpouring of anti-establishment dissidence that issued from the Yes campaign; allied to a critical stance on Scottish nationalism, whether in the mode of Braveheart machismo, Salmond-era Celtic Tiger booster-ism, or Sturgeon-era cosmopolitan nation-branding (which, we argue, are not as divergent as either 'side' of the nationalist internal war would have you believe).

A final note: *Scotland after Britain* was written before the Russia–Ukraine war and the interrelated cost of living crisis. However, neither factor would substantially change our analysis or our proposals. Neil was, like ourselves, a critic of Vladimir Putin's efforts to carve out a Russian sphere of sub-imperial influence, and would have been appalled by the 2022 invasion. But he would also have been sceptical of decontextualised, ahistorical and (let's be blunt) hypocritical outrage. Neither Anglo-American foreign policymakers nor NATO have shown the remotest interest in national sovereignty before 2022. Indeed, they have actively flouted the principle. A lifelong critic of Western 'interventions', Neil, we are sure, would agree with our own assessment that, in terms of moral and logical consistency, those who condemned the NATO occupation of Afghanistan and the disastrous bombing campaigns in Libya are those best placed to condemn Putin's invasion.

The list of our political debts is lengthy; sadly, we cannot list specific names, but you all know who you are. We owe particular thanks to Jamie Allinson, Chris Bambery, Raymond Morrell and Alex Law for offering invaluable feedback on an earlier draft of this book (naturally, any errors are our own). We must also acknowledge our editor, Rosie Warren, for her perseverance, and our partners, Miren and Cat, for their patience. James would especially like to thank Pete Ramand, Umut Korkut, and his colleagues at Glasgow Caledonian University. Ben gives thanks to former colleagues at Common Weal and present colleagues at Brave New Europe. Finally, we extend special thanks to Neil's partner, Cathy Watkins, who was continuously helpful during Neil's fading health and after his passing.

James Foley and Benjamin Wray
May 2022

Introduction: Independence in an Era of Ruptures

This book examines how the Scottish national question emerged from the political fringes to become Britain's most enduring – and at times most divisive – conflict. While Scotland is our focus, we are conscious that any consideration of independence also poses wider questions about the United Kingdom, a postcolonial, multinational state with an outsize role in the world's military and economic affairs. For generations, British politics was dominated by its core functions, with parliamentary conflict centring on voters caught up in the finance-led boom in London and the south-east, and foreign policy dominated by aspirations to be a 'pivotal power' between Europe and America. More recently, with Scotland's 2014 referendum, Brexit and the re-politicisation of the Irish border, the UK periphery has experienced new agency in shaping the state's future.

In one sense, there is nothing particularly 'British' about these provincial revolts. They reflect much wider questions of economic failure, democratic deficits and the unintended consequences of the breakdown of class-based representative politics. 'Populism' is the standard (though inadequate) rendering of this 'problem', according to which 'left behind' voters have abandoned their traditional political affiliations for promises of change and/or rebellion. But since Britain is a peculiar state, these winds have exerted lasting effects that have not only weathered but conclusively restructured the state. Brexit, thus far, is the most decisive of these transformations. Scottish independence and (not inconceivably) Irish reunification could yet follow.

Our interest in these questions has evolved over a decade of study. It grew, at first, from a personal investment in reviving Scotland's socialist traditions, and from an optimism, on solidly internationalist grounds, that the breakup of the British state could help unleash democratic energies within and far beyond our borders. While much of what follows will criticise dominant articulations of Scottish nationalism, our enthusiasm for a certain type of Scottish independence has, if anything, only grown with the writing of this book. For all its flaws, the independence movement has been an inspiring example of how popular mobilisation in peripheral and working-class communities can redraw the map of state power. Leftists everywhere would be foolish to ignore this break with a generation of fatalistic capitalist realism, epitomised in Margaret Thatcher's phrase, 'there is no alternative'.

But as the independence movement peaked and faded after the Brexit referendum, our interest has become more analytical. Scotland has provided a vantage point on a much broader set of problems – namely, the interacting crises of capitalism and (social-)democratic politics that followed from the breakdown of the neoliberal certainties that dominated in the 1990s and 2000s. Much of this book tells the story of the left's early successes and ultimate failure to reckon with this era of disruption and the types of political mobilisation it inspired. In part, it is about what went wrong, and what it might take to put it right.

Peter Mair, the late Irish political scientist, imagined contemporary politics as a 'void' separating the state from citizens and their organised social interests. The result was a 'non-sovereign people' detached from public authority, and an equally detached governing class administrating the hollow remains of democracy. As we understand it, Scotland's national movement has been both a reaction against this void, and an ironic demonstration of its persistence. On the one hand, it produced a passionate, mobilised mass-participation movement, perhaps the most extensive and most enduring in Scottish history, arrayed against the Westminster establishment. That movement transformed the Scottish National Party (SNP) into an overnight mass party, with a sudden, post-referendum influx of 100,000 members making it one of Europe's biggest political forces, proportional to the population. On the other hand, the SNP in practice, according to its army of former members, has come to epitomise what Mair called a 'cartel party', holding the reins of patronage and servicing an army of lobbyists and dependents who orbit the parliament.[1] Scotland's ruling party is thus a pregnant unity of agency and stasis – servant of a mobilised movement and manager of stagnation. This tension dominates Scottish elections and everyday political management.

Still, few can dispute that a section of Scotland feels newly empowered since the referendums of 2014 and 2016. To outsiders, the parliament appears to enjoy a new agency that speaks with the authority of a budding nation-state. Many observe that Edinburgh's nationalist government is now the Westminster government's most worthy adversary and the most proximate threat to the interests surrounding Britain's hegemonic Conservative Party. Those who pine for the 'stability' of pre-Brexit Britain are thus just as likely to look to Scottish nationalism for leadership, rather than the Labour Party. Scotland's first minister Nicola Sturgeon functions as a stock stylistic contrast with the excesses of a British populism that appears unassailable in England. At the height of Brexit, the *Guardian* stated, with only a hint of irony: 'Sturgeon speaks for Britain' – an extraordinary plaudit for a lifelong Scottish nationalist.[2]

Meanwhile, Westminster's official opposition has endured a terminal identity crisis. After bruising defeats in its Scottish and northern heartlands, Labour Party activists are increasingly reconciled to the fact that any future non-Conservative government should be a 'progressive alliance', perhaps involving Liberals and Greens but certainly involving Scottish Nationalists. Not long ago, this seemed unthinkable: Ed Miliband, by many accounts, lost the 2015 election because English voters could not conceive of a 'coalition of chaos' with Sturgeon's predecessor Alex Salmond. The contrast with today, when the mere thought of a 'one-nation', governing Labour majority strikes many as archaic, serves to illustrate a qualitative divide in history. Labourism no longer has the clout to crowd out other oppositional forces.

The newfound confidence in Scotland thus also testifies to a growing despair in progressive British politics. A system designed in theory to ensure strong governments has been irreparably fractured by decades of attacks on the foundations of collective representation and institutional solidarity. The SNP's vitality – the flipside of Scottish Labour's necrosis – has transformed opposition politics, and broken the two-party pendulum on which the democratic legitimacy of Westminster depends. Regardless of whether the 'breakup of Britain' is formally realised, Scotland, in a sense, is already 'after Britain', insofar as no British project seems likely to form a unifying frame for political action. What remains is an incoherent battleground of at least four national projects, patchworked together by a Labour Party rooted in cities, universities and tech towns with vanishing links to the provincial working class.

The outcome of this last decade has been a dual crisis of Britain, simultaneously a crisis of the state and of the left. Three years of Brexit shenanigans is perhaps sufficient proof of the haemorrhaging of legitimacy on all sides by a parliament that failed to satisfy anyone. But even after the decade of political emergency, Conservative restoration has not reinstated normality or pacified the periphery. Supposedly sovereign Westminster governments are now forced to accept humiliating limits to their power. This was well illustrated in 2021, when the people of Pollokshields in Glasgow mobbed and turned away a Home Office patrol attempting to impose the UK's draconian immigration laws.[3] That event symbolised how little applies of the old rules about delegated and absolute authority: even in policy areas supposedly 'reserved' to Westminster, Scottish communities (and, to a lesser extent, the Holyrood government) freely ignore London's prerogative. Much of Scotland – not just Glasgow's fashionable Southside – has abandoned even the pretence of cultural and political deference to British institutions. And this example testifies to the crisis at its most mundane: events in Scotland pale next to the never-ending problems of the Irish border.

As with Northern Ireland, an element of mobilised Britishness may well survive in Scottish communities. But increasingly it does so in the mode of subcultural rebellion against Holyrood's 'progressive' agenda. With the collapse of Scottish Labour's intermediary role, Britishness has retreated to the red-white-and-blue margins, to the 'No Surrender' Protestantism that continues to form the foundation of all Scotland's cultural backlashes. Far from demonstrating resilience, this only reinforces the ultimate loss of esteem for Scotland's unionist bloc, and the doubts about how it could construct a viable challenge to the SNP. Any open display of 'progressive' Britishness carries the risk of being swamped by a more deep-rooted and culturally relevant reactionary communitarianism. What remains of moderate Scottish unionism is a passive inheritance, rooted in pessimism (too wee, too poor . . .) and unmoored from any ambitions for winning devolved power.

If the British state is experiencing a persistent crisis of authority, the British left, in its mainstream incarnations, suffers from a crisis of purpose. Efforts to 'redefine Britishness', with promises of 'progressive federalism', satisfy no one, and have the appearance of sticking plasters on a broken limb. They fail to address root grievances with Westminster, and assume that top-down, ameliorative reforms can solve problems of agency, accountability and democracy. The problem with British politics is not just one of maldistribution, but a more fundamental crisis of legitimation.

Many liberals and leftists, who span much of the media, the Scottish Green Party and even some of the intellectuals orbiting the Labour left, have responded by throwing in their lot with nationalist Holyrood and its promise of 'independence in Europe'.[4] Any boundaries between Scotland's campaigning ecosystem and the Edinburgh government are increasingly permeable. Academics, NGOs and professional-managerial interests – the heartlands of contemporary leftism – find it easy to access Holyrood's corridors of power. But assimilation and insider status have come with costs. Often, the pro-independence left is no clearer in its purposes than its British unionist counterparts. There are growing questions over its de facto incorporation into a government enjoying unchallenged power.

Scotland's national question excuses a multitude of sins. Leave aside the constitution, and the SNP has done little in power to advance the interests of its (often steadfastly loyal) working-class supporters. On many real measures of poverty-related alienation, Scotland remains near the bottom of European league tables; there has been little reckoning with inequality in education and health; and promises of 'green jobs' have come to nothing.[5] Of all the gruesome statistics, the most tragic is that Scotland has by far the continent's highest rate of drug deaths.[6] Cynics might call this a record of empty rhetoric and broken promises not dissimilar to those of the SNP's predecessors, Scottish Labour. Unlike Labour, the SNP has a readymade excuse (Westminster as the plausibly demonised antagonist) and a sense of purpose to explain away failings in the present (*after independence*, of course . . .). This formula has proved extraordinarily effective in weathering a succession of political storms. If there is a weak link, it is the SNP's dependence on mobilising faith in that vision: unlike Labour, it cannot afford to retreat from missionary purpose into cynical, post-democratic governance. Having no trade-union funding or big business backers, even its financial foundation rests on the personal conviction of its members. Nationalist parties are nothing without mobilisation. Retiring into technocracy is the temptation of devolution, but it carries the risk of demoralisation and political failure. Without a plan for substantive breakthroughs, it will always be a matter of how long the party can stave off the inevitable.

For all their apparent invincibility, SNP leaders have found contesting elections far easier than developing a coherent vision of independence. The flipside of their success is thus a growing reluctance to talk about the party's basic purpose at all. As agency in the party has been centralised under Sturgeon and her husband, SNP chief executive Peter Murrell, efforts to keep independence off the agenda at party conferences have become increasingly neurotic. This reflects a basic contradiction in the party's philosophy. While it has been the beneficiary of an era of democratic upsurge and economic decline, its vision of what independence means belongs to the era of apathetic post-democracy and competitive market globalisation. The contradictions are sharp, and for that reason the party leadership has sought to prevent any encroachment on its programme by a frustrated membership.

Independence, as the SNP imagined it, was never meant to emerge in an era defined by the breakdown of capitalism. Indeed, many of its key thinkers held this to be impossible. For the devolution-era generation of Scottish nationalism, rising economic optimism was both a necessary and, in cruder moments, a sufficient condition for independence. The enduring hold of unionism, it was argued, was all about a sense of Scotland being 'too wee, too poor, too stupid' to govern itself; but such negativity would melt away as Scottish companies prospered in the rising global economy, with countries like Ireland and Iceland demonstrating the benefits of competitive nimbleness in wider market spaces. In Tom Nairn's words: 'After a long period during which bigger was in some ways better, with the initial rise of industrialisation and the diffusion of global commerce, globalisation may have inaugurated another, in which smaller is, if not better, then at least just as good (and occasionally with the advantage over the erstwhile great, the muscle- and hidebound).'[7]

Since then, established grounds for optimism have evaporated. This had already begun before 2008 – the collapse of the dot.com boom and the EU's eastward expansion effectively signalling the death of Scotland's 'Silicon Glen' electronics boom. But the financial crash was the real killer, taking down the two banking behemoths, RBS and HBOS, that dominated the Scottish economy, and crushing some of Salmond's cherrypicked models of economic success, including his favoured benchmark, the Irish Celtic Tiger. Subsequently, things would only get worse. After the 2014 referendum, Scotland's already declining oil industry suffered from a catastrophic crash in prices. The Scottish government has been forced into a series of emergency nationalisations of failing parts of Scottish infrastructure – Prestwick Airport, ferries, shipyards – much against its own vision of market-led success. All of this was long before the coronavirus pandemic, and none of it is exceptional: these are the standard travails of European capitalist economies.

Many in Salmond's team were sceptical about their prospects in the 2014 referendum, precisely because economic optimism seemed so distant. Received economic wisdom gave the Yes campaign no chance. The *Economist* published a front-page depicting 'Skintland', with Scottish towns and landmarks 'humorously' renamed to reflect their economic failures: 'Edinborrow (twinned with Athens)', 'Glasgone', 'Aberdown'. 'Project fear' may have been a deliberate strategy constructed by operators in the unionist elite of politics, business and media, but that should not obscure the hostility of aggregate capitalist opinion: by all the established neoliberal rules, independence did not add up. Project fear, in that sense, was really a Scotland-specific expression of the mantra of capitalist realism: there is no alternative.

But democratic instincts resisted this neoliberal economic fatalism, and thus none of the above has stopped rising support for Scottish independence. Quite the opposite. The long decade of declining living standards and failing businesses has been boom time for the cause of independence. The biggest surge of support came during the most intense period of referendum campaigning, when economic narratives were bleakly set against the Yes campaign. The 2020 pandemic – arguably the biggest ever peace-time collapse of capitalism – has seen further consolidation. The SNP has thus built a platform of public consent for independence out of an era of economic failure.

Yet while the SNP has been superficially well adapted to the political moment, its case for independence remains imprisoned in an earlier consensus. Salmond's argument in 2014 was, in retro-spect, the last gasp of an era of western European nationalism, where, for smaller nations, the question of independence largely centred on 'competitive' cuts to business taxation and regulation. This was the essence of the positive case that Salmond contrasted to project fear: an optimistic neoliberal argument for investment against a pessimistic neoliberal case for austerity. But since 2014, any notion of rising living standards for all has looked increasingly like a feature of the capitalist past: the contours of the Scottish economy, such as its oil dependence, reinforce the point.

Sturgeon has discarded some of the Celtic Tiger, corporate tax-cutting enthusiasms of the Salmond era. But the economic prospectus that has emerged has the potential to impose an even harsher version of neoliberalism and (just as importantly) far tighter restrictions on popular sovereignty. The 'Sustainable Growth Commission', which remains the SNP's last word on a post-independence economy, was an effort to resolve doubts about the 2014 economic plan, particularly on the question of currency. Andrew Wilson, the Commission's orchestrator, is a one-time SNP politician turned associate of the controversial Charlotte Street Partners – a lobby group whose principal function is to draw a discrete link between Scottish nationalist governance and corpo-rate Scotland. In its original incarnation, the Commission's report was an almost undiluted reflection of the capitalist take on inde-pendence. The report begins by thanking the 'wide range of inter-ests' consulted in its preparation: among those, seventeen out of twenty-three were business lobby groups, and none were trade unions, environmental organisations or representatives of marginalised communities. While its findings were watered down to appease internal critics, it still committed Scotland to 'sterlingisation': the unilateral use of the UK's currency without the formal institutions of a central bank, without lender-of-last-resort facilities, and without control of monetary policy. Such arrangements are almost unheard of in advanced economies with large financial sectors.

Leftist critiques of the Growth Commission have centred on its implications for public spending. Despite official denials, the document does imply sweeping cuts (or tax rises), and some of Scotland's leading economists have presented sterlingisation as a route to austerity.[8] Given how heavily the SNP leadership has leant on its anti-cuts credentials, critics have been quick to note the obvious, superficial ironies. Even so, the Commission's critics have arguably missed the more insidious consequences for democracy. The problem is not simply that the Growth Commission entails a roll-back of government spending, with all that implies for growth, poverty and inequality; the problem is that, in the name of stability and order, it imposes restrictions on public power that would be almost impossible to vote away. It radically limits what governments might do – and, more importantly, what the public might command them to do.

When neoliberalism was ascendant and unchallenged, the proposals might have appeared like just another madcap, think-tank-generated idea to limit the state in the name of markets. However, the Growth Commission appears exceptionally anachronistic in our era of crises centring on climate and coronavirus, when nobody any longer denies capitalism's dependence on discretionary government spending. Even if Sturgeon (as seems inevitable) does concede the flaws in the Commission's methodology and statistical modelling, three questions will remain. Firstly, why did the case for independence, for all its origins in an anti-austerity social movement, become so intellectually dependent on untested libertarian blueprints dreamt up under the leadership of corporate lobbyists? Secondly, what replaces the Growth Commission as the mainstream vision of independence? While Wilson's social and intellectual roots are worthy points of criticism, he was grappling with real problems for the governance of Scottish capitalism. Given the Commission's indisputable inadequacy in post-Brexit, post-pandemic circumstances, there is an intellectual gap at the core of the independence movement. Thirdly, if Sturgeon continues to postpone a reckoning with the Growth Commission's intellectual collapse, it raises questions about the SNP's intentions. Even if we allow the maximum of good faith, would any government seriously contemplate establishing a new state without any coherent plan for currency? If the answer is no, it is unlikely the SNP is planning for independence. That itself is a democratic problem, given how heavily the SNP leans on the national question in mobilising its members and the public.

Equally, critics of the Growth Commission are mutually divided and lacking in coherence. Scotland's small unionist left has seen the Growth Commission as conclusive proof that independence means austerity. Its existence means that no further thinking is required: the democratic failures that led to the crisis of devolution and Labourism are absolved by the peril of post-independence cuts. Independence is either deemed impossible or so radically awful that nobody would seriously contemplate it. The whole phenomenon can be written off as an outbreak of mass irrationalism. Equally, mainstream pro-independence critics are no clearer. The Scottish Green Party has long opposed sterlingisation, but it also entered into an effective coalition with Sturgeon, an alliance whose rationale rests on achieving independence within the next parliamentary term – and the SNP's neoliberal vision of life after Westminster never emerged as a controversy in negotiations. Either independence is not being seriously contemplated within the parliamentary term, or the Greens have postponed reckoning with a fundamental problem for the sake of formal unity.

The question of what follows the Growth Commission is central to two further questions about Scotland's governing parties, both of which have compelling implications for democracy. Firstly, is their vision of independence truly an advance for popular sovereignty relative to Westminster governance? There is a not irrational argument, for instance, that, in terms of the crucial question of monetary policy, Scotland would have *less popular control* under the Growth Commission proposals. Secondly, are the governing parties serious about independence – or will they continue to trade on the passions of a polarised electorate and the coffers of a mobilised base to maintain the status quo?

But the Growth Commission also raises questions about the left, by which we mean, the extra-parliamentary remains of the radical left. One question is whether this group will continue to give cover to the SNP–Green coalition, despite a prospectus for independence that is both anachronistic and dangerous for democracy. A bigger question is what the left means by its criticisms of the Growth Commission. Anti-austerity politics can become its own type of comfort zone, for both supporters and opponents of independence. Certainly, the Growth Commission's proposals would have severe implications for public services and everything associated with them, from tackling poverty to investing in green infrastructure. But the central issue is: How much control can the public exert on institutions of economic power? Rather too often, the left has been diffident and divided on these questions. Economics becomes a strategic battle that focuses exclusively on maximum public spending. This misses the worst and most enduring impact of the neoliberal era: curtailment of the capacity of the working class to exert collective control over workplaces or politics.

The panic over Brexit allowed the SNP leadership to evade hard questions about what it means to establish a nation-state during a deep, systemic crisis of capitalism. How will the SNP reconcile EU Single Market membership with the currency policy of sterlingisation? How does the EU weigh against the UK internal market, given that England is by far Scotland's biggest trading partner, and

Single Market membership could very well entail a 'hard border'? How will Scotland, having declared a 'climate emergency', manage the transition away from North Sea oil without devastating losses of well-paid working-class jobs? How will they break the deadlock of Conservative and Labour opposition to a second referendum at Westminster?

However, discomfort on these questions is clearly symptomatic of a deeper pessimism about prospects for national independence. This obviously applies to established neoliberals like Wilson, but there have been parallel shifts on the left. In what used to be the essential article of socialist wisdom on nationalism, the Edinburgh-born Irish revolutionary James Connolly remarked, 'If you remove the English Army tomorrow and hoist the green flag over Dublin Castle, unless you set about the organisation of the Socialist Republic your efforts will be in vain . . . England will still rule you.'[9] The point is not simply that supporters of the SNP leadership have embraced the opposite premise: that independence should ideally involve little more than a formal handover and a changing of flags. A deeper problem is that many self-declared socialists feel queasy about challenging this 'internationalist' logic. A similar discomfort attaches itself to any claims for popular, majoritarian self-rule – a more maximalist form of national sovereignty than the stripped-down neoliberal version. In the current ideological climate, any national framing of politics risks being written off as an irrational, right-wing error.

This embarrassment is deep-rooted, since decades of politics, commentary and social research have been dedicated to rubbishing aspirations for national independence as a nostalgic, retrograde, even xenophobic longing for redundant imagined communities. Few concepts, perhaps excepting social class, have been considered so passé, or so frequently held up as a foil for more fashionable ideas. Sociologists like Ulrich Beck spoke of a 'politics of post-nationalism' in which 'the cosmopolitan project contradicts and replaces the nation-state project'.[10] The dominance of such sentiments on the broadly defined academic left has been reflective of numerous factors, but most especially the failure of Third World bids for post-colonial autonomy and the triumph of American-style market capitalism after the collapse of the Berlin Wall. American individualism fostered American academic thinking on the left, marking a sharp break with popular European traditions of social democracy and class politics.

Today, the conditions sustaining the triumph of neoliberal globalisation have long passed, but the implications have barely been processed. Intellectual progress has lagged behind practical developments. Particularly after Covid-19, nation-states have engineered a sudden turn towards planning and large-scale intervention, in a spirit of panic, to save the capitalist system from collapse. But there has been no reckoning with the built-up legacies of the neoliberal era. Sturgeon's top-down, technocratic vision is very much a product of the limits of imaginative responses to this crisis from the left. Indeed, it should not escape notice that, among contemporary world leaders to achieve any manner of sustained electoral success, she is among the most left-wing.

Supporters have therefore concluded that Sturgeon's liberal vision is the maximum of what can be achieved. Our claim, conversely, is not simply that more can and should be achieved, but that the SNP's post-democratic vision is unsustainable. Three factors are converging that will inevitably force a fundamental rethink of national independence: the failure of global capitalism to deliver rising living standards or hope for the future; the democratic deficit; and the persistent question of climate change. All three may be regarded as blowback from the early success of the neoliberal era in dismantling working-class collectivism and reducing the space of ideological debate to questions of cultural preference.

The prospect of Scottish independence, contrary to the leadership's self-image, belongs to a historical era of political and economic ruptures, reflecting the persistent failure of capitalism to raise living standards – and of the left to gain popular consent for meaningful change. Theoretically, these premises should hardly be controversial. Few can seriously deny that the 2008 bank bailouts, climate change and now coronavirus make any return to 'normality' impossible – nor, more to the point, would it be desirable. However, the independence question has a confused relationship to the wider political crisis. It is clearly a product of an era of anti-establishment revolt; yet it has allowed a party representing all the old complacency to consolidate power and entrench the status quo.

For all these flaws, there are reasons why the prospects of Scottish independence should enthuse critically minded leftists everywhere, whether in Scotland itself or elsewhere. Firstly, it opens necessary questions about state power in the United Kingdom. For centuries, wherever progressive forces have made serious gains, the British state has backed the restoration of reaction. Whether sponsoring the rise of Islamism to break Arab nationalism, arming Saudi Arabia against Yemen and Indonesia against East Timor, or undertaking 'regime change' in the service of America's oil interests, Britain has all too often been on the wrong side of history. In its postcolonial guise as the right hand of American empire, with a permanent seat on the UN Security Council and a worldwide network of defence contractors and spies, the UK plays a key role in punishing governments, parties and movements that show any inclination to break from the straitjacket of exploitation. Imperial interests are baked into the British political order and, as Jeremy Corbyn discovered, defying them imposes debilitating costs. The persistent presence of Trident nuclear weapons not far from Glasgow serves as a costly reminder of Britain's unsavoury world role. This may or may not matter 'on the doorstep', but it should matter to any internationalist worthy of the name.

Equally, there is little to love about the internal organisation of the British state. An unjust electoral system has systematically empowered middle-class preferences and disenfranchised the working class. Regional inequalities are among the worst in Europe, thanks to the overweening influence of London in the economy and the state. A host of anachronisms, from the House of Lords to the Stormont parliament to the Windsors, are periodically 'rebooted' to conform with the fashions of the day, without ever delivering constitutional coherence. Brexit emerged against a backdrop of frustrations in England and Wales; but its aftermath has disenfranchised Scottish institutions, leaving a toxic, unresolvable legacy of two nationalist governments facing off in Holyrood and Westminster. There can be little hope of a coherent democratic recovery from this mess. Scottish independence will not resolve these problems at a stroke, but it will reopen crucial questions of democracy and power that the normal course of Westminster debate suppresses.

Scottish independence is also about fidelity to what we call 'working-class agency'. In 2014, the referendum was designed to have a prearranged outcome. Nobody anticipated anything but a resounding No: this, indeed, was why David Cameron agreed to it in the first place. All of the Westminster leadership, the business lobbies, the newspapers and even a few trade unions were mobilised to defend their investments in the status quo. Add to all that Barack Obama, European officials and the international high command of capitalism more broadly, and the impression should be clear: voters were told that, while a referendum was happening officially, any impression of meaningful choice was an illusion – economics precluded independence. This explains why 2014 was worth fighting for: voters asserted a positive choice against coordinated resistance. Having been told that choice was a box-ticking formality, that there was no alternative, they imposed their will to create a historical opening that redefined British history. Class, in such cases, ceases to be a passive sociological category, becoming instead a political force. That Scottish Labour was its primary victim only made it more interesting. No party has been more remote from its electorate or more expectant of power; the punishment imposed on it was thus entirely deserved.

Since that referendum, a largely left-wing and working-class social movement has fought to keep the independence cause alive when the leadership has sought to push it off the agenda. These demonstrations attracted crowds unprecedented in Scottish history. We write in sympathy with this movement, which has too often been disparaged by polite Scottish opinion (Sturgeon, tellingly, has never joined the demonstrations). A common, and patronising, impression is that the marches are 'apolitical'. Yet listening to the speeches from the stage, there is far more gutsy radical politics than would normally feature at a civic Scotland, NGO or Labour conference: there are frequent calls for abolishing nuclear weapons, for solidarity with Palestine and Catalonia, and for radical redistribution of wealth and income.

Nonetheless, our respect comes with caveats. The movement's overriding flaw is its faith that arguments about the content of independence can be postponed until Independence Day. Their sovereigntist perspective implies that the crucial questions of currency, Europe, Nato, and so on, will be opened to the scrutiny of the Scottish electorate as soon as independence has been achieved. Until then, unity should prevail. This narrative has equally been promoted by the more cynical elements that circle the SNP leadership, and for good reason: it allows them to keep awkward questions off conference agendas and away from the scrutiny of the membership.

But there are simply no historical grounds for any of these beliefs. When states are formed, the most important work happens well in advance of formal independence. Even today, without so much as a referendum having been called, the 'nation' is being mobilised behind project Scotland. While popular sections of Scotland have assembled on the streets, Scotland's boardrooms have been meeting and greeting Sturgeon's entourage, hoping to impose their own agenda. Their vision is of a Scotland fully constrained by the discipline of market forces – excepting, of course, those instances when capitalism itself needs a bailout. Charlotte Street Partners has been essentially writing the crucial economic documents, such as the so-called 'Sustainable Growth Commission'.[11] Equally, Sturgeon handed the big thinking about

Scotland's post-pandemic recovery strategy to former Tesco Bank CEO and current head of Buccleuch Estates, Benny Higgins, while the board of the strategically crucial Scottish National Investment Bank has been staffed with escapees from Shell, the UK Treasury, JP Morgan Chase, and a host of asset-strippers from the world of high finance.

In 2014, Scotland's upper class effectively snubbed independence all but unanimously. This left the working class, the lower middle classes and the social movements to take up the slack of imagining the new nation. Grassroots institutions like Common Weal have continued that legacy – but they have been excommunicated from Sturgeon's elite inner circle. In any future referendum, elite attitudes will be more sanguine: in the wake of Brexit, many are happy to entertain the idea of independence if it is to their liking. But that now poses the risk of complacency. Having built the groundwork with its endeavours, the independence movement risks being subsumed by the thoroughly elitist tendencies circling the provisional Scottish state.

None of this makes us cynical or resigned. These are the risks that real struggles for political power always pose, and responsibility lies in accepting these stakes without illusions. Our aim with this book is thus to give a clear-sighted account of what independence is about, where it came from, and why the risks might be worth it. By approaching these difficult questions with intellectual honesty, we hope to rediscover the excitement raised by the working-class social movement of 2014, and to reopen in a Scottish context the global questions of capitalism, class and sovereignty that will continue to define politics after coronavirus.

1

2016 and All That: Global Britain and Its Aftermath

Few anticipated that the 2016 referendum would end with the UK electing to leave the European Union. The word 'Brexit' may have been coined on the model of 'Grexit', but, unlike Europe's devastated southern periphery, Britain led a seemingly charmed life in the European order, with privileges including a generous rebate, preferential opt-outs and, crucially, none of the ramifications of Eurozone membership. For these reasons, British elites were largely agreed on the benefits of participation – if not out of actual enthusiasm, then as a calculation of self-interest.

Indeed, elites on both sides of the Channel pictured the referendum debate precisely as David Cameron had intended: as a lever to extract new concessions on behalf of core Conservative backers (most especially, in ironic retrospect, the City of London). Even Boris Johnson, by Cameron's recollection, thought the purpose of the referendum was to enhance the UK's bargaining position inside the EU, not to exit the world's largest trading bloc. When the results ultimately showed a narrow victory for Leave, reactions thus ranged from bemusement to incredulity. 'Germans watched . . . with stunned disbelief', notes John Kampfner, one of the UK's leading foreign affairs journalists. 'They could not

understand how the Mother of Parliaments, a country synonymous with stability and predictability, could have descended into
such chaos.'[1]

The shock, as Kampfner suggests, was not that someone had
aimed a kick at the EU. Politically conscious Europeans knew of
Britain's historic Eurosceptic leanings; and continental voters
had their own, often more valid reasons to distrust the EU technocracy. What they struggled to grasp was why Britain of all
countries had chosen such an uncharted, chaotic, risk-laden
path. The result defied what many thought they knew about
British liberal democracy, what Kampfner's Germans had called
its 'stability and predictability'. As this suggests, many Europeans,
certainly at elite level, had seen the UK as a bastion of political
order, the antidote to the continent's appetite for revolutionary
shifts in state power. 'As an English resident of Rome, I never
cease to hear middle-class Italians singing the praises of a
"normal country" – Britain', observes David Broder. 'Seen from
Italy, ours is a land of efficient bus services, friendly locals offering up trays of tea and cakes, and earnest professionalism in
public life.'[2] To Italians, who saw an entire political class decapi-
tated by corruption in the early nineties, and the subsequent rise
of Berlusconi; or to Greeks, many with a historical memory of
fascism, labouring under an openly venal elite; or even to middle-
class French reformers exasperated by workers' strikes, Britain
stood for an imagined security. When Brexit rudely disrupted
this cosy image, it was traumatising for elites, both domestic and
continental. If this paragon of order could fall to the mob, they
asked, who, what or where was safe?

Yet if Brexit transformed the UK's image, in other ways it
strengthened the underlying mythology. Or, rather, a successor
myth emerged in which an otherwise well-managed political
regime had been struck by a thunderbolt of plebiscitary madness.
Brexit was commonly spoken of as an incomprehensible 'act of
self-harm' – a stock phrase used by just about everyone, from
world leaders to the leading parliamentarians of an earlier era:

whether Gordon Brown and Tony Blair, Paddy Ashdown or John Major.

Conveniently for that earlier generation of big beasts, the 'self-harm' narrative served to absolve the architects of the UK consensus they had overseen, the peak neoliberal years lasting from Margaret Thatcher through New Labour to David Cameron. That era had seen extraordinary inequalities between classes and between regions. It was no accident that the pro-Brexit vote, like the vote for Scottish independence, was concentrated in some of the most afflicted communities. Yet Britain's pro-EU intellectuals (with honourable exceptions like Anthony Barnett) showed little remorse for recent history. Brexit, indeed, soon led them to revel in a nostalgia for the 1990s consensus that began in irony and ended in deadly earnest. Symptomatic was the rehabilitation of excommunicated figures like Peter Mandelson, or his former colleagues Tony Blair and Alastair Campbell – the ideological architects of everything from foundation hospitals to the Iraq invasion. Cheered on by columnists in the *Guardian*, the *New Statesman* and the *Independent*, they re-emerged as central players in the drama that unfolded between 2016 and the general election of 2019, as leaders of the 'People's Vote' movement.

The fiction of a stable pre-Brexit order suited many agendas. It allowed domestic elites to whitewash the earlier epoch of British history, and European elites to construct a populist bogeyman to keep their own polities in line. Strange as it may seem, it even suited Scottish nationalist leaders who, during the neoliberal years, had been the most honourable critics of the British state's world role. Yet the new narrative also brought them newfound respectability. Suddenly, Britain's most unfashionable cause was all the rage. Its pariah status cast off, nationalist first minister Nicola Sturgeon toured the globe telling the story world leaders wanted to hear, of how one of the world's most distinguished political classes had fallen prey to the madness of crowds. With this story to tell, Sturgeon was suddenly a peer of Angela Merkel, Jacinda Ardern and Emmanuel Macron, the last of the old-fashioned centrists.

Yet the collateral damage of this narrative was the movement for which Sturgeon herself had been the figurehead. After all, if Britain had suddenly gone wrong in 2016, what had become of the Yes revolt two years prior to that wrong turn? The 2014 result likewise had to be reinterpreted as an act of plebiscitary self-harm. And much of Scotland's elite, including those who made careers from the 2014 movement, began heading in precisely this direction. SNP leaders and their media operatives actively distanced themselves from the Yes social movement. Some nationalist MPs went further, conceding that the referendum had been shaped by 'Russian interference'.[3] Even those who avoided conspiracy theory began to relegate the popular movement from its heroic, historic role, rendering it a mere footnote, as Sturgeon handed the economic project to the corporate lobbyists and neoliberal economists who would lead the Sustainable Growth Commission. Respectability among the new peer group was contingent on cutting off some embarrassingly populist relatives.

But, given subsequent experience, surely it was 2014's No voters, political leaders and commentators who had drowned themselves in a national mythology. They had voted for a stability that turned out to be a fable. They failed to appreciate that three decades of British political consensus had left a powder keg of contradictions. The notion of British stability itself has a history, and really begins, not in the late seventeenth century, but rather in the late 1980s, with the country's vanguard role in neoliberal globalisation and its success in forging elite consensus around that agenda. Neoliberal globalisation rescued British capitalism from the gloom of its post-war period, when it had the moniker of the 'sick man of Europe'. But what the world experienced in 2008 was precisely the collapse of neoliberal globalisation – at least insofar as it raised expectations of rising living standards beyond the elite. Britain's accelerated role in that order left it peculiarly vulnerable. Older traditions of loyalty to the state had been smashed, deliberately and vigorously. The earlier regime had nothing to offer except buckling down to austerity to restore 'competitiveness'. But popular consent had evaporated: few preserved the old faith in globalisation as a national project of trickle-down wealth-creation.

If part of the story is Britain's overdeveloped identification with the old order, there is another question to consider. Why did Britain's crisis concentrate so squarely on constitutional relationships, while elsewhere 'populism', for all its success, had been more unfocused in its grievances with the governing establishment? To understand this, we must engage in a deeper consideration of the dynamics of British state power. The problem was not just the extent of neoliberalism in Britain, measured by inequality and privatisation, but also the way in which it was implemented – and particularly how it mapped on to older elements of state formation. What becomes clear is that precisely those elements that produced the illusion of bipartisan stability have served to deepen the intractability of the crisis, leaving Britain as an unusually fractured polity. The flipside is that, in problematising the question of popular sovereignty, the UK's four nations might also accelerate their escape from the lifeless, post-democratic interregnum that followed the 2008 collapse.

British Foundations

What type of state is the United Kingdom? Without pandering to any type of British exceptionalism, the state form has three distinguishing characteristics. Firstly, the UK is an unconquered state, whose ruling class survived two world wars having never suffered the humiliation of invasion – or, for that matter, decapitation by revolution. This class can thus trade on a degree of deference and the prestige of lineage. It has absorbed democratic challengers without processing the implications of their challenge: Labour has rarely seen any contradiction in the idea of 'monarchical socialism'. Secondly, it is at the same time a postcolonial state, with the historical baggage of having once ruled colonies across the world, and then lost them. This continues to inform foreign policy, and accounts for Dean Acheson's barbed remark that the UK had 'lost an Empire and not yet found a role'.[4] Lastly, it is a multinational state of the type that dominated Europe prior to the Bolshevik Revolution and Wilson's articulation of his Fourteen Points. The national units have not only competing jurisdictions, competing identities and competing interests, but also today, in Northern Ireland's case, separate trade arrangements with the EU. In everyday contexts this remains a source of national confusion, as when we switch unconsciously between saying 'the United Kingdom' (which includes Northern Ireland) and 'Britain' (which does not).

These characteristics do not necessarily make Britain's ruling class better or worse than others; but they do have consequences. Having escaped invasion and revolution since the seventeenth century, political institutions have evolved gradually, without fundamental reforms. This in itself does not ensure 'stability': it would be myopic to forget that British capitalism, as recently as the seventies, was met by uncontainable industrial unrest and menaced by the threat of coups by discontented aristocrats. The foundation of recent stability was the state's adoption of emergency powers to violently suppress the trade unions. Still, there were always peculiarities. In Britain, near-insurrectionary class struggle often proved compatible with business as usual in party politics. For all the alarmism about Tony Benn in the eighties, and even Harold Wilson in the sixties, Labour remained within the grip of its right-wing rather consistently across the Cold War period and beyond. Indeed, the state form experienced its most radical overhaul, ironically, under Tony Blair, who enacted a 'modernisation' that was a patch-up job by an elite who no longer feared class struggle from below.

The British state has survived intact thanks to its history of seeing off the most determined challenges, such as Chartism, while incorporating, emasculating and finally gutting the remnants. Ruling elites have found that deference to tradition is often most pronounced among rising social classes. This is best illustrated by the most industrially radical of movements, the Red Clydesiders which, propelled by the class struggles of 1915–19, threatening the core of the wartime and post-war state. Yet Davie Kirkwood, leader of the Clyde Workers Committee, was reduced to sublime tears by the House of Commons and the good manners of its honourable members. 'To me it was full of wonder', he gushed. 'I had to shake myself occasionally as I found myself moving about and talking with men whose names were household words. More strange was it to find them all so simple and unaffected and friendly. In the House of Commons there is no snobbery.'[5] A similar story is told of Manny Shinwell, Clydeside's greatest union agitator, who would ultimately put his firebrand persona to more estimable uses as the right-wing's attack dog in defence of British imperialism. By the time he became Baron Shinwell, he had resigned the Labour whip protesting the excessive leftism of the pacifist (but Falklands War–supporting) liberal Michael Foot. Those who stuck to leftist principles on issues of state power, such as James Maxton, John Wheatley or even Keir Hardie, ended their lives effectively excluded or sidelined from Labour: Jeremy Corbyn will likely encounter a similar fate.

Some anti-establishment firebrands, like Kirkwood, are simply absorbed through their deference to power. But elsewhere, parties formed of outsiders find self-interested reasons to cling to the status quo. Consider the first-past-the-post (FPTP) electoral system, a peculiar Anglo-British tradition which disenfranchises working-class electorates at the expense of middle-class 'swing voters'. Theoretically, in Britain's party-political system, the body that should protest this injustice is the Labour Party, once considered the institutional bedrock of working-class interests. But it also had the least incentive to protest, since the blackmail worked (certainly until recently) to Labour's advantage – or at least enabled its lethargy, as elections would boil down to a choice between Labour and Conservatives, ensuring its re-election in 'safe seats' effectively unchallenged, without engaging the electorate in serious political debate. Labour's leftists (with honourable exceptions) were just as complicit, moralising this democratic deficit as a means of keeping UKIP, the SNP and other populists out of the electoral arena. It was in these terms that the inheritors of the Chartist cause became the most avid defenders of the UK's latter-day rotten boroughs.

On foreign policy, Britain has long observed an effective bipartisan consensus for liberal Atlanticism. Labour governments have gone out of their way to emphasise that they will govern 'in the national interest', observing standard protocols of imperial rule, the Cold War and the post-1989 new world order. Lying behind this posture are elements of immovable architecture that shape the British state's world role. These include a strategic arms industry, served by a global network of 'diplomacy' that usually involves a great deal of toadying to the world's right-wing dictatorships, who are always in the market for 'defence'. Britain's seat on the United Nations Security Council, a remnant of its imperial past, has helped ensure the persistence of imperial ambitions. The so-called Special Relationship with America – special only from a British standpoint – is baked into numerous institutions, including the nuclear weapons system which, far from being a guarantee of British sovereignty, is effectively useless without US command. Even under the pacifist Corbyn, Labour was unwilling to drop nuclear weapons from the party programme.

Historically, there have been some small windows of exception. Nuclear disarmament, in Peter Mandelson's recollection, was 'part of the glue that held Old Labour together', though Mandelson himself found it 'one of our most entrenched and electorally perverse policies'.[6] Even if this was a barely plausible account of 'Old Labour' history, New Labour nonetheless made a great ceremony of excising the ghost of Bennite anti-imperialism.

From this emerged the enduring myth, articulated by Mandelson, that 'Old Labour' had been relentlessly pacifist, perfidious – and thus unelectable. In truth, foreign policy was arguably the area where New Labour was most closely aligned to Old Labour tradition; the anti-nuclear stance of party conferences was far from a reflection of that tradition. It was, instead, the 'New Left' using conference to assert its will against an 'Old Labour' that remained, after the collapse of the ILP, uninterested in foreign affairs, or else committed to state power in its existing form. Even under the pacifist Ramsay MacDonald, nobody seriously expected Labour to threaten the empire – although, ironically, the first Labour government was brought low by a (falsified) accusation of collusion with Soviet Russia. That Red Scare was traumatic enough to ensure that Labour would never again contemplate anything so treasonous as opposing British foreign policy.

Instead, Labour's social base found its own reasons to support state power at its most irrational and perverse. When Britain's political economy, remodelled by Thatcher, decimated outlying, traditionally Labour communities, arms production and military recruitment moved in to soak up surplus populations. 'Defence', very often, is what remains of British manufacturing, offering well-paid jobs to working-class youths without a postgraduate education. While Labour's union affiliates often oppose foreign wars, they have found it much harder to coalesce around a pacifist industrial strategy. The union movement remains divided even on renewal of the costly Trident nuclear missile, whose cancellation, given austerity conditions, could surely release funds for more productive social uses. Yet the reasons for this are obvious enough. After Thatcherism and Blairism, good manufacturing jobs are scarce, and fear of losing them overpowers optimistic visions of political change. While the system is irrational by any substantive calculation, working-class communities are understandably distrustful of any political agenda that threatens jobs.

Jeremy Corbyn's period as Labour leader in effect destruction-tested the architecture linking parliamentary politics to state power. Not that Corbyn, by the standards of historical social democracy, was especially radical, either in his proposals (mild economic reform) or his ideology (mild Bennite pacifism). Certainly, the issue was not Corbyn's economic programme – a necessary response to a decade of capitalist crisis that has largely continued under Sir Keir Starmer, and arguably been surpassed, at least in terms of the scale of public spending, in the Johnson government's response to the coronavirus. Corbyn's 'crime', instead, was to challenge unwritten rules of foreign policy. 'To say that most [Labour MPs] loathed Corbyn would be an understatement', notes Tariq Ali.[7] Almost from the start, therefore, they made extraordinary efforts to remove him, measures that would be traitorous if even whispered about under any other leadership. They could only be rationalised because Labour MPs believed that electing Corbyn was itself a violation of the British constitution. Responsibility to the 'national interest', they reasoned, had to transcend party democracy. This becomes more comprehensible when one considers that the national interest in Britain has long meant elite liberal Atlanticism rather than British popular sovereignty. Corbyn's treason was to combine, in the softest of terms, support for the latter with old-fashioned international solidarity of the tea-flask and pin-badge variety. He was relentlessly prosecuted for this non-conformity, not only by the tabloids and the Blairites but also by influential sections of the Labour left, proving that the state's defence mechanisms run deep.

The final distinguishing mark of the UK state is its multinational character, which has become perhaps the main source of rancour today. In the absence of serious Westminster opposition, commentators regularly refer to Nicola Sturgeon as Britain's 'real' opposition leader. Equally, Theresa May's plans for Brexit were effectively held hostage by the Protestant fundamentalists of the Democratic Unionist Party (DUP). This is not the first time the state has nearly come apart over the Irish question. By contrast, Scotland, a senior partner of the British Empire, its surplus populations serving as both foot-soldiers and professional administrators, was a historical source of British stability until the last decade. There may have been an identifiable (if much mythologised) Scottish resistance to Thatcherism. However, the Scots provided the bulwark of the New Labour regime of neoliberal consolidation: even Tony Blair received his private education at Fettes, in

Edinburgh. The early Holyrood administrations were likewise models of complacency. Moderate noises of dissent from the likes of Scottish Labour leader Henry McLeish quickly led to excommunication. Holyrood was expected to be, if the phrase may be forgiven, New Labour's loyal little Ulster.

How Scotland emerged as the central contradiction of British politics is a story told in other chapters. Crucially, the multi-national character of the state has always theoretically left a channel for grievances to assume the form of the national questions. There was no guarantee this would happen. In earlier historical moments, nationalism was effectively sidelined by the benefits of the Union (proceeds from the Empire or freebooting globalisation) or by the promise of collective emancipation (through the British road to socialism). The disintegration of these various state projects has produced the present historical moment of irreconcilable national differences.

Britain and Neoliberal Globalisation

All accounts of what makes Britain different owe something to Perry Anderson and Tom Nairn, who originally rose to fame with a singular account of the British exception. The Nairn–Anderson thesis, promulgated at the tail-end of the post-war era, held that Britain was declining due to the aristocratic backwardness of its ruling political and economic elite. Having stopped short of full capitalist revolution, Britain had never rid itself of the parasitic old regime, which lingered on through the public school system, Oxbridge and the financial sector. As a result, Britain was stuck, mired in 'decline' and incapable of modernisation.

While much in their methodology was insightful, reflected in Anderson's later investigations of national cultures,[8] their claims about British decline largely failed the test of historical prediction. Under Margaret Thatcher's leadership, the British state emerged as a tigerish exponent of capitalist modernisation. The elements of

British backwardness identified by Nairn and Anderson were transmuted into articles of cosmopolitan contemporaneity. London's financial sector was converted from a gentlemanly extension of the golf course to the apex of predatory capitalism. Oxford and Cambridge became centres of world-leading, semi-privatised science as much as dusty refuges of the humanities. With Charles and Diana, the Windsors came to embody a trashy celebrity culture pitched at American tourists and tabloids. Even Britain's public school system today caters increasingly to the offspring of Russian oligarchs, Arab oilmen and American celebrities.

All of the above may still be symptomatic of British decadence; but, if so, it was a decadence drawn from advanced capitalism in its mutated neoliberal form. Nairn and Anderson, like most of their generation, had failed to grasp the implications of the cultural tensions that led from modernity (celebration of newness and development) to postmodernity (celebration of kitsch). Britain was on the bleeding edge of this global trend. It was in this era that Britain threw off its notoriety as the 'sick man of Europe' crippled by industrial unrest, and gained its reputation as a beacon of 'stability'.

Of course, Thatcher's 'modernisation' of Britain equally entailed an assault on the (always limited) cultural, economic and political forces of innovation. The BBC, having been a purveyor of sometimes provocative, modernist and working-class dramas in the Dennis Potter mould, became a haven for public-school and Oxbridge graduates, specialising as time wore on in insipid period dramas for the American market. Manufacturing trade unionism was smashed in the emergency mode of state violence, hammering the agency of Britain's industrial and post-industrial regions, which were effectively punished for voting Labour with doses of mass unemployment. Labour leftism was likewise crushed, with extraordinary personal attacks on Tony Benn as an individual, and institutional attacks on the Greater London Assembly, accused of promoting 'loony leftist' causes such as anti-racism and lesbian theatre groups. These were part of the foundations of what became 'Cool Britannia'.

There is always a risk of exaggerating the degree to which

Thatcher transformed the British state. Many apparent innovations, such as radical tax cuts, were contextual responses to the inflow of North Sea oil revenues. While privatisations cut deep, Thatcher did not reduce the state's involvement in the economy as dramatically as either her supporters or her enemies like to imagine. She neither got government off people's backs (the repressive state grew markedly) nor destroyed the welfare state; indeed, arguably her New Labour successors were significantly more daring in their experiments with privatisation. In fact, Thatcher did not achieve much of an economic renaissance either: growth rates were not much superior to the sluggishness of the preceding decade, which had helped usher in Britain's neoliberal experiment.

Her legacy lies chiefly in the field of social class, rather than of state power or the economy per se. Thatcher's success was in dismantling structures that allowed workers in private industry and manufacturing to exert power over their managers: her project, as she put it, was 'management's right to manage'. Her (counter-)reforms helped to hasten transformations in the geography of British capitalism. Most notably, a hard monetary policy, buttressed by oil monies and accelerated by deregulation and privatisation, dismantled provincial British capitalism to the benefit of a voracious City of London. The dark irony was that North Sea oil revenue, presented in the 1970s as the lubricant of a Scottish industrial renaissance, probably helped obliterate what remained of Scotland's manufacturing sector.

Global elites watched the Thatcherite experiment with envy. In the wake of the post-1968 incursions of workers and the left, they were equally eager to restore management's right to manage. And while Thatcher often cut an isolated figure on the European stage, her reforms were the inspiration for what is now the central institution of the EU. The figure behind this was Lord Cockfield, a free-market zealot and Thatcher appointee to the European Commission who is rightly dubbed 'the father of the Single Market'. What Cockfield realised was that, in imposing market globalisation on reluctant populaces, a transnational bureaucracy could be more effective than a sovereign state hamstrung by democratic account-ability. The European Project thus established the consensual move to neoliberalism, imposed through top-down legalism and obscure trade rules, rather than parliamentary battles or the heavy hand of police violence against picket lines. This caused a deep rift with Thatcher, who was abandoning her early Europhilia for Euroscepticism, just as an increasingly middle-class left was making the opposite journey. This rift ranked alongside the Poll Tax rebellion among the factors that led Conservatives to dump Thatcher as Conservative leader so unceremoniously.

Thatcherism, then, was a pivotal moment in the relationship between democracy and the British state. On the one hand, it unleashed the blitzkrieg of neoliberal globalisation that would dismantle the agency of regional Britain, trade unions and any notion of the left as the bearer of a systemic ideological alterna-tive. Quite aside from a heroic rise in economic inequality, Thatcher served to weaken democratising forces in society. Conversely, in a crucial sense, Thatcherism was the last disrup-tive moment in British parliamentary democracy before the referendums of 2014 and 2016, and the brief window of Corbynism. Indeed, somewhat in contradiction to the New Left view, Thatcher demonstrated some residual strength in British parliamentarism, whipping the Sir Humphreys into shape and imposing the will of certain (albeit reactionary) social forces on the state. Thatcherism showed that parliamentary leadership could tame the bureaucracy for social and political ends. It was a struggle to hold state power accountable to a social base repre-sented by a parliamentary party. And, of course, for those with authentically 'progressive' aspirations, these are precisely the aims to which a meaningful left should aspire, albeit in reverse.

Symptomatically, the Thatcher period produced cabinet figures who were objectionable, often licentious, and certainly far from 'ordinary', but who nonetheless remained pivotal to public life. The contrast with what followed is stark. Thatcher's transformation of

British politics paradoxically ushered in a new era in which bureaucratic power was restored at the cost of the draining of any meaningful political content from parliamentary combat. Bureaucracy, in effect, was normalised as neoliberal. The parties would compete over the pace of 'reform' and 'modernisation', each seeking to outdo the other on 'competitiveness'. Combat at the ballot box thus centred on means rather than ends. The idea of parties as servants of social classes was replaced by a 'void' separating all politicians from all voters, while party leaders struggled to correct this 'apathy' by adding more consumerism to public-service delivery. The result was a post-Thatcherite parliament of empty (if ambitious) suits, speaking in corporate bromides rather than the combative language of the Iron Lady herself. Thatcher's ultimate achievement for British politics was to usher in a new era of lethargic, complacent consensus.

Britain's Economy

If the story of Britain between 1979 and 2008 could be summarised in a word, that word would be financialisation. As the economist Ben Fine has suggested, financialisation was the motor driving globalisation and neoliberalism, and the UK was an exceptional exponent of it.[9] Even in a worldwide epoch of frenzied speculation, Britain left competitors in the shade. Between 1975 and 2009, American banking assets rose from 80 per cent to 100 per cent of GDP; the equivalent UK figure rose from 100 per cent to an astonishing 550 per cent. By the 2008 global crash, Britain was the most highly leveraged of the major economies. During those years, private debt trebled relative to the underlying economy, peaking before the financial crisis at 190 per cent of GDP. Considering that ratio never rose higher than 72 per cent in the century between 1880 and 1980, the transformation was extraordinary.[10]

The debt-and-speculation economy thus ran rampant, cheered on by politicians of all parties, and would ultimately reconfigure politics itself, as state power became ever more intertwined with and dependent on a booming City of London, which shared a revolving door with both the Treasury and the Bank of England. The appearance of British dynamism in the neoliberal era was inseparable from this boom in mortgages, credit cards, currency brokerage and gambling on complex financial instruments. The high-wire act of City trading gave the impression of bleeding-edge innovation. Beneath this activity were layers aspiring to a middle-class lifestyle, built on new debt instruments but supported by the security of house prices rising annually, in many fashionable post-codes by double-digit percentages, having lost even notional touch with underlying productivity.

Today, long after the bankruptcies and nationalisations, few would deny that these were years of hubris. Nonetheless, it is equally impossible to ignore how thoroughly Britain's economy was transformed. For all the later penalties it imposed, the numbers still have a dizzying quality to them, testifying to economic but also cultural and political transformation.

This is best illustrated by the extraordinary rise of inequality. In a single generation, Britain transitioned from one of Europe's most equal countries, almost equivalent to Sweden, to one of its least equal. In 1978, the bottom 90 per cent of earners accrued 72.2 per cent of total income; by 2007, this had fallen to 57.4 per cent, a demonstrable social regression.[11] Party-political shifts made little impression: inequality peaked not under Thatcher, but under New Labour. The share of the richest 1 per cent likewise was at its highest under the centre-left, at 9.6 per cent. 'Tony Blair was the king of income inequality', notes Danny Dorling. 'No British prime minister since Stanley Baldwin had seen the bottom 90 per cent take so little as they did under New Labour.'[12] Britain also emerged as the most regionally unequal economy, with a gap surpassing more famous cases such as Germany's east–west or Italy's north–south divide. The Institute for Public Policy Research claims the UK is the most regionally unequal country in the developed world, with London recording the highest gross value added in Europe, while the Scottish Borders, south Wales and Cornwall can only match the GVA of southern Italy.[13]

Labour's response was a characteristically 'Third Way' mixture of trickle-down economics and redistribution. Provincial cities were encouraged to imitate the 'London model of globalisation' (Edinburgh and Newcastle took up the offer with gusto, to the vast eventual cost of the UK taxpayer). And Chancellor Gordon Brown actively celebrated deregulation: 'No inspection without justification, no form filling without justification, and no information requirements without justification, not just a light touch but a limited touch.'[14] The rationale was that letting London rip was in the national interest, as government skimmed the top off soaring financial profits and subsidised a declining Britain through stealthy cash transfers or by moving back-office jobs to areas less adapted to the new competitive climate. New Labour saw all this as evidence of 'trickle down' in action. If London's dynamism was raising aggregate incomes, why object? What was good for the City was good for the UK. The effect was that Labour, albeit with different motives, was just as invested in financialising the economy as Thatcher had been.

Labour's programmatic dependence on the City persisted long after the simultaneous collapse of British living standards and Blairite politics – even after the election of a 'Marxist' leadership. As shadow chancellor, John McDonnell opened a 'City surgery' to reassure bankers about his plans for government.[15] Twelve months before Jeremy Corbyn and John McDonnell were ousted, Labour had 'cooled on plans to nationalise or break up RBS', Reuters reported, with the party now not seeking to exercise day-to-day control or introduce a financial transaction tax.[16] There is no need to moralise this point. McDonnell could plausibly claim that these were the best tactical moves to prevent capital flight, reassure middle-class voters and protect the Labour left base – which, after all, was itself concentrated in London, where Corbyn, McDonnell and Diane Abbott held their seats. However, the deeper problem it illustrates is that the financial bloc was so entrenched that it had been naturalised and depoliticised even by the most radical left elements within the Labour Party. Indeed, after the Brexit vote, the City had become almost a quintessential part of 'the British left', reimagined as supporters of Atlantic globalisation against Brexiteer isolationists.

In Scotland, the range of leftist cases for the Union are likewise built on redistribution of the City's incomes. The source of regional inequality becomes the answer to it. Indeed, as the Labour left imagines it, the growing scale of regional inequality only deepens the need for the Union as a mechanism for fiscal transfers such as those administered via the Barnett formula. Former Glasgow North-East MP Paul Sweeney has stated this premise directly: 'London essentially generates the wealth, and it is re-distributed to other regions of the UK.'[17] Chris Giles of the *Financial Times* has also made this case, arguing that 'if London was a nation state, it would have a budget surplus of 7 per cent of gross domestic product, better than Norway . . . the idea that London sucks the life out of other parts of Britain is absurd'.[18]

This viewpoint has been heavily contested, not least because it elides wealth production (where labour value materialises) with wealth registration (where wealth appears in final company accounts). Economic geographers including Doreen Massey have argued that the City of London extracts more wealth out of the rest of the UK than it gives back via fiscal transfers.[19] As one report to a UK parliamentary inquiry into regional inequality put it, 'the very obvious one-way flow of wealth as evidenced by London's tax and budgetary and jobs contribution, is only the most visible part of a more complex, less visible, two-way flow, with powerful and troubling regional implications'. Using the example of a PFI police college in South Lanarkshire completed in 2002, the authors show that Scottish taxpayers are paying £111 million over twenty-six years on a building with a value of just £17 million to a 'financial superstructure' almost all of which ultimately leads back to one address in the City of London.[20]

The deeper problem with the Labour left's conception of redistribution is that it depoliticises 'the British economy'. London's

precise impact may be contested among national income account-
ants; but certainly, decades of political preferences for City of
London interests and financialisation more broadly were built out
of the predatory dismantling of regional Britain. The current relationship of dependency represents the effective elimination of the
agency of provincial England, Scotland and Wales – until the
austerity regime drove those regions to embrace more radical
solutions to the democratic deficit, whether in the form of Brexit
or independence. Labour's response, when not simply cocking a
snook, has been to double down on Gordon Brown's model of
regional redistribution, with the aim of demobilising and depoliticising grievances (characteristically, the Scottish Labour left has
reclaimed Brown as a secular saint).

This represents an instinct opposite to that of the Corbyn
project at its best – an agenda Bhaskar Sunkara framed as 'class-
struggle social democracy'.[21] In Sunkara's formulation, what
distinguishes Corbyn and Bernie Sanders from the twentieth-
century parliamentary left is their realistic understanding of the
barriers facing a socialist policy project. Thus, both leaders are
said to be pursuing economic reforms as a means rather than an
end: a mechanism for raising political consciousness among the
working class and spurring it to mobilise in common cause.
However, even when viewed within this framing, there was
significant unevenness even within Corbyn's core base. If the
project was highly mobilised in London, it was flaky elsewhere,
especially in Scotland, where fear of nationalism among Labour
activists fuelled a regression to top-down Fabian solutions, often
dressed up in communitarian rhetoric that imagined (long after
this was remotely plausible) that Labour could restore itself as
the 'voice of the doorsteps' purely by proposing ameliorative
reforms. By contrast to Sunkara's formulation, the aim was
rather precisely to halt political mobilisation in favour of a
return to 'normal politics', whereby Labour would deliver
services to Scotland's working-class communities. Socialist-
sounding ideas of redistributing wealth from London, whether

feasible or not, were thus built on an underlying conservatism: an instinct to depoliticise that often came rather close to advocating a return to the New Labour era.

None of the above should obscure the fact that the victims of London's exorbitant power are often the capital's own residents. The Grenfell Tower fire of 2017, which killed seventy-two working-class people not far from some of the UK's most upscale residences, was a reminder that London is one of the developed world's most unequal cities. Grenfell itself was a somewhat solitary holdout against the waves of gentrification that have seen working-class Londoners pushed further out towards the city's periphery. The contrast between London and provincial Britain thus disguises how central the City has become to class domination as such, and its ongoing dependence on waves of cheap labour flowing to the capital.

Britain's World Role

If the myth of British stability was built on shallow domestic foundations, it becomes altogether risible when applied to the world stage. Through the neoliberal period, Britain and America together were characteristic 'revisionist powers', seeking not just to defend their existing privileges, but to reorder the world in their own image, to the point of openly violating their own 'norms'.[22] Britain's postcolonial militarism emerged in successive waves. Phase one involved the reassertion of British power under Thatcher, the New Cold War alliance with Ronald Reagan, and the first Gulf War under John Major. The second phase was defined by 'humanitarian' warfare, with the US–UK coalition as policemen of virtue, rolling over governments that transgressed imagined moral boundaries. Finally, the terminal stage, which is still ongoing, was the War on Terror. This has dominated security policy for decades and, far from liberating the world from the yoke of terrorism, the collapse of state authority in Iraq and elsewhere facilitated the rise of depraved fundamentalist groups like Isis – a fact frankly acknowledged even by Tony Blair himself.[23]

The overall story has been one of continual blowback, as the UK's pursuit of its 'national interest' – by treading on the sovereignty of others – has served to make the country (and the world) more vulnerable, generating further 'interventions' in overseas affairs. In almost all cases, the official nemeses of British foreign policy are erstwhile allies promoted, funded or sold weapons by UK governments. The most obvious case is the jihadi cause. 'British governments, both Labour and Conservative, have, in pursuing the so-called "national interest" abroad, colluded for decades with radical Islamic forces, including terrorist organisations', notes Mark Curtis.

> Governments have done so in often desperate attempts to maintain Britain's global power in the face of increasing weakness in key regions of the world, being unable to unilaterally impose their will and lacking other local allies. Thus the story is intimately related to that of Britain's imperial decline and the attempt to maintain influence in the world . . . The US has been shown by some analysts to have nurtured Osama Bin Laden and al-Qaida, but Britain's part in fostering Islamist terrorism is invariably left out of these accounts, and the history has never been told. Yet this collusion has had more impact on the rise of the terrorist threat than either Britain's liberal culture or the inspiration for jihadism provided by the occupation of Iraq.[24]

A similar story may be told of Saddam Hussein. The one fact that everybody now knows about Hussein is that he had no chemical weapons in 2003. However, in earlier decades Hussein did undoubtedly breach the norms of warfare, using chemical weapons on the battlefield – especially against the Iranians (which few in Britain cared about) but also against the Kurds (which provoked endless handwringing but zero soul-searching). But it was Britain that had authorised the sale of the materials, and indeed given financial support to the company doing so, despite warnings of a 'strong possibility' that they would be used to produce mustard and nerve gas, trade minister Paul Channon arguing: 'A ban would do our other trade prospects in Iraq no good.'[25] This was just one incident in a long and positive relationship between the Thatcher government and Hussein. He was welcomed as a trading partner, and the Anglo-Americans backed him through his most egregious abuses during the Iran–Iraq War, where the estimated death tolls begin at 1 million. It took the invasion of Kuwait for Thatcher to decide that her erstwhile ally was 'acting like Hitler' (rather as the *Daily Mail* had labelled Gamal Abdel Nasser 'Hitler on the Nile'). In the interregnum between the Gulf War and 2003, sanctions would kill half a million children. After Hussein was overthrown in the US-led invasion, the vacuum was soon filled by terror groups and competing regional interests, principally Iran, against whom Britain had built up Saddam in the first place.

There is a less obvious but perhaps even more darkly ironic story of meddling and blowback in eastern Europe. After the Cold War, Britain and the United States worked in tandem to ensure that Nato was not only preserved but expanded towards Russian borders. Russia itself was subjected, under British and American tutelage, to brutal 'shock treatment' consisting of sudden privatisations and market reforms, causing one of the biggest peacetime economic meltdowns ever recorded, and in turn political chaos. The outcome was the rise of the Russian nationalist Vladimir Putin, initially welcomed as a source of order but ultimately emerging as the latest phantasmic enemy of Western foreign policy. With little hint of irony, Euro-American liberals now blame Putin not only for the chaos in the Middle East, but also for their own post-2008 political meltdowns and the rise of 'populism'. Wide sections of the British elite have pinned the blame for Brexit on Russia. At the height of the conspiracy fad, a billboard appeared in London featuring a winking Vladimir Putin, reading, in a Russian font, 'Let's celebrate a red, white and blue Brexit' (depicting the Union Jack colour scheme overlapping with the Russian flag). Few of those peddling British nationalist narratives about a country under attack by 'foreign agents' ever mentioned Britain's endless intrusions into the elections and other affairs of states of sovereign nations.

Britain's pursuit of the 'national interest' – or, rather, of post-colonial trade, prestige and control by meddling abroad – has consistently made ordinary people, not least British troops, more insecure. Radical Islamists, Saddam Hussein, or Vladimir Putin have all been useful bogeymen for those who view Britain as a benign imperial power under attack from external actors. But few credible political scientists buy the narrative that Putin bought the Brexit vote. The threat of Islamist terrorism was real enough, but far outweighed by the panicked overreaction and massive crackdown on civil liberties, especially though not exclusively in Muslim communities. And Hussein, in retrospect, posed no threat at all except to his own people, whose lives Britain somehow conspired to make worse. The resulting misery spawned the rise of Isis, a terror network more brutal, irrational and indiscriminate even than Al-Qaeda. Certainly, the trillions dedicated to the 'War on Terror' hardly served to lessen the terrorist threat.

The implications of the relative decline of American empire remain unclear. The United States underwent a unique phase of adjustment under the successive reigns of Obama and Trump – both, uniquely in post-1945 US history, elected on anti-war tickets. Their preference for military isolationism modified by drone strikes left little room for coalition-building around 'regime change'. The upshot was that Britain was rarely pressured to play a role in American imperial policy – the disastrous (but largely ignored) Libyan 'intervention' being an exception. This is part of the story of how a certain idea of cosmopolitan Britishness imploded: military-led globalisation was central to asserting a united, post-Thatcherite British identity, particularly under New Labour. Public war-weariness, and the apocalyptic collapse of post-invasion states in Iraq and Afghanistan, served temporarily to exclude this mode of Britishness. Nonetheless, the UK's post-Brexit isolation has already led to pressure to join future American 'interventions' aimed at restoring hegemonic order against rising Chinese competition. The 'Aukas' submarine pact between Australia, America and the UK suggests a revived confidence, and the liberal left's growing tendency to talk up conflict with Russia presents another avenue for a reassertion of American empire. 'Anglobalisation' may be out of fashion, but its temptations remain.

Questions of Sovereignty

If British nationalism from Thatcher to Cameron was framed around competitive adjustment to globalisation, recent British history has been dominated by rival claims of sovereignty. The refrain of the Scottish government's White Paper on independence was 'Scotland's future in Scotland's hands'; two years later, the Leave campaign led with 'Take back control'. Of course, these slogans imply different ideological and moral perspectives. The Leave slogan, as many conceived it, was a 'dog whistle' to lure soft anti-immigrant voters; the Scottish government, by contrast, claimed that the powers of independence would allow Scotland to attract *more* immigration. The racialised messaging of the Dominic Cummings–led official Vote Leave campaign, which warned that the whole population of Turkey could imminently be immigrating to the EU, could not have been in starker contrast to 'Yes Scotland', in which the most edgy slogan about international affairs was 'bairns not bombs'. These distinctions are important, partly to guard against uninformed notions of independence as a 'Little Scotlander' movement, and partly to emphasise – contrary to the antidemocratic liberal biases in journalism and academia – that popular control does not always imply the reign of bigotry. But neither should this obscure the underlying commonality between Leave and Yes. Both sides were seeking to bring democratic scrutiny to an issue currently controlled by remote, unaccountable elites. And both were thus intended as claims of sovereignty.

This word, of course, carries many ambiguities. In international law, national sovereignty is the principle that states should not interfere in the affairs of others, except for reasons of emergency. It can offer a legitimation of war (self-defence against a threat of invasion), but equally acts as the framework for opposing war (Saddam Hussein's Iraq posed no threat to the UK or the United States; the invasion thus violated Iraqi sovereignty). Nationalists might also oppose globalisation in the name of sovereignty, evincing a preference for decisions to be taken within the nation-state. These were the constitutional parameters of the Brexit debate. On one side, Brexiteers appealed to the sacred principles of British parliamentarism. In this context, 'Take back control' meant restoring powers to Westminster. On the other side, Remainers dismissed criticisms of the EU as a category error, suggesting that they misconstrued the nature of political power in an era of 'pooled sovereignty'.

Few considered that the problem might be less about *national sovereignty* per se – British autonomy from Brussels regulations – and more about *popular sovereignty* – the ability of the democratic public to hold politicians to account. But, more than a preference for British politicians over 'Eurocrats', the Brexit vote represented a kick against all established political authority. Unwillingness even to conceive of this, or to understand the connection between the two, betrayed ingrained prejudices of power. In this respect, Brexiteers and Remainers alike were guilty of similar errors. Far from the EU being an all-powerful superstate, its staff is no larger than some urban administrations. Its 33,000-strong bureaucracy is dwarfed by the UK's 400,000 unelected civil servants. The problem, then, is less that the EU tramples over the sacred authority of national parliaments than how member-statehood transforms domestic relations between parliaments (or, more properly, state power) and the public. The winners from 'pooled sovereignty' are national governments and transnational corporations; the losers, as far as democratic accountability goes, are the national populace.

Consider the tragic case of Burntisland Fabrications (BiFab).[26] Traditionally, in Scottish industrial history, the decision to bankrupt a key component of the Scottish supply chain in the century's most important emerging industry (green energy manufacturing) would have brought insurrectionary protests. Environmental activists and the left would have linked arms with defensive nationalists, trade unionists and the beleaguered workers and communities of Fife. However, because the Scottish government cited impersonal EU state-aid laws, a sense of fatalism descended on any such nascent coalition. While there were many complaints, and a critical vote in parliament, there was never any serious prospect of overturning the decision. EU membership thus empowered the Scottish state, or what passes for one, to fend off outraged workers, the communities and industries they serve, and even a critical parliament. The only unusual thing about BiFab was the extent of its politicisation; more commonly, member-statehood in the EU has so normalised the rules of market competition that few even deign to question its authority. Effectively, the EU functions as a mechanism for depoliticising economic (and political) decisions.

If this highlights weaknesses in the liberal Remain coalition, it also shows the weaknesses of the Brexiteers. Boris Johnson's slogan in the 2019 general election, 'Get Brexit done', caught a mood of exasperation with parliamentary shenanigans on both sides of the aisle. But it also invoked a demoralising, demobilising notion. A truly interesting Brexit would have begun a popular process of reshaping state power *within Britain*; instead, it was rebranded as a one-off event where powers would simply be restored to a Westminster elite that would take matters in hand and deliver on behalf of the people. Even the British parliament was barely 'empowered' at all. If 'Take back control' was properly embraced, it could have meant rethinking the imposition of an impersonal, bureaucratic, depoliticising state power that was the ironic outcome of the neoliberal era. But little was done to embrace the potential of departure from the regime of EU member-statehood. A classic British settlement was achieved – a halfway house epitomised by the absurdity of the new arrangements for Northern Ireland.

Among the principal culprits were the British left. Many abandoned their critical faculties altogether and embraced not just the
EU as an institution but also a coalition with the old regime of
New Labour, the Liberal Democrats, and the Cameronite
Conservatives. But even leftist critics of the EU struggled to articulate what they stood for, or even what they were against. Their
vision usually boiled down to top-down economic reforms,
exploiting openings around state aid and public procurement
to reinvigorate regional economies. This vision was arguably
predicated on wishful thinking: it required not just the unlikely
prospect of a leftist coalition in Westminster, but an even more
implausible leftist coalition dedicated to shifting power away from
London – home to Corbyn, McDonnell and Abbott, and the only
secure base of Labour leftism. More fundamentally, it missed the
principled argument, which was less about economic planning
than about the denigration of democracy under neoliberalism.
Brexit was in many ways a missed opportunity to rethink popular
control over state power.

A small group of scholars, including Christopher Bickerton and
Phillip Cunliffe, developed a more sophisticated account of why
Brexit mattered.[27] This was based on the core concepts, also developed throughout this book, of popular sovereignty, democratic
accountability, and an older tradition of internationalism that
departed from the neoliberal cosmopolitanism that dominates
much of the left. Their position was more intellectually serious and
less prone to wishful thinking in suggesting why Brexit, even if it
did not lead to progressive economic policies, could foster the
conditions by which a fundamental altering of the relationship
between state and citizen is politically viable. That Brexit posed a
true and interesting crisis situation is not in doubt. As Susan
Watkins observes,

The Brexit vote constituted a further dimension of crisis, this
time for the political establishment as a whole. Operative respect
for democracy would run counter to the entire cast of

government policy and state administration, involving a wrenching re-orientation of the Whitehall machine. The liberal intelligentsia was devastated, far more so than it had been by the ravages of Thatcherism or by Blair's mad-dog wars.[28]

Intellectually, the above perspective has real strengths, not just in identifying the crux of possibility in Brexit, but also in conceptualising the role of the EU in the contemporary political malaise, conceived as a new type of relationship between state power and citizens that Bickerton calls 'member-statehood'. However, this account arguably paid less attention to the internal dynamics of the British state itself. While adopting brave and principled stances on republicanism, House of Lords abolition and Irish unification – matters which, incidentally, scarcely arose in any Remainer narrative beyond the Scottish independence movement – these critical supporters of Brexit never seriously addressed Scotland's democratic deficit. The problem was not simply that 62 per cent of Scotland voted against Brexit; it was also about the composition of that coalition, which was far from the stereotype of the middle-class 'Remoaner' agonising about Pinot Grigio, Erasmus programmes and holidays in Tuscany. Scotland's democratic discontents were working class in nature, and concentrated on Westminster rule. Among Scotland's Remain voters were many who would otherwise have sympathised with opposition to the EU, but would never endorse a regime led by Boris Johnson.

The EU should be conceived as both undemocratic (its parliament has no powers to initiate legislation) and antidemocratic (it erodes democratic scrutiny at the national level). The problem is that similar problems also afflict the devolved UK state. The half-hearted transfer of sovereignty to Edinburgh, Cardiff and Belfast has simply created new layers separating the public from political accountability. In these crevices various opportunists have nested. The Conservative regime of David Cameron found that the multiple layers of the UK state were an excellent mechanism for imposing austerity – indeed, his advisers had a term for this: 'devolving the axe'.[29] Public anger would be diffused between multiple agents and competing layers of government. Scottish Nationalist control of Holyrood, far from breaking the wheels of the machine, has in a sense made it more effective. Sturgeon blames problems on Westminster, and promises final resolution with independence; but she uses that posture to enact an endless postponement of any reckoning with Scotland's daily injustices. This forms the central paradox of Scottish politics: pervasive discontent with public services and the social order combines with unprecedented support for the national leadership – a sure sign of a failing democracy. The general conclusion should be that the EU was afflicted by a wider neoliberal void of accountability, which was likewise installed in the devolution process. Political accountability was transferred upwards, to the inter-governmental and EU bureaucratic level, but also downwards, to Holyrood and its sister parliaments. But this was all predicated on a complacency generated by rising living standards. The collapse of the debt economy led to a collapse in consent, and a constitutional mess.

British politics has long passed the point where 'the people' have the institutions to mobilise around a common process for redesigning the state. Even under Corbyn, the Labour Party never showed any capability of relating to Scotland's democratic grievances. Under Keir Starmer, as Tariq Ali has observed, Labour has abandoned any effort to relate to the public, settling instead for the old Napoleonic procedure of not interfering while your opponent is making a mistake.[30] Labour now hopes that the two-party pendulum of British politics will passively generate exhaustion with the Conservatives, who have now been in power for over a decade, allowing Labour space to restore centrist 'normality'. Starmer's core audience is thus composed of businesses, bureaucracies and broadsheet journalists. Rather than standing for a distinctive vision of Britain's post-EU future, Labour has settled for the more familiar role of being 'not the Conservatives'. Starmer is the politician of demobilisation, who licenses all the complacencies of the middle classes who are his chief supporters.

Paradoxically, for Brexit to foster popular sovereignty, the breakup of Britain would be required. Only on this basis can there be a reckoning with the national level of democratic renewal. Worthy-sounding proposals for federalism are always predicated on demobilisation, on finding new payoffs to nationalist sentiment, on postponing the settlement of grievances through an increasingly nebulous appeal to British identity or national solidarity. Proposals that federalism should involve anything more radical than a further devolution of taxation run into similar problems as 'Lexit': they are predicated on magical thinking, and pay little heed to existing political forces. Would Labour, of all parties, ever seriously contemplate abolition of the House of Lords or removal of the Windsors?

At a deeper level, the federalist slogan reflects anti-political pessimism. Economic interconnection, Labourists believe, makes independence logistically impossible (the same was said of Brexit). Thus, a technocratic compromise within the existing order offers far less risk and inconvenience. This argument should be resisted because it simply postpones any reckoning with ultimate political responsibility. While a patch-up might temporarily stem the tide of support for independence, it certainly will not destroy the SNP, which will exploit all the same inconsistencies in British state power for decades to come – precisely because Labour is incapable of articulating a coherent British national project.

Of course, this picture is more complex. The logistics of democracy, trade and state power have changed after Brexit, and the SNP leadership has yet to address the consequences with any intellectual depth. Andrew Wilson, architect of the party's existing economic strategy, was embarrassed on these basic questions during an interview with former BBC journalist Andrew Neil, which bears repeat viewing.[31] Equally, there is every prospect that, with independence, Scottish voters would choose to hand their newfound sovereignty to the EU – or, in effect, to their own political class. Naturally, this prospect forms a core component of the SNP leadership's programme.

Nonetheless, it is impossible for Scotland to have a true debate about the EU and popular sovereignty while it remains under Westminster rule. Much of Scotland will never take seriously the idea of self-rule under a Conservative-dominated parliament, regardless of the permutation of powers that might be transferred to Holyrood. This leads many to regard the EU as a protector of Scottish rights – a conclusion that might be dubious given the fate of the Catalan independence movement, but which retains real resonance thanks to the longstanding failure of the UK state. Scotland can only consider the democratic implications of Europe when the debate is properly framed around the national project – and this requires the dismantling of the Westminster regime.

A final complexity – though a potentially positive one – is the English question. Most of the English left has continued to cling to a state identity (Britishness) and to reject any project centred on England as an inherently corrupt and reactionary notion. For all the moralism that attaches to this position, it has countervailing consequences: an unwillingness to criticise and a tendency to naturalise state power, undergirded by the kind of metropolitan snobbery expressed in former Labour foreign secretary Emily Thornberry's infamous sneering tweet of a white van and an England flag in Rochester (Thornberry represents the fashionable London borough of Islington South and Finsbury). A certain status quo bias was also involved. Since Britain was the existing identity of state power, it stood for permissiveness, or for postponing awkward national questions in favour of 'more fundamental' issues. Even when Britishness was invoked in support of endless neo-imperial projects, this rarely shook such liberal passivity. Britishness was not good; but Englishness was always imagined to be worse – so inherently terrible, in fact, that the goal of leftism must be to engineer it out of existence.

But circumstances have conspired to render this position untenable. Brexit, and the subsequent collapse of the Red Wall, made it impossible for the left to ignore the democratic deficit in northern

England and the Midlands. Meanwhile, Labour can no longer count on the passive acquiescence of Scotland, as it did for more than half a century. Scotland's departure would seal the need for a fundamental rethinking of postcolonial identity. But even some bodged halfway house – as with the federalist proposals dreamt up by Labour Party intellectuals – would depend on somehow addressing the English question. In terms of population, England represents the vast majority of the United Kingdom, and any blue-print for federalism would somehow have to accommodate this reality without defaulting to the notion of Westminster as England's parliament. So far, most options fall foul of an absence of democratic imagination. 'North West England' might be a bureaucratic identity, but it will not form a base for political mobilisation. Nonetheless, Britain – or what remains of it – must somehow bridge its aching democratic voids.

In Britain especially, the question of public control of state power will ultimately boil down to that of taming an out-of-control capital city. The left has found rather too many self-interested reasons to ignore the overweening dominance of London in the nation's economic, political and cultural affairs. Simply calling for a more vigorous redistribution of London's monies is no longer an answer. It will repeat the mistakes of the past, ultimately serving to weaken economic and political responsibility further north, while reinforcing London's economic dominance under the guise of transferring power. The fundamental democratic task is to control London's dominance. But that dominance is so entrenched that a challenge to it requires a triggering event – and a bigger one than Brexit. Scottish independence is the last viable progressive project inside the UK dedicated to a real shake-up of state power, and the most feasible route to a rebalancing of Britain's power structures. The route back to a united working-class identity might lie through the separation of its national units.

2

Nationalism, Internationalism and Independence: Contemporary Applications of Socialist Theory

A decade of continuous political emergency, starting with the Conservative–Liberal coalition and concluding in the mishandling of the pandemic, has seen Britain dismissed as the 'sick man of Europe', and even a 'failed state'.[1] While these phrases are meant in all sincerity, the problem with diagnosing Britain as abnormal is where to set the barometer for normality. In the years when Brexit was paralysing British politics, the French government faced effective civil wars with Gilet Jaunes protestors every Saturday, while the forces of the Spanish state were breaking heads in Catalonia; and that is before considering Trump's America, Salvini's Italy or Kaczyński's Poland. Britain's crisis has special characteristics, but they are ultimately symptomatic rather than exceptional. They are one chapter of a wider story about the breakdown of public faith in the institutions of neoliberal globalisation.

The beneficiaries of this legitimacy crisis, we now know, have not been the anti-capitalist left but various strains of nationalism. This nationalist surge has served to expose crucial weaknesses in the left's armoury. Leftist critiques, rooted increasingly in moral categories of goodies and baddies, tend to see nationalism as the work of the outside agitator bringing problems into otherwise peaceable working-class communities, rather than as symptoms of wider systemic failure. With traditional parties of the left losing power and influence, the intellectually lazy answer was to pin the blame on what former Scottish Labour leader Johann Lamont called 'the virus of nationalism'. The result, rather too often, was a moral panic that failed either to capture the underlying problem or to address it.

Here we offer an alternative account. By excavating older leftist traditions of the critique of nationalism, with all their nuances, we aim to provide a foundation for understanding the complex relationship between national ideology and the crisis of neoliberal globalisation. The old dualisms of class versus nation, nationalism versus internationalism, and so on, have been strategic crutches serving useful functions in the left's everyday tactical dilemmas. However, their utility has been compromised by the decay of old social-democratic parties – which extends far beyond Labour – and by the breakdown of internationalism from above. The task, in these circumstances, is to rescue international solidarity from the wreckage of that old order. In Scotland, where nationalism runs up against the postcolonial state, there are further, pressing issues. With much of the left, and at least half of society, supporting independence, we must carefully untangle that cause from a nationalist outlook that postpones all questions of inequality until 'after independence'.

Marxism and (Inter)Nationalism

The Marxist tradition may seem like a peculiar starting point for assessing the dilemmas of nationalism. Famously, for Tom Nairn, 'the theory of nationalism represents Marxism's great historical failure'; for Benedict Anderson, it is Marxism's 'uncomfortable anomaly'. More broadly, a generation of post-'68 radicals had developed a settled critique of Marxism's failings, which they saw as doctrinaire internationalism, class reductionism and a failure to grasp the emotional, meaning-constructing side of human nature. In later years, many would take these initial provocations further: materialists, according to the emerging cultural sociology, needed to abandon economic abstractions and make room for new modes of identity construction. Nationalism itself, crucially, was framed as part of a progressive rainbow coalition involving other emerging identity-based social movements, such as feminism, environmentalism and LGBTQI+ liberation (this approach is adopted, for instance, in Ernesto Laclau and Chantal Mouffe's still influential reading of populism).[2]

Recently, however, the consensus has shifted markedly. The nation, regarded as a site of crude majoritarianism where marginal identities face attacks from an intolerant public, is now contrasted to the rainbow coalition, while Marxist analysis, in this new context, finds itself attacked from the opposite direction. Increasingly, materialist accounts, because they attempt to provide sociological explanations rather than moral censure, are charged with giving nationalism *too much sympathy*. In one widely feted book, Sivamohan Valluvan warns that, while the old mode of Marxism has been accused of denigrating nationalism, 'The real trouble lies in those instances where nationalist politics is read [by Marxists] as a misdirected anti-capitalist politics ripe for socialist capture.'[3] Any effort to give an objective account of the social foundations of, say, Brexit or Donald Trump – in other words, anything but an abstractly moral attack on the right wing – can be seen as tantamount to complicity with the worst excesses of the post-2016 critics of liberalism. Symptomatically, even pro-migration, anti-war nationalisms like Scotland's frequently end up being condemned by the same standards, especially insofar as they have a working-class support base.[4]

In academia, as in activist circles, efforts to understand the Marxist approach to nationalism have been plagued by out-of-context quotations and the substitution of moralised categories for historical analysis, by supporters just as much as by critics of the materialist method. Given these confusions, the original texts are a necessary starting point. While Marx and Engels contributed only indirectly to an explicit theory of nationalism, an emerging body of scholarship has begun to reconstruct the basic contours of their intellectual, moral and tactical approach. By the standards of contemporary morality, their example is far from blemish-free, but analytically it still makes for a much richer perspective than their critics on both sides might allow.

Politically, Marx and Engels's account is certainly more nuanced than many appreciate. Consider, for instance, their most celebrated (and disparaged) statement of internationalism: 'The working men [and women] have no country.' This has become one of the best-known refrains of the socialist tradition, and, for some, analysis begins and ends with that sentence. Yet, as if to highlight the prospects for confusion, the text adds, 'Since the proletariat must first of all acquire political supremacy, must rise to be the leading class of the nation, must constitute itself the nation, it is so far, itself national, though not in the bourgeois sense of the word.'[5] The implication is that turning the numerical dominance of the working class into political dominance will begin from a national framing: national politics will not be the final destination, but it is the point of departure.

Nationality thus becomes a battleground for class politics. In Solomon Bloom's rendering, 'Every class had the tendency to picture the nation, and sometimes the whole species, in its own image. It then proceeded to worship that image. For each class there was a different "fatherland".'[6] Even Trotsky, often framed as an arch cosmopolitan, was dismissive of doctrinaire internationalism. 'If, in your self-education study group, with the aid of the methods of Marxism, you have freed yourself from various national prejudices, that is, of course, a very good thing and a very big step forward in your personal development', he remarked.

But the task confronting the ruling party in this sphere is a more far-reaching one: we have to make it possible for the many millions of our people, who belong to different nationalities, to find through the medium of the State and other institutions led by the Party, practical living satisfaction for their national interests and requirements, and thereby enable them to get rid of national antagonisms and prejudices – all this not at the level of a Marxist study group but at the level of the historical experience of entire peoples.[7]

Similar ambiguities will be discovered by examining their practical record as political activists. For all their undoubted influence in shaping internationalism, in practice Marx and Engels supported many national independence movements, of all shapes and sizes and varying shades of historical advancement. Equally, to draw simplistic moral lessons from this – as if they offered *unconditional* licence to any and all national projects – would be just as misleading. Their support was not based on moral absolutes but rather on a tactical assessment of how to advance the interests of the working class and accelerate moves towards socialism.

Nineteenth-century nationalism, as much of the left conceived it, was essentially concerned with breaking apart absolutist states and confused layers of feudal sovereignty so as to lay the foundations for the modern capitalist order. At this stage of development, nationalism had yet to gain its later connotation of 'narrowness' – indeed, building nations was a process of expansion. As Hobsbawm observes, 'it seemed clear that small, and especially small and backward, nationalities had everything to gain by merging into greater nations, and making their contributions to humanity through these'.[8] Nations needed to demonstrate 'viability' – to achieve a certain threshold of size to thrive. For this reason, Giuseppi Mazzini, the nineteenth century's chief apostle of liberal nationalism, did not envisage independence for Ireland: its small population and backward economy meant it simply was not viable as a separate entity. In the conception of Mazzini, the map of the future nation-states of Europe would be formed of large states that we would now call multinational.

At times, Marx and Engels supported nationalism for similar reasons, as a solvent of feudal and absolutist modes of sovereignty. Engels in particular became overzealous in his application of the threshold position. However, their support for Irish separatism and anticolonial movements highlights an approach that transcended the cruder, teleological theories of progress of their liberal contemporaries. As always, Marx and Engels based their judgements largely on the geopolitical consequences of a nationalist breakthrough. In these cases, they thus supported national movements not merely to 'prepare the ground' for capitalism, but also, where the capitalist social order had advanced, as a disruption to bourgeois rule.

As their analysis evolved, they also paid growing attention to how peripheral nationalist movements might condition the class consciousness of workers in the metropolis. Irish nationalism was thus seen as breaking down the ties that bound the working class of England to their state:

> For a long time, I believed it would be possible to overthrow the Irish regime by English working-class ascendancy. I always took this viewpoint in the *New York Tribune*. Deeper study has now convinced me of the opposite. The English working class will never accomplish anything before it has got rid of Ireland. The lever must be applied in Ireland. This is why the Irish question is so important for the social movement in general.[9]

The importance of this point cannot be overstated. In subsequent generations, Marxism would go on to shape the mass working-class parties of the early period of parliamentary democracy. But the Second International vastly overemphasised the underlying resilience of their internationalist pieties. Panicked by initial working-class enthusiasm for World War I, almost all of them would end up siding with their imperial states in recruiting for mechanised warfare. Thus, as mass working-class politics became the main strategic problem for the capitalist class, a central problem for Marxism became how to address the lure of imperial chauvinism in larger states.

The limitations of Marx and Engels's approach have been pored over by a generation of social scientists. Certainly, they never define an absolute moral foundation for deciding which nationalisms are good and which are bad. There is no recognition of an abstract right of self-determination. Instead, their position on national conflicts was largely tactical and 'consequentialist', based on an analysis of whether a particular side's victory would hasten the fall of feudal or reactionary powers, or weaken the ideological power of a bourgeois state over its workers. Their iconoclastic distrust of liberal moralisers would sometimes bleed into contrarian language. Thus, on India, Marx lampooned the defence of pre-industrial hierarchical society: 'I share not the opinion of those who believe in a golden age of Hindostan':

> England, it is true, in causing a social revolution in Hindostan, was actuated only by the vilest interests, and was stupid in her manner of enforcing them. But that is not the question. The question is, can mankind fulfil its destiny without a fundamental revolution in the social state of Asia? If not, whatever may have been the crimes of England she was the unconscious tool of history in bringing about that revolution.[10]

Here we see the potentially brutal rhetoric of a consequentialist position, which can sound like an endorsement of cruelty and plunder. Yet he also remarked, 'The Indians will not reap the fruits of the new elements of society scattered among them by the British bourgeoisie, till in Great Britain itself the now ruling classes shall have been supplanted by the industrial proletariat, or till the Indians themselves shall have grown strong enough to throw off the English yoke altogether.'[11] While Marx was no purveyor of pious liberal concern, his tactical sense of the international situation led him to support anticolonial national movements.

The weaknesses of Marx and Engels's position are also, in certain contexts, a strength. The omission of moralism in determining good and bad nationalisms can bring renewed attention to how claims of nationhood function in the struggle for class domination. 'National ideology', Erica Benner emphasises, 'appears in this context not as a fixed or monolithic mechanism of a single class's ascendancy, but as a key doctrinal arena in struggles for political power.'[12] Equally, the Marx–Engels approach focuses on the effects of independence movements on the truly international context, where states spar with one another for influence.

For all the criticisms that have been levelled at Marx and Engels, in the particular case of Scotland these remain the crucial strategic stakes for the left. In a word, Scotland's questions are tactical. What will be the impact of independence (versus the alternative prospect of ongoing union) with regard to the class consciousness of workers? What prospects are there for working-class influence – and for weakening ruling-class dominance – in the national movements? And what impact would the breakup of Britain have on the international order of states? As we will explain, efforts to moralise the question of independence – to make it, for example, into a question of 'oppression' – have had contradictory consequences, and have tended to perpetuate historical myths.

The Useful Myth of Self-Determination

In search of firmer grounds for assessing the moral claims of national independence movements, a common but often misleading starting point is the 'right of nations to self-determination'. First coined in 1917 with the twin declarations of Woodrow Wilson and Lenin, self-determination would become the central legitimating principle on both sides of Cold War geopolitics. Today, it continues to provide the ethical justification for the international system of competing states. Many nations claim to trace their statehood to this right: there are thus statues to Wilson (where once stood statues of Lenin) in Poland and Bulgaria, symbolising those people's ethical claims to national independence.

Yet, for all the term's mystical aura, and for all that it persists as a theoretical claim in the UN Charter, self-determination, as an abstract moral claim, is often unenforceable. Indeed, as Catalonia has discovered, it often has no authority at all; and transnational institutions with an ethical remit, such as the EU, may actively collude in suppressing it. There are no instruments to distinguish legitimate from illegitimate claims, and there is no ultimate sovereign to decide – except, in practice, the United States, which, thanks to its superiority of force, usually settles the benefit of any doubt. Most cases of the actualisation of self-determination are thus a product of the total collapse of transnational states and empires. Hence the peculiar status of Scotland and Catalonia, whose claims are pressed within nominally powerful and even successful states.

This all makes a mockery of the supposed Wilsonian right of self-determination, according to which powerful states (or the 'international community') ensure respect for the claims of would-be nations. It is a founding hypocrisy, as clearly illustrated by the world system's failure to provide justice for the Palestinians. Conversely, Israel's foundation and subsequent expansion illustrates the real grounding of sovereignty: military victory against a colonial power and/or mentoring by the great powers. In other words, the 'right' provides a moralising gloss to the real basis of the system of states, which is founded on the successful prosecution and monopolisation of violence, whether colonial or anticolonial (or, in Israel's case, both).

The principle thus serves as the mythological foundation for explaining why some states exist and others do not. Its moral force alone is rarely adequate to the task of state-making. The consequence of this, of course, is that there is little precedent for movements, like Scotland's, that are not founded on a deeply felt sense of national oppression, and where there is every expectation that independence will be achieved without a single shot being fired.

Nonetheless, it would be wrong to reduce self-determination to its hypocrisies. Acknowledging that self-determination is effectively a myth does not abolish its role as a moral guide to leftist strategy. Its mystical allure has real-world effects. The myth was powerful enough that both Ho Chi Minh and Fidel Castro actively solicited the support of the United States, the country of Woodrow Wilson, for their claims of national freedom, and were – in good faith – shocked to discover that liberal America backed old-fashioned colonial reaction. Equally, Lenin's rendering of the right is not founded in illusions about the state system. It is designed instead to guide the tactics of working-class movements, and (contrary to its function today) to challenge state power, both in relation to coercion and consent internally, and to the international system of states.

However, Lenin's formulation left numerous ambiguities. At some points he seems to imply that self-determination and independence are one and the same: '[T]he self-determination of nations means the political separation of these nations from alien national bodies, and the formation of an independent national state.'[13] This leaves the nation little choice in the matter. Lenin's loose formulation thus arguably does little to distinguish itself from the philosophically nationalist view that nations and states must correspond. The ambiguities in Lenin's formulation have never been adequately resolved. For some, Scotland's self-determination simply equates to independence; for others, it means that Scotland's membership of the UK is based on consent, implying the possibility of divorce but also the choice of ongoing union.

Such ambiguities allow for endless trickiness in practice. Theoretically, even UK state managers have conceded the right of self-determination. During the general election of 1992, John Major asserted: 'No nation can be held within a Union against its will.'[14] Shortly after the general election of 1997, when preparations for the Scottish and Welsh devolution referendums were underway, Donald Dewar noted that 'the only way [the Scots] could move to independence would be if people voted for independence. That is clearly their right.'[15] However, as Michael Keating has noted, 'successive British governments have recognised' that Scotland is a self-determining nation within the Union, but 'then tried to deny the consequences'.[16]

In these cases, the question is less the principle itself – which has effectively become a monotonous platitude, superficially adhered to by all except when it has real-world consequences – than the details of its application. National movements like those in Scotland and Catalonia have few precedents for pursuing their claims, and must rely on assumptions of good faith from successor states (the remainder of the UK or Spain) and the always nebulously defined 'international community'. Equally, expressions of solidarity from outside the nation will inevitably appeal to the principle of self-determination – Scotland's right to choose its future – rather than explicitly 'telling' Scotland to vote one way or another. Self-determination is thus a useful myth from many angles, and serves many purposes.

Crucially, in Scotland itself the debate over the right to decide (whether through a referendum or by other means) serves to reproduce an ultimately conservative consensus under the guise of a dispute. One side insists it has numerous mandates (but is powerless to enact them) while the other wields state power to impose what it regards as its own mandate (the 2014 result). Questions relating to the nature of independence or of the British state are effectively shielded from politics by proxy battles over procedures and prerogatives. Rather often, talk of self-determination thus functions in the opposite sense to that intended in the Leninist tradition: far from radicalising debates about state power and solidarity, it serves endlessly to defer them. Conversely, though, if Scotland *were* to achieve independence, it would radicalise debates about the state across Europe, establishing a precedent that would serve to galvanise movements in Catalonia, the Basque Country, Ireland and elsewhere. This illustrates once again that Scotland

stands on a knife-edge between the radical implications of independence and the conservative reproduction of nationalist governments under the devolved UK order.

Oppressed and Oppressor Nations

The Leninist tradition made a second contribution to the national
question in drawing a distinction between oppressed and oppressor nations. Even in countries where Marxism had a limited
profile, these criteria have shaped leftist debates about the comparative merits of nationalist movements. Scotland has not been
immune: indeed, scholarly debates about Scottish history have
often been coloured by the sort of motivated reasoning necessary
to force reality into these categories. The result, most frequently,
has been the unnecessary misrepresentation of complex historical
situations.

Insofar as the distinctions have any meaning, there should be
no doubt that Scotland, as a central partner in the British Empire,
was an oppressor nation. Much of early Scottish nationalism
during that period was about a demand for Scotland to enjoy equal
sovereign status among plunderers. Equally, the almost total
absence of Scottish nationalist sentiment until the 1960s may
partly reflect the status that came with belonging to an empire,
which was central to certain forms of Protestant identity that cut
across class lines.

And it would be mistaken to assume that Scotland's role in
oppressive global systems ended there. It has become intellectually
convenient to imagine that, with the rise of American empire,
Britain entered a persistent decline into ever greater irrelevance. In
truth, there was no consistent pattern. British military technology
and power would experience a revival after the initial shock of
decolonisation. Scots, such as the quasi-fascist operator Colonel
David Stirling, founder of the Special Air Service (SAS), would
play a central role in that revival. More recently, a whole gamut of

Scottish New Labour figures have played equally prominent roles in advocating for American adventurism: Gordon Brown, John Reid and Jim Murphy are three vivid examples. At the risk of labouring the point: insofar as the British state has been and continues to be an oppressor, Scots have more than played their part.

The real question is whether this is still relevant in adjudicating Scotland's national question. Today, no side of Scottish nationalism's factional war claims that Scotland was historically oppressed. Alex Salmond, for example, explains: 'Scotland was never oppressed, or at least not all of Scotland. There were parts of Scotland [that] obviously had a rough time within the Union, the highland clearances. But Scotland wasn't an oppressed nation . . . It was a partner in Union as opposed to being colonised or planted [like Ireland] so it is a different history and different experience.'[17]

Nicola Sturgeon's stance has been even more unequivocal. So demonstrating that Scotland is not oppressed is hardly likely to preclude support for independence. Indeed, a central socialist motive for independence relates precisely to consciousness of Scotland's role as an oppressor with a disproportionate historical role in both the British Empire and the contemporary nuclear strategy of US imperialism. Independence may not prove a mortal death-blow to these institutions; but it would unambiguously damage the imperial foundations of a powerful and reactionary state, regardless of whether these are the conscious motives of nationalist leaders. By contrast, even Jeremy Corbyn, the extreme case of a dedicated pacifist taking over Labour, was forced to accept the usual routine of British state power – Nato, nuclear weapons, alliance with Israel. Undoubtedly, he would have been forced into yet more embarrassing climbdowns if he had ever assumed power.

Conversely, proving that Scotland is an oppressed 'colony' would not necessarily demonstrate the case for independence. Indeed, in the 1970s it was relatively common to find socialists defending the Union precisely on the grounds that Scotland, being a colony, was too weak to stand alone. In these accounts, Scotland was so severely oppressed that it lacked the basis for autonomy: under independence, its oil would inevitably become the plaything of the City of London and global capitalist forces. These traditions have persisted, particularly in Stalinist accounts, but also in a wider milieu surrounding Scotland's Labour left and trade-union bureaucracy, through networks such as the Red Paper Collective.

Rather than any category of victimhood, the true tactical question should be that of agency. What relationship with state power gives the greatest chance for working-class and democratic forces to exert meaningful political choice against established interests? Unionist critiques based on the 'unity of the British working class' must gloss over the fact that, for several decades, the repressive British state has effectively worn trade unionism down to a nub of service provision, while the party-political order has systematically disenfranchised working-class voters. In other words, it has reduced working-class participation to little but consumer choice. Scottish independence, by contrast, emerged from a political moment, the 2014 referendum, which was an organised revolt against the logic of 'there is no alternative', built on a demand to be treated as active citizens rather than passive consumers. Whether independence achieves these aims is an open matter, but reversing decades of political reaction requires an appreciation of the scarcity of working-class agency, and that it be taken seriously where it emerges.

British Patriotism versus Scottish Nationalism?

For all the undoubted risks in nationalism, abstract anti-nationalism often functions as the alibi of powerful states and social classes. This is best illustrated by the Anglo-American practice of contrasting one's own patriotism with the nationalism of others. 'The vast majority of American authors employ the term "nationalism" whenever they write about other nations and "patriotism" in the context of the history of their own country', notes Miroslav Hroch.

'Any book that speaks of "American nationalism" is generally likely to have been written by a non-American writer. Put very simply: we are patriots, the others are nationalists. The matter is even more complicated in the case of British nationalism and British patriotism.'[18]

While George Orwell did more than anyone to popularise this dualism, there is something ironically Orwellian about contrasting the good patriotism of world-straddling empires with the toxic nationalism of the little people. Moreover, invocations of patriotism often exert a more coercive influence on public culture than those of out-and-proud nationalism, precisely because the term's apparent innocence leads would-be critics to miss its function in enforcing conformity. When centrist critics demanded that Jeremy Corbyn should 'be more patriotic', they meant, quite explicitly, that he should embrace flag, monarchy, the national-security state and a pro-American foreign policy. They were not calling for him to express a simple love of place and people – 'patriotism' as Orwell defined it – but rather to embrace the practices, rituals and symbols of a state still aspiring to world power. However, their true demand – that Corbyn 'be more nationalist' or even 'more imperialist' – would hardly command the same rhetorical force.

British people thus have a peculiarly confused and inconsistent relationship to nationalism, national identity and state power.[19] Moreover, that relationship has evolved markedly, particularly in the wake of Brexit. It is easily forgotten that, until recently, there was a common notion of British politics as uniquely innocent of nationalistic delusions. In 2006, when Gordon Brown – Nairn's 'bard of Britishness' – proposed a patriotic national holiday, the sceptics included Conservative opposition leader David Cameron. 'I think we should realise that Britishness is a concept that, if grasped too hard, slips away', he argued. 'This coyness, this reserve, is, I always think, an intrinsic part of being British. We are understated. We don't do flags on the front lawn.'[20] In Cameron's rendering, the UK, with its various national identities, was an essentially cosmopolitan state ruled by tolerance of diversity and an underlying rationalism, in contrast to the enthusiasms of the continent or America.

Today, Cameron's 'flags on the lawn' narrative is almost as unfashionable as the former prime minister himself. Since 2016, liberals no longer defend British 'patriotism' as unusually unproblematic; they have overthrown Orwell's cosy dualism and are now hyper-attuned to the delusional strains of British and American nationalism. Yet this new awareness involves a dubious tendency to ascribe all the problems of the British state and its national culture to overbearing Little Englanders – and to politicians held prisoner by an ignorant, irrational public majority. Alongside this there has been a search for the hidden folkloric root of British xenophobia, which James Meek has identified in appeals to St George and Robin Hood, and Fintan O'Toole locates in the introverted English nostalgia for empire and 1950s seaside holidays.[21] There is a strong strain of traumatised motivated reasoning in these narratives. In fact, some survey evidence suggests that British citizens, far from being xenophobes, are among the most pro-immigration in Europe.[22] (This tendency, incidentally, has a counterpart in liberal attitudes to America. In earlier decades, it was common to hear people say, 'I love the American people but hate the violence of American state power.' By contrast, in the Trump era, the more familiar framing today has been to exalt representatives of unelected state power, including former Bush administration officials, while condemning the bulk of the population as backward and ignorant.)

The bigger problem is that, in ascribing all of Britain's problems to introversion, most of British history is lost, including several decades that stretch between the start of the Thatcher period and the exit of Blair. It is worth remembering that the term 'little Englander', perhaps the most common epithet hurled at Brexiteers, was initially an insult aimed at Liberals who opposed the expansion of the British Empire. With this in mind, the imagined contrast between cosmopolitanism and racism is especially misleading: the missing link between the two is empire. If there is thus a certain reality of British cosmopolitanism, it is a reflection of the state's imperial ambitions, and subsequently its grandstanding as an auxiliary of US state power. Churchill, in that respect, epitomises the British cosmopolitan outlook – a sense of automatically belonging anywhere in the world that comes with white, English-speaking supremacism. (Equally, it involves no contradiction that Wilson, the founder of American global liberalism, was a segregationist and Klan supporter.)

Romantic imperial delusions were thus a feature of British politics long before 2016. Before that, the sense of historical mission bestowed by the imperial legacy had made Britain's ruling elite distinctively prone to foreign policy adventurism, irrespective of the wishes of populations. Efforts to justify these projects involved an endless stream of racial caricatures – thieving Argies, mad Mullahs, Irish terrorists – supplemented by liberal phrasemaking (humanitarian intervention, making the world safe for democracy, and so on) – all of them hand-crafted by elites in positions of state and media power. And far from being some right-wing aberration, this tendency reached its peak during a period of unparalleled centre-left dominance. 'Century upon century it has been the destiny of Britain to lead other nations', intoned Blair, lambasting his Conservative predecessors for cutting military spending. 'That should not be a destiny that is part of our history. It should be part of our future. We are a leader of nations or nothing.'[23] What thus emerges is an imagined sense of national purpose, defined less by a search for the ethnic foundations of British antiquity than by the residual sense of self-importance in the governing classes after the collapse of empire – given institutional expression by permanent membership of the UN Security Council.

Blair's well-publicised attraction to American neoconservatives is often ascribed to a characteristic servility to power: his post-leadership career, after all, has been as a service provider to various dictatorships. However, there were also underlying intellectual reasons for New Labour to admire Bush's Republican administration. Its agenda, linked to the philosophy of Leo

Strauss and the *Weekly Standard*, was based on a similar dilemma: how to build a unifying national myth in a cosmopolitan, globalised age. Blair and Brown's busy search for the essence of Britishness thus converged on a messianic foreign policy. As for the neoconservatives, this revolved around easily caricatured Bond villains, inevitably based on thinly disguised ethnic stereotypes, and inevitably involving some dubious revisionism about the British Empire. Much of Britain's transatlantic cultural elite bought in to this vision: witness the tragic final decade of Christopher Hitchens, or (Glasgow-born) Niall Ferguson and his endorsement of 'Anglobalisation'.[24]

Thus, with respect to British nationalism, the new prevalence of liberal critique disguises an underlying one-sidedness. Valluvan's *Clamour of Nationalism*, a book-length consideration of the vices of British national identity with a particular focus on the othering of Muslim communities, only makes two passing mentions of Iraq; Afghanistan and Libya are not spoken of at all. Indeed, with the exception of border policy and Brexit, there is little mention of foreign policy. This is despite what we know from the best of historical scholarship, Linda Colley's *Britons* being a prime example: Britishness asserts itself primarily against enemies defined by foreign policy.[25] Liberal scholarship has been marked by the importation of American campus categories of race, which (for all their anti-empire rhetoric) assess racism within self-contained national silos, framing an opposition between the morally awakened and the ignorant, rather than mobilising categories of class, state power and imperialism.

These biases have palpable consequences. The narrative that prevails in much of liberal commentary suggests the public imposes its ignorance on mainstream politics, flouting much of recent history, in which politicians and media operatives have constructed propaganda profiles to manufacture consent for what seemed to be an unending war effort. Ultimately, this one-sidedness leads to a failure to understand Brexit itself, even if we consider the Leave campaign with the most cynical eye. The turn to Brexit among a fraction of the

British elite reflected the exhaustion of national identities built around decades of fighting increasingly obscure foreign-policy foes, in which the British state was converted into a martial arm of globalisation, remaking the world in the image of Anglo-America. Britain's approach to that project exposed an underlying emptiness of national identity, and a pessimistic resignation about the limits of military power. This coincided with austerity: another project centred on limiting the ambitions of the state.

In understanding nationalism more broadly, there are dangers both in the cosmopolitan defence of Britain and in nationalist critiques of it. Britain, many claim, has no cohesive national identity, lacking an underlying sense of ethnic particularism (even the English language is global). The deeper truth disguised in this account is that all nations are, to a degree, invented by nationalism. While Britain is composed of diverse parts, it has arguably been historically more unified than, say, France, where only a minority spoke the national language until the twentieth century; or Germany, unified only in the late nineteenth century, which spent the Cold War divided and today has an essentially federal system; or Italy, a historical hodgepodge of languages and sovereignties where separatists have recently occupied government; or Spain, where regions preserve distinct languages and the Catalan independence movement is just as powerful as the Scottish. What has defined Britain is less its multiple ethnic components than its ongoing search for imperial aggrandisement – even if that has meant junior-partner status.

The Crisis of Internationalism from Above

All forms of contemporary nationalism around the world are shaped by the breakdown of neoliberal globalisation. Many, particularly on the left, continue to defend a cosmopolitan outlook on cultural grounds, but few now make the argument that imposing new rounds of 'economic reform' and 'open markets' will deliver rising living standards. Most are keenly aware that the earlier prosperity was an illusion built on a debt bubble. As voters desperately cast around for alternatives that might restore their power in a world of zero-sum competition, the result is political volatility. Nationalism's plausibility among groups on the political periphery, particularly rural and rust-belt voters, thus emerges from the breakdown of 'internationalism from above' (and from the vacuum where internationalism from below might have been). Britain, as an overdeveloped case, is no different; nor, for all the SNP's cosmopolitan affectations, is Scotland.

The crisis has been disorientating for much of the media and political establishment. Throughout the nineties and noughties, the free-trade, free-market, free-society regime seemed to score successes on all fronts. Ideologically, entrenched distinctions between left and right collapsed: Thatcher was correct to say that her greatest accomplishment was New Labour. Meanwhile, profits rose; and, despite rising inequality, voters embraced the new opportunities for debt-financed consumerism and home owner-ship – in any case, they had few other options. Today, by contrast, there are few takers for the old belief that the onset of a 'borderless world' will bring rising living standards for all. If a decade or so of stagnant living standards were not proof enough, the coronavirus crisis has confirmed that the old methods of neoliberal globalisa-tion cannot restore expectations of rising living standards to pre-crisis levels.

Nonetheless, what has emerged is less an optimistic vision of the future than a sense of resignation to inevitable decline. 'Capitalist realism', as described by Mark Fisher, has retained an imaginative hold, insofar as 'polarisation' in politics only rein-forces a collective failure to imagine a future beyond the endless present. Pessimism has often led the radical left to cling precisely to the institutions most implicated in the collapse of the old order. The obvious example is the EU: its role in crushing Greek popular sovereignty and imposing a punishing compromise on the leftist Syriza government in 2015 seemed only to reinforce leftist

Europhilia, as the EU was framed as a last bastion against the breakdown of civilisation into bankruptcy and civil war.

The crisis of neoliberal globalisation thus reinforced a link between activism and professional elitism, while also, with Syriza's capitulation, demonstrating the radical left's weakness of will and political agency. It would be wrong, of course, to suggest that working-class people across Europe uniformly oppose the EU. But whereas many voters see it as a necessary evil, the left has also tended to see it as protection against the perceived illiberal attitudes of the public, and thus embraces a European identity as a counterweight against the national framing of politics. This attitude carries inevitable markers of social class. While upper-professional and bourgeois identities often take European form, there have never been corresponding moves in working-class consciousness and democratic party-political structures.[26] This should hardly be surprising: democracy at the national level was hard-won; European 'democracy' was merely imposed. Working-class investment in Europe, so far as it exists, is depoliticised and essentially instrumental. The activist left's neuroticism about the risks of any national framing of politics has thus led to convergences with the Davos agenda of globalisation, just as the latter faced institutional collapse.

Scotland's role in this crisis is more complex than it might appear to the country's various ideological factions. Contrary to the remarkably persistent 'little Scotlander' stereotype, Scottish nationalism, as one of the family of European neo-nationalist movements that emerged in the 1970s, is both a product and a catalyst of globalisation. As Nairn has observed, cases like Scotland do not belong among earlier phases of nationalism that sought the autonomy to pursue a forced march towards industrialisation. Emerging at the tail-end of industrial capitalism, with elite business organisation moving towards multinational norms, neo-nationalist movements sought a 'seat at the table' within transnational spaces.[27] Far from 'retreating', they aimed to enhance the nation's competitiveness in wider markets. Even when the

movement was formally opposed to Nato and the EEC, it represented an ambition to break free of the limited bounds of Britain
and assert Scotland in larger bodies and spaces. Anyone remotely
familiar with recent SNP history would know this – which has not
stopped critics bemoaning Scottish parochialism.

Of course, while the SNP fully embraced market globalisation,
it displayed notable local quirks. Salmond was never a consistent
enthusiast for the US–UK mode of imposing liberal norms by
armed force: indeed, he was an acerbic critic of 'humanitarian
intervention' discourses even when the intelligentsia had fully
embraced them.[28] This reflected a strain in Scottish Nationalist
tradition, built up during years of outsider status in British politics, of identifying with anti-imperial movements. More recently,
for all its protestations, the SNP has been among the biggest beneficiaries of the crisis of neoliberal globalisation. Particularly in the
immediate aftermath of 2014, it drew support from the political
disenchantment of post-industrial housing estates facing punishing austerity at the hands of the Cameron–Clegg government –
which, it should be remembered, was a characteristically cosmopolitan version of the neoliberal revival. The SNP's messaging
response to crisis and austerity remains focused on combining
themes of national unity and strength; it has consistently fought
elections with the slogan, 'Stronger for Scotland'.

Yet critiques of the SNP that rest entirely on anti-nationalism
have a tendency to fall flat, partly because, after Brexit, Scottish
Nationalist leaders are licensed to play the same game. Indeed,
Sturgeon asserts,

> What those of us who do support Scottish independence are all
> about could not be further removed from some of what you
> would recognise as nationalism in other parts of the world. So
> the word is hugely, hugely problematic sometimes for those of
> us [for whom] Scottish independence is about self-government,
> it's about running your own affairs and making your own mark
> in the world.[29]

Before considering the prospects for rescuing internationalism from the wreckage of the global neoliberal order, the first step must be to develop a critical stance towards the Sturgeonite narrative – that is, to demonstrate its limits. Sturgeon is surely correct, in the outline above, to assert that self-government and 'running your own affairs' do not automatically equate to xenophobia. But the unanswered question is: What are the prospects for self-rule given the overweening influence of international economic forces and powerful states? While the traditional socialist left has always been the most consistent, especially in hard times, in opposing racism and building international solidarity, it has also been the most consistent in defending important national interests from forces of external control, whether military or economic. As Antonio Gramsci observed,

> The more the immediate economic life of a nation is subordinated to international relations, the more a particular party will come to represent this situation and to exploit it, with the aim of preventing rival parties gaining the upper hand ... From this series of facts one may conclude that often the so-called 'foreigner's party' is not really the one which is commonly so termed [i.e. the Communists], but precisely the most nationalistic party – which, in reality, represents not so much the vital forces of its own country, as that country's subordination and economic enslavement to the hegemonic nations or to certain of their number.[30]

Even at its seemingly most nationalistic, when directly pushing for independence, the SNP has proposed little to reverse Scotland's economic subordination to what the sociologist David Miller describes as the 'nested ruling class network' which is 'based only in part in Scotland'. As he notes, 'The economic and political decisions which affect Scotland are also made in London, in the US, at the EU, the IMF, the World Bank and the WTO.'[31]

The SNP's proposals rest on parcelling away sovereignty to many of these external forces, ranging from the less important (a Windsor head of state) to the more serious (monetary control to the Bank of England, fiscal control to the EU, military command to Nato). In many respects, then, elements of the SNP leadership become representatives of Scotland's subordination, as Gramsci might have predicted. The task of defending self-rule thus falls to the left. This, in fact, is what happens in practice: socialists in Scotland traditionally opposed Nato membership, sterlingisation – and even, in many cases, the EU itself: causes that are all embraced by the hardened 'realists' among the Scottish nationalist leadership. Socialists took this position not because indigenous elites are better people, but because they sought to maximise the prospects for the working class to exert democratic influence over the state and economy.

The Trouble with Nationalism

As a political ideology, nationalism – any nationalism, progressive or reactionary – entails the belief that what unites the national group is more significant than what divides it, class being chief among the latter. But independence does not have to observe this principle. Throughout history, leftists have routinely separated tactical support for independence movements from endorsement of philosophical nationalism. We would furthermore insist that 'internationalism' implies the prior existence of the national framework of politics, as implied in the history of socialist thought going back to Marx. Contrary to the claims of a generation of liberal social theorists, the nation remains the battleground of real political struggles, including those for international solidarity. The final task, then, is to offer a clearer account of why nationalism does pose a barrier to radical political movements.

The reality is of course that many SNP members and supporters are nationalists in the narrow sense. The so-called 'cybernats' – who bend every dispute, domestic or foreign, to fit the narrow opposition between Westminster and independence – rather obviously belong in this camp. The mere thought that state and nation might not coincide is an outrage to their philosophy. More importantly, Sturgeon also belongs in this group, insofar as abstract national unity forms a platform for unchallenged government, while proposals for independence – deferred indefinitely into the future – allow her to postpone any reckoning with the injustices that afflict Scottish society. There is also a growing number of liberal leftists who have such a catastrophist view of Westminster that they will happily shelve debates about the exact form independence should take until after the event. Regardless of how these groups choose to define themselves, all have embraced a nationalist outlook.

The slippery slope view, common since 2016, that equates nationalism with xenophobia, xenophobia with racism, and racism with fascism, must be discarded. Ironically, in the particular case of Scotland, the tendency to monster nationalism has ultimately had a disarming function: crude moralising against the SNP's 'toxic nationalism' collapsed after Brexit; subsequently, Scotland's liberals have lost all critical distance from Sturgeon's (still nationalist) government. This mode of complaint also does little justice to the variety of historical national movements, whether as a description of their functions or as a moral guide. There may be problems with Sinn Féin, the ANC or the PLO, but to dismiss them crudely as representing ethnic fundamentalism would be wrong both morally and factually.

Equally, even where nationalism does indeed draw upon xenophobic sentiments, as in the Brexit campaign and among Donald Trump's base, there is a tendency for abstract moral certainty to preclude deeper analysis. For liberals, the true danger of nationalism lies in its capacity to stoke conflict and its distraction from the 'reality' of globalisation. To address the core problem, these assumptions should really be flipped on their head. If anything, the specific problem of nationalism lies in its capacity to disguise more fundamental social conflict. Naturally, nationalists do make reference to real social injustices – Trump just as much as Sturgeon.

But what further unites Trump and Sturgeon is that they (indefinitely) postpone any reckoning with these problems in favour of deploying their rhetorical powers against other nation-states (or national identities).

Nobody would deny the huge differences between Sturgeon's nationalism and Trump's. Among the many differences, as a populist, Trump focuses on treacherous internal enemies, such as the liberal elite, while Sturgeon speaks of abstract Scottish unity and makes the aggressor, Conservative Westminster, purely external (she rarely, perhaps to her credit, speaks of traitors in Scotland's midst). From a liberal perspective this is Sturgeon's strength; but in other respects it is precisely the sort of tactic that an alert public culture should guard against, because it obfuscates real grievances and diverts them into channels that postpone domestic social change.

Faced with the easily monstered figure of Boris Johnson, Scottish civil society has allowed Sturgeon the room to engage in power grabs that would compromise any other government. Thus, at a central moment of emergency such as the pandemic, Scotland's business elite were given carte blanche to reimagine the Scottish economy. With grievances projected onto Westminster, former Tesco Bank CEO and current head of Buccleuch Estates, Benny Higgins, was invited to speak for Scotland's economic needs, with little protest from either wing of Scottish politics. In this way, the fixation on the evils of Westminster forestalls critical analysis of Scotland's underlying economic forces and power structures.

The risk of nationalism, as we understand it, is that it obscures and mystifies social division, and works to demobilise and incorporate forces of opposition. Nationalism, in this sense, is fully operational in Scotland, and this mode of nationalism is at its most potent precisely in the no-man's-land of devolution, with independence enjoying ideological hegemony yet only half-completed. Full independence would force some kind of reckoning with underlying grievances and injustices. But while independence is tantalisingly near but never realised, and there is an antagonist plausible enough to ensure pacified national unity, all internal problems can be postponed.

In many respects, the tactical questions surrounding national-ism and independence today would have made perfect sense to Marx and Engels. Their assessments always centred primarily on geopolitical consequences, and while Nato, the arms indus-try and British imperialism may not be uppermost in voters' minds (although the lingering impact of Iraq and Trident should not be underestimated), the geopolitical impact of inde-pendence has been pivotal to critical leftist thinking. By contrast, the Labour Party in all of its incarnations – except for that headed by the extremely idiosyncratic Jeremy Corbyn – has rarely criticised established UK foreign policy priorities. Partly, this reflects the fact that Labour imagines itself to occupy the moral high ground of internationalism; partly it reflects its imagined role as advocate for 'concerns on the doorstep' or 'in the communities'. But two decades of political shifts have left Labour in a dubious position to perform that role. Insofar as the term 'internationalism' retains emancipatory connotations, the SNP arguably represents internationalism more effectively; insofar as community sentiment is registered at the ballot box, the SNP is undoubtedly more in touch with feelings on the doorstep. The SNP's success in securing mass consent for an openly pro-immigration and anti-war platform – something Labour has never achieved – seems to rankle with many Labour members who should instead take the opportunity to learn from the SNP's example.

A second question the early Marxist tradition can give us insight into is the impact of Scottish independence on the remainder of the United Kingdom. The English left remains disorientated since Corbyn's departure, and has done little to examine the reasons behind the loss of working-class votes to the Conservatives. Too often, the automatic response to a defeat is to retreat from the struggle for political power, whether into depoliticised community

projects or abstract policy schemes. The pursuit of Scottish independence, by contrast, forces a reckoning with truly political questions of state power and the national frame of politics. For now, the
question of Scottish self-determination, in a context where
Westminster suppresses it, may provide tactical space in which to
reconceive the English left. A yet more exciting question is what
impact independence might have on political struggles in Ireland,
Catalonia, the Basque Country and elsewhere in Europe. As of
today, there are no precedents for the peaceful, democratic moves
towards independence to which much of Scotland aspires. Almost
regardless of whether independence has progressive outcomes, the
mere fact of setting the precedent could re-energise questions of
state power across Europe.

Our central claim is that the Scottish independence movement should embrace its place in a historical context. This will
entail resisting efforts to project problems of the contemporary
nation-state into the past – whether to the medieval period or to
the 1970s. Modern Scottish nationalism is a product of neoliberal globalisation; the post-2014 independence movement is a
product of its state of crisis, reflecting both the immediate effect
of austerity and the long-running democratic deficit. These
forces have collided with a peculiar post-imperial British state to
produce the present political deadlock. The result is a historic
moment of possibility – but one requiring clear-sighted leadership from a movement that has fully detached from the political
consensus of the nineties.

The failure of the anti-capitalist left to exploit the openings
that emerged between 2008 and 2020 hardly needs emphasis.
Too often, as with Corbynism in England and Syriza in Greece,
moments of excitement fizzled out when forced to reckon with
the antidemocratic pressures of internationalism from above.
Securing a remedy for this, and in the process reimagining class
politics, will require us to embrace a truly critical outlook on
nationalism, based on its failure to enact its supposed core principles of sovereignty, self-rule and democratic control. Policy

remedies such as the Green New Deal and the four-day week certainly have their place; so does community activism. But the left derives no credit from politely evading the democratic deficit, which only reinforces the gulf separating leftism from working-class communities.

3

The Emergence of a Movement for Scottish Independence, 2012–14

Conventional wisdom holds that a movement, or at least a campaign, for Scottish independence has been in existence since the middle decades of the last century. James Mitchell writes: 'Debate on Scotland's constitutional status and whether Scotland should be independent have been in the background, and occasionally foreground, of Scottish politics since the 1960s. In this sense, there has been a long campaign dating back decades.'[1]

For some, however, the nature of the movement (or campaign) has changed fundamentally in recent years. In an interview for David Torrance's 2009 biography of Margaret Thatcher, Alex Salmond claimed that the most significant impact she had made on Scotland was her 'politicisation of the self-government movement . . . [T]he movement over the past 100 years had been mainly cultural, and to some extent in the 1970s it was economic . . . She changed all that.'[2] 'Self-government movement' is a typically ambiguous phrase which can refer to supporters of either devolution or independence, or both. The former certainly existed, but the latter did not, at least until several years after Salmond gave this interview. There were members of the SNP and some smaller parties that wanted independence and stood for election on that basis, and there were the people who voted for them; but they did not constitute a 'movement'.

Until 2012–14, there was no 'campaign' or 'movement' for Scottish independence even in the way that there was a campaign against the Poll Tax and a movement against imperialist intervention in the Middle East. Supporters of independence were not organising demonstrations, petitions and debates, or mobilising in any general way. A demonstration on 30 September 2006 called by the short-lived pan-nationalist front Independence First mobilised – according to the organisers – 1,000 people.[3] In the case of the anti-war movement, however, positions registered in opinion polls were also expressed in action. On the demonstration of 15 February 2003, perhaps as many as 100,000 people protested against the Iraq war on the streets of Glasgow – people who had been mobilised over a period of months by local groups throughout the country, many of which remained in existence throughout the occupation that followed the fall of Saddam. In short, apart from a relatively small hard-core group who would have supported independence under any circumstances, most people who have considered doing so showed no sign of being prepared to do anything more than express a vague aspiration in opinion polls. Sometimes they would vote for parties that stood for independence along with – in the case of the Greens and the Scottish Socialist Party – many other things beside. Yet, in an extraordinarily short period of time, the hitherto missing movement for independence had finally taken shape. The neoliberal years created the conditions of possibility for a genuine independence movement, which we will argue was only realised during the independence referendum itself.

In order to appreciate the extent of the shift in popular support for Scottish independence after 2011, we need to begin with the relatively low levels at which it was recorded across the decades beforehand. The first data on support for independence was collected in 1974, on the eve of the neoliberal era, when it was recorded at 21 per cent. In polls where people were presented with a range of options – not simply a polar opposition between support for and opposition to independence – support for independence rose from 7 per cent in 1979 to 37 per cent at the time of the referendum in 1997, after which it fell back to 28 per cent in 1999, and to 29 per cent in 2002.[4] William Miller summarised the trend in relation to the other options: 'Over three decades . . . public support for independence increased by less than 6%, while support for devolution increased by 11%, and opposition to a Scottish parliament declined by 21%.'[5] In short, support for independence peaked at the time of the 1997 referendum and, with occasional fleeting movements in the opposite direction, declined over the following decade.

By a happy accident of timing, the Scottish Centre for Social Research carried out a survey between the Scottish election of May 2007, which resulted in the formation of the first minority SNP government, and August of the same year. It revealed that public support for independence, at 23 per cent, had fallen to its lowest point since the 1997 UK general election, while support for a devolved parliament with tax-raising powers, at 55 per cent, had risen to its highest level ever.[6] The survey confirmed what most people took for granted at the time: that no simple line could be drawn between support for the SNP, for self-government, and for independence.

Two longstanding trends are important here. One is that not everyone who voted for the SNP or the other pro-independence parties supported independence, suggesting that these parties attracted support for other reasons. This trend might appear to be cancelled out by the other, which is that support for independence always registered as higher than combined support for the SNP and the smaller pro-independence parties. Indeed, some polls conducted in the first years of the twenty-first century suggested that over 50 per cent of voters supported independence – an increase of 13 per cent over the previous peak (37 per cent), recorded at the time of the Devolution Referendum in 1997.[7] But the conclusion that inevitably follows is that people who were prepared to express a wish for independence in an opinion poll then voted for 'unionist' parties – above all the Labour Party – in actual elections, even though they knew that these parties were fundamentally opposed to independence. At the very least, this calls into question how strongly they held their views on independence.

Further evidence from this period tends to confirm that support for independence may have been relatively superficial. During the 1997 general election campaign, despite John Major talking up the 'constitutional threat' of devolution, one study of the election found: 'Out of 16 issues "constitutional issues/devolution" ranked 16th in importance with voters.'[8]

The lack of interest in matters constitutional was replicated again during the general election of 2001. One MORI/*Times* poll asked a sample of Scottish voters which issues were very important in helping them decide what party to vote for. Out of seventeen issues, 'constitutional issues/devolution' received the support of 8 per cent of the sample, coming in fifteenth place.[9]

Nor was support for independence consistent. David McCrone and Lindsay Paterson questioned the same cohort annually over the four-year period between 1997 and 2000. Among this group 45 per cent supported independence at least once, but only 7 per cent supported it on all four occasions, and only 14 per cent on three out of the four. The authors concluded: 'there is no stable core for independence', but added 'many more people are prepared to countenance independence if they were persuaded that it would generate more responsive government, and would be likely to produce the kind of society they aspire to'.[10] In short, until 2011, independence was a minority interest.

Delivering the Referendum

In May 2011 the SNP won a shock parliamentary majority. This gave it a mandate to hold an independence referendum; but the constitutional powers to grant one were, then as now, reserved to

Westminster. The stage was set for a showdown on the issue between Salmond and Tory prime minister David Cameron. Cameron sought to set the agenda in early 2012 by announcing that Westminster would legislate for a referendum if certain conditions were met. Central to the prime minister's thinking was the need to knock back Salmond's desire for including so-called 'maximum devolution' – or 'devo max' – on the ballot, in favour of the binary alternative for or against independence.

Simplistic accounts have assumed that the political situation was simply reducible to SNP support for independence and Tory support for the status quo. In fact, the majority of the leadership of both parties would have found devo max preferable, although for different reasons neither could publicly admit it. Devo max was the option overwhelmingly supported by most Scots at this point.[11] Although there are various conceptions of what exactly this might involve, its most complete version would have left the Scottish parliament in control of all state functions (including taxation), with the exception of those controlled by the Foreign Office, the Ministry of Defence and the Bank of England. The SNP leadership also believed that there was not a majority for independence – or at least not one that would survive the transition from opinion poll to voting booth. Devo max was therefore what it hoped to achieve – and more importantly, what they thought they could achieve – in the short-to-medium term. But although Salmond would have preferred three options to have been included in the referendum – status quo, devo max and independence – he could not openly argue for this without incurring the wrath of the 'fundamentalist' wing of his party, for whom anything less than independence would have been a betrayal. What he seemed to want was that enough popular pressure would be expressed through 'civil society' (in particular, the institutions of the Scottish professional and technical-managerial upper-middle classes, plus the Scottish TUC and its constituent trade unions) to have the devo max option included on the ballot paper – but without his direct intervention.

The situation was further complicated, however, by the fact that devo max would probably have been acceptable to a majority of Tories if it was understood as politically necessary. Cameron certainly wanted to win a vote against independence; but he was also aware that, even if this was achieved, the demand for further devolution would have been unstoppable, and would probably have resulted in pressure for a further referendum asking Scottish voters to choose between the status quo and devo max. Cameron effectively conceded this in a speech in Edinburgh on 16 February 2012, when he offered further measures of devolution if voters rejected independence.

In the event, Cameron resisted Salmond's preferred framing. His reason for insisting on a stark alternative between the status quo and independence was simple enough: he wanted to defeat the latter decisively – if not for all time, then at least for the foreseeable future – without allowing voters the escape hatch of devo max. The risks involved seemed small; he was as familiar as Salmond, after all, with polls showing minority support for independence, at around 29 per cent. Cameron was prepared to pay a high price for a one-question referendum. He eventually conceded to the SNP leader his demands for the enfranchisement of sixteen- and seventeen-year-olds, and for the right to decide on the date and nature of the question, thus enabling Salmond to frame his desired outcome as a positive (as opposed, for example, to: 'Should Scotland remain in the UK?'), and campaign for an upbeat 'Yes' outcome. These provisions were all confirmed by the Edinburgh Agreement, signed by Cameron and Salmond for their respective governments at St Andrews House on 15 October 2012. The official Yes campaign, Yes Scotland, was launched on 25 May the next year, and was unsurprisingly dominated by the SNP, with the Scottish Green Party and the Scottish Socialist Party in supporting roles. Its rival, Better Together, appeared on 25 June, uniting the Scottish Conservatives, the Scottish Liberal Democrats and Scottish Labour – the latter providing both the campaign's front man, in the shape of former chancellor Alistair Darling, and the bulk of its activists on the ground.

Some Labour activists sought to minimise their embarrassment at being in league with the Conservative enemy by pretending the entire business was simply a tiresome distraction from the class struggle, involving equivalent cross-class alliances on both sides. Pauline Bryan of Labour's Campaign for Socialism wrote: 'In Scotland we can see that the SNP and particularly the Yes campaign are a broad alliance across the political spectrum, and the referendum has resulted in the Better Together campaign which has the support of the Tories, Lib Dems and Scottish Labour. It takes the politics out of politics.'[12]

This was simply an evasion. The most obvious difference between the two sides can be expressed by identifying the forces which stood behind the No campaign: the supposedly neutral institutions of the British state, in particular the Treasury and the BBC; most British capitalists; UKIP and the British National Party; the Orange Order; the entire press, with the sole exception of the *Sunday Herald* – the more right-wing (such as the *Express* and the *Mail*) the more rabidly unionist they tended to be; President Obama and his ordained Democratic successor, Hillary Clinton; the EU Commission; and the rulers of all nation-states with insurgent nationalist movements.[13] In short, behind the three unionist parties stood the representatives and spokespersons of the British and international capitalist class, supporters of the current imperial ordering of the world system, and reactionaries and fascists of every description.

The Yes Campaign as a Social Movement

To understand the nature of the Yes campaign as it developed, especially in its last six months, it is instructive to compare it with the two previous referendums on Scotland's constitutional position. On the day of the 1979 vote on devolution, monitors reported 'no activity; no cars to polls; no literature; really pathetic . . . Political activity during the referendum campaign was significantly absent.' Similar reports were made in 1997: 'Apart from the media you would not have known there was a referendum ... The campaign was almost non-existent. No opposing campaign [to devolution] at all was evident.'[14]

The contrast between these dismal scenes and the aftermath of the 2014 campaign could not be more striking. Scottish journalist Paul Hutcheon recalled:

> Rather than consisting of activists manning jumble sales, the Yes movement was on its way to creating the 300 local community groups, 50 sectoral organisations and dozens of other spin-offs that would flood the country with pro-independence activity. Tens of thousands of people across the country were now involved: from self-generated local Yes groups, to National Collective and the left-wing Radical Independence Campaign . . . from individuals manning Yes cafes, to new recruits running drop in centres. Yes staffers knew the grass-roots campaign was working when they learned of large community debates they had not organised, run by local groups they did not know existed. Yes Scotland was now almost redundant – it had become a 'central services' resource for groups, providing literature, merchandise and email updates. By May 30 this year, the formal starting point of the referendum campaign, Yes was the biggest grass-roots political movement Scotland had seen.

Hutcheon wrote of 'two campaigns' – one traditional and led by the suits, arguing in conventional set-piece media debates; the other a 'ground war', 'one-to-one', 'door-to-door', 'intentionally bypassing the media'.[15] It was this 'other' campaign that had drawn in people from the previously marginalised housing schemes. In his research into the so-called 'missing million' of Scots who were either unregistered or chose not to vote, Willie Sullivan points out that their reasons were not what was commonly assumed: 'One key point ... is that they are not apathetic about where they live, or about the desire for it to be better. Any suggestion that non-voters are uninterested and broadly disengaged beyond voting was not borne out by the research.' On the contrary, they had perfectly rational reasons for political disengagement: 'Participants recognised that they have a choice in voting, but options arising through voting are set by others who are unlike them, and none of those options are felt to make much sense.'[16] The residents of these housing schemes did become involved in local movements for political activity. For example, organising against the construction of the M77 motorway across the public space occupied by Pollock Country Park on the South Side of Glasgow began in 1978, culminating in the establishment of Pollock Free State in the early 1990s. The problem was that, just as the votes of the inhabitants of Pollock were regarded as irrelevant by those in power, so too was their activity outside electoral politics.[17] But in the case of the independence referendum, there was going to be an outcome – and it was one which they could influence.

Much of the credit for beginning the process of involving these Scots must go to the Radical Independence Campaign (RIC). Starting as a conference in November 2012 attended by 800 people, it had grown by the following year's event to 1,200, and it was from this point that it began to operate as an active part of the campaign rather than simply a forum for discussion. A coalition of the left involving members of the existing left parties (including the Scottish Greens) and the left wing of the SNP, it helped initiate one of the most important aspects of the overall campaign – the voter-registration drives in working-class communities. Two founder members described part of the operation as follows:

The mass canvass took place in over 40 localities. We are now reaching into all major settlements in Scotland. But because we recognised that the poorest, most densely populated communities must bear the most votes and the most ready support for a decisive political and social change, we canvassed these areas the hardest. RIC is also concerned with a scheme for voter

registration and for recording the areas of greatest Yes support
– for remobilisation closer to the vote. We recognised early that
those voters who would buck the polling trend would be those
voters who don't talk to pollsters and hate politicians; those
voters who have told our activists: 'You are the only people to
ever ask me what I think about politics.'[18]

It would be wrong to credit RIC with all activities of this type – in
the north and west of Edinburgh, for example, groups like
Craigmillar Yes also conducted mass registration and canvassing
drives. RIC gave the campaign an initial push towards the left. But
initiative and creativity also emerged independently of any organised group, and in the most unlikely places. Journalist Lesley
Riddoch gives an example of a woman from the village of Farr,
near Inverness, who came to one of her meetings in Aberdeen – a
round-trip of 225 miles:

> She went home and chatted to another mum as they watched
> their children at the playground. Neither had organised a politi-
> cal event before but they enlisted like-minded friends to produce
> hundreds of posters, laminate and nail them onto every road
> junction within a 10-mile radius of the village hall, and replace
> them up to four times to cope with rain and naysayers. On the
> night, the women organised a PA system, got badges, stickers
> and books, produced food and drink . . . and opened the night
> with a fabulous, local all-women band. Around 250 people
> packed into Farr's tiny remote hall and the ensuing talk and
> discussion lasted almost four hours.[19]

Even unionist opinion-makers in the London press felt obliged
to report the packed public meetings, the debates in pubs and
on street corners, the animation of civic life.[20] Sober academic
analysis of the campaign also registered the level of
participation:

From early in the long campaign, grass-roots activists focussed
on registering voters in deprived communities and developing
strategies to ensure turnout was higher in such areas than
normal. Radical Independence campaigners were particularly
active in this respect . . . The degree of public engagement was
partly accounted for by the length of the campaign but also
reflected levels of political activism commentators agreed had
not been previously witnessed in Scotland.[21]

In Colin Barker's discussion of 'collective effervescence' (a term
borrowed from pioneer French sociologist Émile Durkheim), he
describes patterns of behavioural change which many participants
in the Yes campaign will recognise from their own experience:

> Participants in collective action regularly report that they
> 'discover' aspects of their selves, and their capacities, which they
> had not previously tested: speaking publicly, organising, taking
> initiatives which, before the event, they would not have imag-
> ined themselves doing. As a result, they felt 'more alive' . . .
> What was formerly desirable may now seem irrelevant or insuf-
> ficient, what was previously impossible now becomes an issue to
> be actively pursued.[22]

Many supporters of a Yes vote saw the closest parallels for the
campaign not in Scotland's own history, but in contemporary
Europe. As George Kerevan noted, 'By the end, the Yes campaign
had morphed into the beginnings of a genuine populist, anti-
austerity movement like the "Indignant Citizens" in Greece or the
May 15 Movement in Spain. Put another way, it was class politics
– not old-style nationalism – that fired the Yes campaign.'[23] Irish
journalist Peter Geoghegan ranged further in his comparisons:

> There was a carnival atmosphere in Glasgow's George Square on
> Wednesday 17 September 2014 . . . This was Scotland as I had
> never seen it before. The boisterous rally, organised largely on

social media, reminded me of places I had reported from –
Cairo's Tahrir Square, Occupy London, restive nights in the
Balkans – not the country I had lived in for the best part of a
decade. Like the 'occupied' public squares across Europe, the
atmosphere was febrile, driven by smart phones and nervous
energy.[24]

Project Fear and the Ruling-Class Offensive

As the Scottish historian Colin Kidd correctly noted, 'The welfare
state apart, Britishness inspires acquiescence rather than vocal
commitment among "No" supporters. Anxiety predominates.'
Kidd shared these anxieties: '[Salmond] is taking major risks – on
EU membership, cross-border pensions schemes, the currency,
and an economy geared for centuries to an integrated British
market.'[25] It was these issues on which the No campaign focused,
Darling even letting slip that the name that most aptly summarised the objectives of Better Together was 'Project Fear', the
essence of which was to terrorise the population with threats to
jobs, pensions and services.[26]

On 13 February 2014, Conservative chancellor George Osborne
came to Edinburgh to announce that all three unionist parties had
agreed that Scotland would not be allowed to join a currency
union with the rest of the UK (rUK) in the event of a Yes vote.
Salmond was widely mocked for his unwillingness, in the first of
his televised debates with Darling on 5 August, to say what Plan B
for the currency would involve if this commitment was honoured.
In fact, as he pointed out subsequently, there were another three
options – using the pound as a floating currency, adopting the
euro, or establishing a Scottish currency; but his core position was
that refusal would be irrational and self-defeating for rUK. That
may well have been the case (though it is at least debatable), but
from the perspective of the pro-independence left this was the
problem. A nominally independent Scotland would have been

caught between the hammer of the Treasury and the anvil of the Bank of England. As their price, the Bank of England–Treasury nexus would have likely demanded a fiscal compact setting a limit on the size of Scotland's structural deficit, as well as mirroring UK financial regulation (which indeed the SNP government's White Paper on independence was willing to offer). National tutelage beckoned. The arguments of No supporters therefore oscillated between two claims.

One involved pointing out that the SNP was deliberately impos-ing neoliberal policies as a matter of choice – the key evidence for this being Salmond's aim of cutting corporation tax by 3 per cent. This was indeed an odious policy, and one opposed by most Yes campaigners outside the SNP. But it was scarcely convincing coming from supporters of a Labour Party that had itself cut corporation tax by 5 per cent: the 2001 Scottish Labour manifesto even boasted that, under New Labour, 'corporation tax rates [had] been cut to their lowest levels ever'.[27]

The other claim was that the SNP might wish to deliver reforms, but would be helpless in the face of objections by international capital. 'The reality is that the left and labour movement in Scotland, decimated by decades of deindustrialisation and defeats, are currently too weak to shape a new Scottish state', wrote Seamus Milne. 'Instead the SNP and its business friends would be likely to do that – a neoliberal world where small states are at the mercy of corporate power without an exceptionally determined political leadership.'[28] Ben Jackson was similarly depressed:

> If left-nationalists aspire to something more radical than a social-democratic Labour government, then they are of course correct to suppose that no such agenda will be forthcoming from any British government in the foreseeable future. But they are wrong if they think that such an agenda will emerge in an independent Scotland. There is insufficient popular support in Scotland for such radical policies, just as there is insufficient popular support for it elsewhere in the United Kingdom.[29]

On his speaking tour against independence, George Galloway, then an MP for Respect, advanced his own brand of grim left unionism: 'Do you honestly think that a UK company is going to situate in a more socialist Scotland when the Tory government had created the perfect low tax, low regulation, low wage capitalist environment?'[30] But consider the utterly defeatist implications of these positions: if financial markets and capitalist investment strategies would prevent an independent Scotland moving leftwards, that would also be true of the UK. These arguments – if taken seriously rather than being used as a convenient stick with which to beat the Yes campaign – would mean there was no point in even beginning to initiate radical change of any sort, including within the UK as a whole.

The UK elite's sense of post-imperial entitlement was not, of course, foregrounded by Better Together. Though the No campaign got off to an underwhelming start – Darling was a wooden performer; Brown was sulking and refused to participate – this did not really matter, since its real cadre was provided by the media, above all the BBC. An analysis of media coverage halfway through the campaign found that STV's *News at Six* and the BBC's *Reporting Scotland* typically presented the No campaign's scaremongering press releases as if they were news reports, with headlines such as: 'Scottish savers and financial institutions might be at risk if Scotland votes for independence', 'Row over independence could lead to higher electricity bills'. In terms of the running order, the BBC's *Reporting Scotland* would typically lead with 'bad news' about independence, then ask a Yes supporter to respond. Presenters put hard questions to Yes supporters, but passive soft-balls to No supporters. Yes campaigners were consistently referred to as 'the separatists' or 'the nationalists', even when, like the Scottish Green Party's Patrick Harvie, they explicitly disavowed the label. 'Expert opinion' from the UK government side – the Office for Budget Responsibility, the Institute for Fiscal Studies, Westminster committees – was treated as politically neutral, while its

Holyrood equivalents were always signalled as pro-SNP. The Yes campaign was repeatedly associated with the personal desires of Alex Salmond – 'Salmond wants . . .' – while no such equation was made for No figures. Airtime for the No campaign was bumped up by the inclusion of responses from all three unionist parties to any statement from Salmond. Television news reports often ended with particularly wild and unsubstantiated statements – that GPs and patients were planning to move to England (*Reporting Scotland*); that the SNP's anti-nuclear policy would bring 'economic disaster' (STV); that insurance companies were looking at 'billions in losses' and 'potential closures' (*Reporting Scotland*).[31] The result was to radicalise Yes campaigners' understanding of the media, since the experience of their own eyes and ears was so fundamentally at odds with what they saw on TV. One example out of hundreds is the way the BBC ignored a Yes demonstration of 10,000 people on 13 September at the top of Glasgow's Buchanan Street, yet filmed Labour No supporters Jim Murphy and John Reid with perhaps thirty supporters at the bottom of the same street.[32]

The print media were less homogeneous. In addition to Scottish editions of the London press – the *Guardian*, *Independent*, *Telegraph*, *Mail*, *Express* and the Murdoch titles – the 'native' Scottish press consists of the *Scotsman*, the *Herald* and the *Daily Record*, plus their separately edited Sunday editions. Only the *Sunday Herald* called for a Yes vote – and that quite late in the day, although the *Herald* itself, and to a lesser extent the *Daily Record*, were relatively balanced; both Darling and Salmond edited special editions of the latter, for example. Even so, No campaign themes were given overwhelming prominence. Foremost among these were the currency, job losses from companies flocking south, budget deficits leading to cuts in the NHS (a *Daily Record* favourite), anxiety about pensions (particularly for the *Express*, whose readership is mostly over sixty-five), increased taxes (Scottish *Daily Mail*) and rising prices in supermarkets. A sub-theme was security: would Nato still want us? Would Russia invade? Would

Isis blow up the oil platforms? Finally, there was the 'proud Scot' theme: you can be patriotic and still vote No.

While the Scottish press kept up the relentless drumbeat of Project Fear, London's left-liberal unionists painted the Yes campaign as consisting of quasi-Nazis, bringing 'darkness' upon the land. For Will Hutton, Scottish independence meant 'the death of the liberal enlightenment before the atavistic forces of nationalism and ethnicity – a dark omen for the 21st century. Britain will cease as an idea. We will all be diminished.' For the editor of the *New Statesman*, 'the portents for the 21st century are dark indeed'. For Martin Kettle, the 'dark side' of the Yes campaign – 'disturbing', 'divisive' – must not be ignored. For Philip Stephens, Salmond had 'reawakened the allegiance of the tribe'. Polly Toynbee provided the more upbeat rendition of Labour unionism – 'It's no time to give up on a British social-democratic future.'[33]

Darling and Blair McDougall, Better Together's campaign chief, had early on identified the SNP's position on sterling as a weak point. In the face of George Osborne's promise that an independent Scotland would be locked out of sterling, the SNP's unspoken preference for devo max was a major handicap: a really determined new-state project would have prepared fully costed plans for an autonomous currency. The No campaign seized on this weakness and hammered it home relentlessly.

The Moment of Crisis

Complacent and assured of victory for the majority of the campaign, the British ruling class was seized by sudden panic as it entered its penultimate week. A YouGov poll published in the *Sunday Times* on 7 September put Yes in the lead for the first time, with 51 per cent. The reaction was well captured by a headline in the *Financial Times*: 'Ruling Elite Aghast as Union Wobbles'.[34] This has been described as a 'rogue' poll, but it was not quite as isolated as is sometimes represented. Two days later the *Guardian* reported that a new poll by TNS had 'found that support for independence has jumped by six points in the last month, putting the yes vote at 38% and the no vote at 39%, wiping out a 12-point lead for the pro-UK campaign led by former chancellor Alistair Darling'.[35] According to Lord Ashcroft's data, only 48 per cent of Yes voters had made their minds up before the final month of campaigning, and it is at least conceivable that this was reflected in YouGov's findings.

What happened next was instructive about how the British ruling class operates. Downing Street held a reception for business leaders: 'He left us in no doubt we should speak out', said one chief executive who attended. Campaign leaders from the unionist parties made calls: 'Those phone calls can be very persuasive', said one figure familiar with the operation.[36] By Thursday, 11 September, businesses were competing to warn of the dangers of Scottish independence. First the oil companies Shell and BP claimed that jobs were at risk in Aberdeen and Shetland; then a stream of banks and financial institutions including the Royal Bank of Scotland (RBS), Lloyds Banking Group, Standard Life and Tesco Bank announced contingency plans for the departure of their headquarters from Edinburgh to London; finally Asda, John Lewis, and Marks and Spencer threatened inevitable price rises. Many of these companies wrote to individual staff members highlighting the threat to their continued employment in the event of independence – a none-too-subtle hint about how they were expected to behave in the polling booth and a genuine example of intimidation – although it was of course not reported in that light. The example of RBS is particularly interesting in relation to the unity between state and capital in this operation. On the evening of Wednesday, while the RBS board was discussing whether to announce to its shareholders a plan to move its registered office to London, officials at the Treasury were already emailing the BBC about the decision – forty-five minutes before it had been made, although the BBC reported it immediately as established fact.[37] These manoeuvres were in most respects simply an amplification of existing components of Project Fear, but now voiced by representatives of capital themselves.

Rupert Murdoch, no less, was alerted to the potential problem on a visit to Scotland, as Joe Pike recounts:

> Senior politicians in the No campaign believe Rupert Murdoch expected something very different from what he found on his visit to Aberdeenshire and Glasgow 55 days before the referendum. 'I think he arrived with a preconceived vision of Celtic low-tax tiger', said one source. 'Then he saw Trots on the street.' . . . [Murdoch] would later tweet: 'Have to worry about some of Salmond's allies. Far-left socialists and extreme greenies. Must change course to prosper if he wins.'[38]

British ruling-class concerns about independence, primarily geopolitical, were well expressed six months before the vote by a Labour figure: George Robertson. A Scottish MP from 1978, opposition defence spokesperson from 1992, minister for defence in the Labour Government from 1997, and secretary general of Nato from 1999, in 2004 he was finally rewarded for his services to Western imperialism by being elevated to the House of Lords as Baron Robertson of Port Ellen. In a hysterical speech to the Brookings Institute in Washington on 7 April, Robertson said that the 'loudest cheers for the breakup of Britain would come from our adversaries and from our enemies. For the second military power in the West to shatter this year would be cataclysmic in geopolitical terms.' The only beneficiaries, Robertson intoned, would be 'the forces of darkness', among which he appeared to include the national movements in Catalonia, the Basque Country and Flanders.[39]

These are not simply the twilight ravings of a Labour buffoon. The threat of removal of nuclear weapons from Scotland was real, and there are virtually no other deep-water bases on the UK coastline where the submarines that carry them can be docked. Peter Hennessy, historian and member of the House of Lords, confided to his Referendum diary on Friday, 5 September his concerns about the fate of the UK's nuclear arsenal – concerns which no doubt reflected those of his confidants in Whitehall: 'There's still no contingency planning happening on Faslane/Coulport . . . To replicate the base somewhere in remainder of the UK would take 20 years and [add] an extra £20 billion to the cost of keeping ourselves a nuclear-weapon state . . . the Ministry of Defence is sans plan, sans costed options, on any of these things.'[40]

In fact, the Ministry of Defence did eventually calculate the potential cost of relocating Trident from the Clyde to the south of England at £35 billion; elsewhere in Whitehall, other concerns of a non-financial nature were being voiced. The Foreign and Commonwealth Office regularly expressed fears that the UK might be removed as one of the five permanent members of the UN Security Council – with the power of veto that position confers – as the result of an Argentinean conspiracy backed by other Latin American states and India, which would be well placed to inherit the position of its former colonial master.[41] Serious organs of ruling-class opinion made similar judgements in the final weeks of the campaign. 'Unionists elsewhere in the UK should admit more than a modicum of self-interest', wrote Phillip Stephens in the *Financial Times*: 'The loss of Scotland would diminish Britain in almost every dimension one can think of.'[42] The *Economist* agreed: 'The rump of Britain would be diminished in every international forum: why should anyone heed a country whose own people shun it? Since Britain broadly stands for free trade and the maintenance of international order, this would be bad for the world.'[43] In other words, Scottish secession would at the very least make it more difficult for Britain to play its current role in the 'international order', if only by reducing its practical importance for the United States.

Finally, the British ruling class was also aware that an immediate consequence of a vote for Scottish independence would be to place a question mark over the existential viability of Northern Ireland, since the Union has always been with Britain, not England, as Ulster unionists of all varieties were perfectly well aware. The rump of the British state might thus be reduced still further.

New Labour's Rescue of the British Nation-State

The possibility of a Yes victory arose because of shifts in attitude among two groups: former non-voters who were registering in order to vote Yes, and Labour voters who were disregarding their instructions to vote No. By this point, the British ruling class genuinely believed that a Yes vote was possible, and the burden of responsibility that weighed on the Scottish Labour Party to save the Union was therefore immense. But the panic of 6 September also resulted in a new theme being introduced into the rhetoric of Better Together. This theme was not exactly Hope – always a dangerous emotion to arouse if your intention is ultimately to bury it beneath new waves of austerity – but Vaguely Uplifting if Unspecific Sentiments about Our Shared Past, Present and Future. One figure was absolutely central to this endeavour: Gordon Brown.

Immediately prior to the referendum, psephologist John Curtice told the *Economist*: 'The truth is that David Cameron is reliant on Gordon Brown to save his skin.'[44] Brown certainly did his best. During a speech at a Labour rally in Maryhill on the eve of the poll, he strutted and fretted his hour upon the stage, impressing metropolitan journalists with his 'passion': 'And what we've built together with solidarity and sharing, let no narrow nationalism split asunder.'[45] As George Monbiot justly remarked,

> There's another New Labour weasel word to add to its lexicon (other examples include reform, which now means privatisation; and partnership, which means selling out to big business). Once solidarity meant making common cause with the exploited, the underpaid, the excluded. Now, to these cyborgs in suits, it means keeping faith with the banks, the corporate press, cuts, a tollbooth economy and market fundamentalism.[46]

The overblown and barely coherent verbiage to which Brown treated his audience was mainly for internal Labour consumption, to stiffen the sinews and summon up the blood of the waverers; but he had other admirers. Tory intellectual Allan Massie called Brown's speech 'the rhetorical highpoint of the debate. It gave renewed heart to Unionists of all parties.' Tory MSP Murdo Fraser spoke of how there had been 'an urgent need for the No campaign to stop this leakage of Labour support and who better to address this but Gordon Brown'.[47]

Brown's most important intervention in relation to the outcome was actually made on 8 September, when he – a back-bench opposition MP – announced a fast-track timetable for further devolution, beginning on 19 September, in the event of a No vote. In doing so he was merely consolidating the desperate promises made by all three of the unionist party leaders after the YouGov poll showing Yes in the lead. Sure enough, on 16 September, Cameron, Clegg and Miliband all appeared on the front of Labour's loyal (at this time) Scottish tabloid, the *Daily Record*, their signatures adorning a mock-vellum parchment headed 'The Vow', confirming that the Scottish parliament would indeed be granted further powers if only the Scots would consent to stay within the Union. It is worth pausing for a moment to consider the meaning of this episode. Cameron, it will be recalled, had been so anxious to exclude a third option of further devolution from the ballot paper that he gave Salmond everything else he demanded in order to achieve it. Now, facing the unthinkable, he and the other unionists had effectively changed the nature of the question within a fortnight of the ballot taking place. From being a choice between the status quo and independence, it had effectively become a choice between devo max and independence – even though tens of thousands had already used their postal votes, unaware that the terms of the referendum would shift.

On the basis of Ashcroft's polling, the majority of No voters (72 per cent) had already decided on their position before the final month of campaigning; and among this group, reasons for doing so included concerns about the pound (57 per cent), pensions (37 per cent), the NHS (36 per cent) and defence and security (29 per cent).[48] What the Vow seems to have done was shift a fraction of the undecided towards voting No, while giving some existing No voters – particularly in the Labour Party – a justification for voting No that was not simply based on fear. As we noted earlier, when the referendum was first announced, the majority position was for devo max. What happened in the course of the campaign was that, having no way of expressing their position in the ballot, voters in the devo max camp polarised, the majority opting for independence as being closer to their desired outcome. The late reintroduction of devo max as the alternative to independence was enough to sway a sufficient number of voters into retreating from their recent conversion. The very success of the Yes campaign had pushed the political leadership of the British state into side-lining Better Together by offering their only remaining induce-ment: constitutional change short of independence. But it is almost certain that the unionist parties would have offered this anyway.

On 11 September, sixty English and Welsh Labour MPs arrived at Glasgow Central Station on the so-called 'Love Train' or 'Save the Union Express'. They were met not only by their Scottish colleagues but by Yes supporter Matt Lygate, who accompanied them along Buchanan Street on a rickshaw with a sound system playing 'The Imperial March' from *Star Wars* and declaiming through a loudhailer: 'Our imperial masters have arrived!' and 'People of Glasgow! Welcome your imperial masters!' One notably humourless target of this comedic highpoint of the campaign complained: 'The implication is that Scotland, like Kenya or India, is just another colony, at last seeking its rightful independence.'[49] In fact, most Yes supporters are perfectly aware that Scotland was not a colonised or oppressed nation. The point was more about Labour's attitude towards its supporters – the assumption that they could simply be summoned to vote in obedience to the leadership's wishes – than Scotland's position in the world order. But there is a sense in which describing Labour as 'imperial masters' is wrong; it is of course not the master but the ever-eager servant of Empire.

Participation and Outcome

By the time the electoral register closed on 2 September 2014, 97 per cent of the Scottish population had registered to vote – 330,000 for the first time, including 109,000 of the sixteen- and seventeen-year-olds specially enfranchised for the occasion. This was the highest level of voter registration in Scottish, or indeed British, history since the introduction of universal suffrage: 118,000 people registered in August alone. By the time the ballot closed on 18 September, 84.6 per cent had voted, compared with 63.8 per cent in the 2010 British general election and 50.4 per cent in the 2011 Scottish parliamentary election. The most recent general election with comparable levels of Scottish voter participation to 2014 was 1950 – the first to follow the Second World War and the establishment of the welfare state – when 83.9 per cent of registered voters submitted a ballot. But turnout in 2014 was also significantly up from the 60.4 per cent who had voted in the 1997 referendum, leading to the establishment of the Scottish parliament. Shortly after that event, Eric Hobsbawm remarked: 'We would have thought it impossible, 20 years ago, that only 60% of the citizens would vote in the first election for a Scottish parliament in three hundred years, an election supposed to realise the historical ambition of the people of that country.' He went on to contrast the behaviour of the Scots unfavourably with that of black South Africans in 1994, before drawing this general conclusion: 'Elections in the West are increasingly events managed by minorities, which do not involve majorities, at the cost of the integrity of the political process.'[50]

Whatever else might be said about the outcome of the referendum, no one could claim that it was determined by a minority in conditions of generalised apathy. 'Turnout was lowest in Glasgow', notes James Mitchell; but even there, 'at 75% it was still higher than it was at any election in Scotland as a whole since 1992.'[51]

Yet the nature of the outcome cannot be evaded. After such extraordinary levels of voter registration, and only marginally less impressive turnout, Scotland ultimately opted against establishing its own state by 55.3 per cent to 44.7 per cent. Only four regions out of thirty-two voted Yes – although, as we shall see, their location and composition were highly significant. Other than the number of votes for each side, and their breakdown at regional and constituency levels, what else do we know about the result? Here a certain amount of impressionism is unavoidable. Two opinion polls were carried out during and immediately after the referendum.[52] Beyond these, we have had to rely on a combination of personal participant-observation, information from others involved in the campaign, and media reports. In spite of the difficulties, a number of tendencies are relatively clear:

Age: Over-forty-fives were most likely to oppose independence, and particularly the over-sixty-fives, among whom between two-thirds and three-quarters voted No. Young voters (between sixteen and twenty-four) were almost evenly split and, while Ashcroft's claim that 71 per cent of the newly enfranchised sixteen- and seventeen-year-olds voted Yes is unsupportable because of the smallness of his sample, it is nevertheless clear that they did not form the anti-independence bloc that had initially appeared possible. The only age cohort with an unambiguous majority for independence was those between twenty-five and thirty-nine, although (since the polls measure overlapping age-ranges) this may also have been true of those between forty and fifty-four.

Gender and ethnicity: Between 3 and 9 per cent more women voted No than men – though that may partly have reflected female predominance in the older age groups; the extent of female opposition to independence in any case reduced over the course of the campaign. Based on pre-referendum polling, as many as two-thirds of Scots of Asian origin may have voted Yes – a fact of some significance in Glasgow, where this group has long been regarded as loyal to Labour.[53]

Class: Data compiled by John Mellon in June 2014 showed the level of support for independence to be highest among supervisors, small business owners and routine workers (assembly-line workers, waiters and cleaners, and so on), with intermediate workers (secretaries and computer operators) and senior managers showing the lowest support for independence.[54] As this suggests, the Scottish bourgeoisie was overwhelmingly against independence. With a handful of exceptions – notably Brian Souter of Stagecoach and Jim McColl of Clyde Blowers Capital – large-scale capital was committed to the Union. Yes-supporting businesses tended to be small- or medium-sized concerns whose owners and employees were on the borders of the petty bourgeoisie proper, relying on local markets and suppliers. Yes-supporting employers, mostly grouped in Business for Scotland, were criticised in the unionist press precisely because of their lack of support among big capitalist firms.[55] The contrast between them and the businesses supporting No – including Keith Cochrane of Weir Group, James Lithgow of Lithgow's and Ian Wood of Wood Group – could not be more stark.[56]

The middle classes were also largely united in voting No, their bohemian and cultural wings being the main sources of dissent. The tendency in middle-class areas was clear. Peter Geoghegan reported from a canvass in Bishopbriggs, one of the leafier parts of Glasgow, late in August:

The streets were lined with neatly manicured lawns, and pebble-dashed semi-detached houses. There was little sign of the referendum. Unlike other parts of the city, the living room windows were free of posters; there were no flags or stickers in the back-seats of cars. This was the land of 'the quiet No's', softly spoken but firmly against leaving the Union . . . As we left, one of the canvassers totted up the scores in the rapidly fading light. No: seven. Undecided: three. Yes: zero.[57]

But the working class – still the overwhelming majority of the Scottish population – was deeply divided. Support for Yes came most strongly from the poorest and most precarious communities, often in the peripheral housing schemes – indeed, it was from this group that most of the new voters emerged. The Scottish Referendum Study found those who 'fear[ed] unemployment', were in the lowest quarter of income earners, and were social-housing tenants were more likely to be correlated with Yes support, while mortgage owners and those in the top quarter of income earners tended to vote No.[58] The testimony of one Yes campaigner in Edinburgh about his experience on the day of the referendum backs this up:

> I visited two areas to get the Yes vote out. The first one was Dryden Gardens [in Leith] which was made up of mainly well-paid workers and pensioners living in terraced houses. On the knocker half of them had changed their vote [to No] or were not prepared to share their intentions with me. I remember being thoroughly depressed by the experience. Following this, I walked round the corner to some Housing Association flats that were more blue-collar with a large number of migrant families. Every Yes voter I spoke to had held firm and had already voted or [was] waiting on family to go and vote together. It was very uplifting.[59]

The social geography of the vote bears this out. The No heartlands lay in the rural districts – Dumfries and Galloway (66 per cent No), Aberdeenshire (60 per cent) – and in traditionally conservative Edinburgh (61 per cent).

One striking feature of the working-class Yes vote was that it was concentrated in what had formerly been the great heartlands of Labour support. In Dundee and Glasgow, the Yes vote reached, respectively, 57.4 per cent and 53.5 per cent, with similar results recorded in North Lanarkshire and West Dunbartonshire; Inverclyde came within eighty-seven votes of a Yes majority. These five regions alone accounted for over a quarter of Yes votes. Partly because of these shifts in the Labour heartlands, the final result for the Yes side was better than had seemed possible when the campaign began in 2012. Of the fifty-one polls conducted between 1986 and 2012, thirty-nine showed support at between 30 and 39 per cent, and only three showed it above 40 per cent, while nine showed it below 30 per cent. Crucially, however, the majority of the latter were conducted after the establishment of the Scottish parliament in 1999 – in other words, the lowest support for independence was found nearest to the decision to hold the referendum.[60] As recently as May 2013, two pollsters associated with Ipsos Mori had claimed that, with two-thirds of voters intending to vote No, the outcome was not in doubt.[61] In this context, the result was a miraculous turnaround, only possible because of the sudden emergence of a mass independence movement that began in 2012.

British Nationalism Rejoices

The concerns of Scottish historian Colin Kidd about the prospect of a Yes vote, noted above, were followed by this response to defeat: 'The relief was visceral . . . coming to at 4.00 a.m. I experienced a calm I hadn't felt for months. I sensed that the nationalists [sic] had lost. Total silence: the sound of the quiet Unionist majority celebrating.'[62]

His relief was widely shared, and not only by this silent majority. No sooner was the result beyond dispute than markets began to rally: the value of stocks in Scottish-based financial companies, which had been in freefall during the final stages of the campaign, soared by £2 billion, with RBS and HBOS leading the way. The FTSE 100 index rose by 18.6 points. Even sterling reached a two-year high against the euro and a two-week high against the dollar, before falling back. According to Cameron, the monarch 'purred' with delight on being told the result. The prime minister himself knew that he would not now go down in history as the modern Lord North, responsible for 'losing' Scotland as his predecessor had 'lost' America – but also, more importantly, that he had averted what one *Telegraph* columnist described as 'the biggest constitutional crisis in the nation's history', a crisis which would have engulfed not just the coalition government, but the entire British political system.[63] Nor was the relief felt only in the UK itself. Ulster Loyalists relaxed. In Washington, Obama and Clinton could rest easy in the knowledge that their client's nuclear arsenal would remain safely ensconced on the Clyde. Spanish prime minister Mariano Rajoy no longer worried that independence movements in Catalonia and the Basque Country would be able to draw sustenance from the Scottish example.

As the counts were declared, Labour activists had exulted alongside their supposedly hated Conservative enemies. The *Observer*'s Scottish columnist Kevin McKenna quoted a conversation with his daughter Clare, who had become a Yes activist during the campaign: 'So many on the side of the rich and powerful must have been cheering themselves hoarse about the no vote and there were Labour people, our very own, cheering and dancing with them.'[64]

Early in the evening of 19 September, this book's authors took part in the first of many discussions about the future of the Scottish left following the referendum. Davidson had to catch an early train home and, after leaving us in a café on Ingram Street in Glasgow's Merchant City, wandered into George Square, which in the weeks prior to the vote had been the site of daily mass gatherings of Yes supporters – not to listen to formal speeches or participate in rallies, but to meet, discuss, sing, or simply to make visible the size and diversity of the movement. It was as if people who were canvassing, leafleting or flyposting – activities that tend to be carried out in small groups – had to return to the square to refresh themselves in a public space over which they had regularly taken collective control. It was in these days that Glasgow most resembled the Greek and Spanish cities during the Movement of the Squares – to a far greater extent than in the relatively small-scale Scottish manifestations of Occupy.

But on this evening Yes supporters were scattered, most of them overcome with grief. The square was filling with triumphant Orange Lodge members, minus their regalia, alongside the outright fascists of Britain First and the Scottish Defence League, singing 'Rule, Britannia' and 'God Save the Queen', waving Union Jacks, burning Saltires, throwing Nazi salutes and howling homophobic, racist and sectarian abuse. The poisonous pus was seeping from the wounded, fever-ridden body of the threatened state, the monstrous id of British nationalism awakened by the menace of Scottish self-determination.

4

The Collapse of Scotland's Red Wall

The year 2015 was marked by a historically disastrous general election for Scottish Labour. As the party once synonymous with Scotland lost thirty-nine of its forty constituencies, the electoral map was transformed overnight, from an autumnal pattern of Central Belt reds (Labour) and Highland oranges (Liberal) to a wall of yellow (SNP) disturbed by a small intrusion of rural blue (Conservative). Labour's presence was all but invisible, and journalists busy reporting heavy losses in the party's 'heartlands' could thus be forgiven for overlooking a solitary red dot in Scotland's capital city. This was Edinburgh South, where Labour not only won but even increased its share of the vote.

In understanding Labour's underlying weaknesses, however, that one victory may be just as revealing as dozens of defeats. Edinburgh South is said to typify 'the elegance and grace of bourgeois districts', and contains such fashionable property hotspots as Morningside and the Grange.[1] Solidly Tory for seven decades going back to World War I, it was held until 1987 by Michael Ancram, a hereditary marquess and Bullingdon Club veteran. Ancram would even beat the future prime minister, Gordon Brown, who contested his first election there before being

promoted to the then safely Labour, working-class seat of
Dunfermline East. Nonetheless, for Brown and other east-coast
modernisers like Alistair Darling, taking Edinburgh South was
truly symbolic of their ambitions. It represented an aspiration to
become Scotland's 'one nation' party, able to speak imaginatively
for everything from Keir Hardie's Lanarkshire heartlands to
Morningside, the home of Scotland's first Waitrose.

Edinburgh South thus foreshadowed the social class coalition
that led the New Labour project. The 2015 election, by that logic,
represented the collapse of that coalition under its own contradictions. Edinburgh South was now not merely the 'safest [Labour]
seat in Scotland', as Brown observed, but also their only remaining
safe seat: the party's new heartland.[2] Here was a clear realignment
of class politics: Labour clinging to the capital city's establishment
as working-class voters turned to an SNP energised by the democratic spirit of the 2014 referendum.

If this may appear an exaggeration, subsequent events have
done little to correct the impression. After an initial recovery –
Scottish Labour won back six seats in 2017 – the party slumped
again in 2019, beaten back to one seat: Edinburgh South. Worse,
the tendencies that had seen the party lose swathes of Scotland
now ran rampant across the party's 'red wall' in Northern England
and Wales. Thus, while class and regional inequalities are just as
much of a feature of British sociology as ever, Labour's role in
representing these forces has shifted. Even a radical lurch to the
left did little to correct the problem: Chris Bickerton suggests that
while 'ideologically, Corbynism was a break from New Labour
centrism . . . sociologically, it was more Blairite than Tony Blair'.[3]

Across Britain, the geography and social composition of Labour
voting has shifted under the pressure of one crisis of capitalism
and two referendums on the future of the British state: in all three
cases, the party had defended the status quo and underestimated
the complex grievances of its working-class electorate. It would be
wrong to say that the outcome made Labour a middle-class party:
the electoral landscape is too fragmented to make that a fair

assessment. But it would be correct to say that decades of deliberate 'modernisation', combined with underlying economic changes, had left Labour with a disorganised relationship to its working-class traditions, unmoored from any base of tribal loyalty. Its new social base reflected the post-neoliberal, atomised, individualist society that New Labour had done so much to promote. But these problems only became apparent when Labour had to ask its voters to observe loyalty to the constitutional status quo during a wrenching era of austerity. That precipitated a final breach between the party and its social foundation, with ongoing implications for Britain's state form.

New Times and Heartlands: The Social Roots of Scottish Labour Decline

Whole generations of Scots were raised to believe that voting Labour was intrinsic to national consciousness and working-class traditions. These principles formed a core part of Scottish identity during the Thatcher years, even to outright Scottish nationalists, who brandished Scotland's anti-Thatcherite voting patterns as evidence of the nation's moral vigour without forgiving the 'feebleness', in Salmond's words, of the country's actually existing Labour representatives. This trope of the loyal Scottish voter betrayed by the party – the flipside of Labour hegemony – persists to this day. Mhairi Black MP, who took working-class Paisley and Renfrewshire South from the New Labour apparatchik Douglas Alexander, used her maiden speech to say she had come from a 'traditional socialist, Labour family', but felt that 'it is the Labour Party that left me, not the other way about'.[4] Although the Scotland–Labour link is surprisingly recent in historical terms, dating perhaps to the 1960s, it has defined a broad-based Scottish mythology of democracy and 'social justice'.

In retrospect, however, it is easy to see that, by the time of the 2014 referendum, the social base of Labour loyalty had been decaying for decades. The final breach was postponed as voting patterns persisted, despite the underlying erosion: indeed, Scottish Labour's electoral hegemony was arguably strongest when its social foundations were at their weakest (the reason, as examined below, being that Scotland's right wing suffered a far more calamitous decline). The party and the social base are therefore governed by relatively autonomous logics, and Gerry Hassan and Eric Shaw have made the useful distinction between Scottish Labour, the party, and its semi-mythologised social background, 'Labour Scotland', which describes 'the society and institutions that the party gave encouragement and support to so as to allow its dominance to be strengthened and reproduced'.[5] Though we highlight flaws in their political assessment of the *meaning* of Labour Scotland's decline, its basic causes are not in dispute, and these authors were ahead of the curve in recognising underlying problems.

To illustrate how far Labour collectivism has fallen, the obvious starting point is the story of Scottish housing. As Christopher Harvie notes, 'Public control of housing and subsidised rents were . . . pillars of Scottish Labour politics until the 1960s' – and arguably for some time after that.[6] Historically, this circumstance emerged quite abruptly: in 1914, just one in a hundred Scottish families were housed by local authorities; and its consequences transformed Scotland's everyday consciousness.[7] Even today, the proud story of rising from a council house to a position of power represents the legitimising narrative of a host of national leaders, including Nicola Sturgeon.

The reverence paid to council housing reflects the role of extreme urban deprivation in Scottish history, which created an unusually broad social basis for collective housing solutions. Prior to the revolutionary Wheatley Act of 1924, Scotland had been a global byword for squalor and slum landlordism. Even compared to England, conditions were five times more overcrowded, and Scottish people were nearly eight times more likely to live in single- or two-room houses, reflecting a legacy of rapid urbanisation, a resulting pattern of low and unstable incomes, and a building code that encouraged sardine-packed populations.[8] Famously, this was the background to the Red Clydeside Rent Strikes that were every bit as threatening to Scottish elites as Glasgow's famous industrial militancy. Enthusiasm for council housing emerged from these extreme conditions. In the mid seventies, an extraordinary two-thirds of Scottish households were accommodated by local author-ities.[9] This was arguably the biggest structural difference in class relations between Scotland, on one hand, and England and Wales on the other, where the comparable proportion was only one-third. This marked collectivism provided most of Scotland with an everyday, bureaucratic link with local authorities that, crucially, constituted the pre-devolution powerbases of Labourism.

Even in Scotland, though, social housing declined precipitously under Margaret Thatcher. By the time Labour's period of devolved rule ended, it had fallen still further, from 31 per cent in 1999 to 25 per cent in 2007. This decline entailed a marked transfer of power away from local authorities to arm's-length housing associations. Devolution thus made little practical difference. Housing was one of the Holyrood parliament's chief legislative competences, and played a key legitimising role in Labour history; but Scottish Labour administrations showed little appetite for a break with post-Thatcherite norms. There was no collectivist turn: in the Labour–Liberal years from 1999 to 2007, just 340 council homes were built. Private-sector builds accounted for 84 per cent of house completions, compared to between 3 per cent and 7 per cent in the 1950s (largely under Conservative governments).[10] Thatcher's flag-ship Right to Buy programme remained intact – until it was cancelled under a Scottish Nationalist administration.

The second pillar of Scottish Labourism, trade unionism, presents a similar story. Unions represented 55 per cent of Scottish workers in 1980; in 1999, at the time of devolution, this figure stood at 35.4 per cent. Today, trade union density stands at just 28.1 per cent: higher than the UK average, but about half the proportion of the early Thatcher period. While these numbers are bad enough on the surface, they only hint at the scale of social, economic and cultural transformation in union membership. The stereotype of Clyde-built men, still a feature of Scotland's union ideology, is barely discernible in the statistics. Today, Scottish union membership is dominated by women, with large concentrations among professionals and graduates; it is also overwhelmingly a feature of the public sector, which has a union density of 61.3 per cent (compared to 15.3 per cent in private-sector jobs). Scottish people with managerial, foreman or supervisor status are more likely to belong to unions than those working beneath them. Density is higher among better-off Scottish workers with gross weekly pay between £500 and £999 than among the lower paid (though this partly reflects the practical benefits of union membership).

While the proportion of unionised workers may have halved in Scotland, the most remarkable change has been in the number of strikes, in which unions actively stand for working-class agency. There are no reliable historical figures for Scotland, but the UK numbers give a general indication of the trend. During the post-war years and the peak of Thatcherism, the total number of strike days lost rarely dipped below 2 million. In particularly militant years, like 1972, 1979 and 1984, the numbers surpassed 20 million. However, since 1991 the figure has only exceeded 1 million on four occasions, and recently there have been a succession of record lows. Although, much to the surprise of mainstream sociologists, working-class identity remained remarkably solid throughout the Thatcher and New Labour years, workplace conflict rarely took organisational form. This had a major qualitative impact on class consciousness: historically, strikes had fostered not just union recruitment, but also the development of organic leadership cadres and a sense of collective identity – an 'us and them' solidarity. While Labour always distanced itself from class struggle, throughout its history the party had nonetheless depended on trade-union militancy to a far greater extent than its leaders would ever acknowledge.

Labour's collective foundations had thus been declining for some time. Nonetheless, if the facts are not in dispute, their political implications have grown in complexity during the ideological crisis of neoliberalism. Hassan and Shaw, citing Eric Hobsbawm's thesis in *The Forward March of Labour Halted?*, fall back on the established notion of Scottish Labour's failure to modernise. '[T]imes have fundamentally changed', they warn, 'the old politics will not work anymore.'[11] Yet the irony of this assessment is that, far from going gently into the good electoral night, the remains of Labour Scotland – council house residents, deprived communities, Irish Catholic voters – saw a resurgence in their political agency precisely in opposition to their traditional party, Scottish Labour. Even if the story of the unions is more complex, their independent agency in Scottish politics has likewise grown (or, in the STUC's case, experienced a partial recovery) as they have gradually distanced their agendas from London's central union offices and from Labourism. The breach between party and social base, when it came, thus empowered the latter more than the former. This fact calls for some caution in the traditional narrative shared by Labour modernisers of both right-wing and left-wing persuasions: that Scottish Labour was the victim of an excessive traditionalism.

The problem with Hassan and Shaw's assessment is an underlying ambiguity about the meaning of 'old politics'. It carries at least two distinct and sometimes contradictory meanings. One is the now decades-old call for the left to shed its class-based reductionism and embrace the new era of neoliberal globalisation – a thesis with both hard-left and Blairite formulations. But 'old politics' can also refer to New Labour itself after its post-2008 failures, as Hassan and Shaw concede: 'The "Third Way" model of social democracy is clearly – post the financial crash – intellectually and politically exhausted.' This exhaustion, however, is only marginally a function of the party's failure to attract swing voters; Labour suffered the most intense backlash in so-called 'heartland' communities, where long-ignored voters, faced with punishing austerity, were searching for new mechanisms to exert power and influence.

Whether in Northern England or in Scotland, Labour has presented its former voters as bamboozled by nationalism. Yet there is an underlying rationale to those voters' search for political autonomy, even in crudely economistic terms. It is worth contrasting Thatcher's hegemonic strategy with the ephemeral nature of New Labour's dominance. Though this factor is sometimes exaggerated, Thatcher did shape a social order that weakened her opponents by giving individuals a 'stake' – a selfish interest in the perpetuation of a market economy. And she delivered not just electoral victories, but also empowerment for the key institutional supporters of Conservatism: British finance capitalism. By contrast, the New Labour era saw only the further erosion of collectivism. The unions – the party's chief financial backers – emerged from thirteen years of centre-left dominance further weakened. Even its policy successes in alleviating poverty were precisely the sort of cash transfers that created dependence rather than autonomy, and were thus easily rolled back under succeeding Conservative administrations.

Most strikingly of all, according to Danny Dorling, the benefits of voting Labour *accrued to Conservative-voting constituencies*, while the most loyal Labour seats barely saw any improvement in life expectancies, income or wealth.[12] Thus, arguably for the first time in British history, voting 'progressively' had ceased to bring rewards, even during an era of economic boom and unparalleled centre-left dominance, to the supposed beneficiaries of progressive policy.

By contrast, Labour's last holdout in 2015, Edinburgh South, reflected the success of a generation of carefully tailored appeals to 'swing voters' in the professional and managerial class – the broadly liberal graduates with most to gain from globalised consumerism. It was thus, if anything, over-adaptation to the neoliberal social and political norms of the 1990s and 2000s that contributed to Labour's collapse in Scotland. This reflects not so much a failure to heed Hobsbawm's thesis as the unintended consequence of its overzealous implementation. Labour's traditional bases of collective support have been in decline for some time. Like all Western social-democratic parties, it cannot simply restore an earlier cultural ideal of masculine industrial solidarity without going through a bracing process of working-class reinvention. Nonetheless, it is increasingly implausible to reduce Scottish Labour's problems to its deference to 'heartlands' and 'core supporters'. The party-political outcomes of neoliberalism have been more twisted and violently disruptive than that.

Scotland's Right and Left

One element of Hobsbawm's prediction did hold: Scotland's electorate would no longer be split into two parties divided by class loyalties. Until recently, however, the outcome of electoral fragmentation was lopsided: the traditional working-class party thrived, while the traditional bourgeois party, the Unionist/Conservatives, retreated to the margins. This unevenness is the chief explanation for Scotland's apparent identification with Labour. Britain's quixotic electoral system created what often felt like a one-party state in Scotland. This was never built on Labour's strength, however, but rather on the weakness of the domestic actors who would naturally form the local foundations of Conservatism. The economic geography of Thatcherism, with its bias towards financial interests in London and the south-east and its indifference to regional unemployment, made matters worse. Thus, Scotland underwent a decade of bracing capitalist reform and industrial slump, after which business interests were barely represented in its politics. This left a party rooted in and funded by trade unionism to rule without competitors, even as underlying working-class organisation receded.

Historically, the collapse of bourgeois Scottish politics was relatively abrupt. In 1955, the right-wing bloc won 50.1 per cent of the Scottish vote – a proportion that betters anything Labour achieved in its history. Even in the Red Clydeside heartland, at the height of global social democracy, nearly half of Glasgow's seats went to the Tories. Richard Finlay concludes, not unreasonably, that 'the Scottish Unionist Party was the most successful organisation in Scottish politics in the period from after the Great War to the mid-1960s'.[13] While the Conservative vote in Scotland fell to less than 25 per cent by October 1974, there was a resurgence in the first Thatcher election of 1979. The extent of Tory decline was only confirmed in 1987, and it took until the first Blair government of 1997 to fully establish Scottish Conservatism's irrelevance. Nonetheless, that result seemed to be conclusive. The Scottish Tories would only show real signs of recovery with the unionist backlash against the 2014 referendum – and even today, as right-wing parties go, they are among the world's weakest, particularly by comparison to the electoral successes of the UK party.

The roots of Conservative retreat are complex. Economically, the collapse of Scotland's heavy industry, which was already well underway in the 1930s, left a vacuum of leadership where native business families had once dominated. As David McCrone observes, these businessmen (they were all men) 'drew their original strength from the imperialist-inclined capitalist class concentrated in west-central Scotland', but 'the transformation of business' as Scottish heavy industries slumped 'destroyed the class coalition which had dominated Scottish politics at local and national level until at least the late 1950s'.[14] Those who replaced them – American, Japanese or English capitalists and their local managers – were no substitute for what had been a globally influential Scottish business class.

With traditional Scottish capitalism on its knees, North Sea oil was reshaping Scotland's national consciousness. The initial burst of enthusiasm for the SNP in 1974, when it won eleven seats and 30.4 per cent of the vote, was won largely at the Conservatives' expense. While the nationalists also gained votes from the left and the working class in Scotland's new towns, their seats were gained from the Scottish Conservatives, whose vote tumbled to 25 per cent. Amid the global economic crisis of the 1970s, there were brief hopes of a Scottish economic renaissance driven by oil-financed state capitalism. These hopes were never realised: the devolution referendum of 1979 failed, since, due to machinations in the Labour Party, the vote was required to gain both a simple majority (which it did) and the consent of 40 per cent of the electorate (which it did not). Paradoxically, in the context of Thatcherism, this outcome boosted Labour's prospects. The economic reality of 1980s Scotland – a chaotic mixture of closures, strikes and dole queues – offered a painful contrast with the elaborate hopes raised by oil. Outright nationalists, bitter and despondent at the lost referendum, split into fundamentalist and gradualist factions and retreated from mainstream politics. Labour rebranded itself as the party of devolution, becoming the vector of a small-n nationalism with substantial support across a Scottish elite disrupted by Thatcherism.

David Torrance has argued that Scotland's frosty relationship with Thatcherism was the product of successive cultural misunderstandings.[15] This interpretation does draw on some truths. Torrance rightly criticises the mythology of heroic Scottish resistance that drove Labour and the SNP into power, only for those parties to adopt a largely Thatcherite economic programme. However, the psychological impact of extreme unemployment and factory closures, set against the hopes raised by North Sea oil discoveries in the 1970s, cannot be ignored. These afflicted other areas of Britain more severely than Scotland. But the interaction was more intense in Scotland, where minority nationalism (or at least national consciousness) provided a platform for resistance, however ineffective.

Scotland, like other British minority communities, became a site of collateral damage in the overthrow of the social-democratic consensus. Thatcher's problem was that, while she was able to gain temporary support with giveaways like council house sell-offs, her core economic programme never enjoyed popular consent, even in England. She could easily have lost to Michael Foot in 1983 if the election had been decided on economics alone, rather than culture and the Falklands War. Winning majorities thus depended on reaching an untapped 'silent majority', targeting specific social groups (single mothers, immigrants, youths) but also minority national blocs. Drawing from Enoch Powell's playbook, Thatcher portrayed Labour as beholden to minority nationalisms. She fanned grievances at supposed concessions to Scottish 'special interests' – institutions, for example, like the Scottish Development Agency that were associated with west-of-Scotland Labourism. This meant Scotland gained little special consideration when faced with a blitzkrieg of factory closures and redundancies. Or, rather, it received far less than Scotland's local managers and grandees, the so-called Scottish Lobby, had traditionally come to expect, making them look spectacularly feeble.

The central paradox, for many sociologists, lies in the mismatch between Scotland's social attitudes (which are not noticeably differ-ent from England's) and its electoral behaviour (which inclines strongly to the left). However, this puzzle becomes easier to manage when we consider the insights of Corey Robin, one of the leading analysts of right-wing political behaviour.[16] Robin considers that right-wing parties exist for little purpose other than to defend exist-ing wealth and privilege from equality-based encroachments from the left. The strength of right-wing feeling and mobilisation there-fore tends to correspond to fear of the left – or, rather, of the left insofar as it pursues a substantive agenda of equality.

Thus, one explanation for the weakness of Scottish Conservativism is that Scotland's social elements that would have feared a substantively leftist agenda had simply never been threat-ened by the recent incarnations of Scottish Labour. With nothing to fear, they had nothing to organise around, and no incentive to engage seriously in the political fray. In that sense, Scottish Labour's electoral strength may always have been founded on underlying weakness: it worked to incorporate and neutralise threatening social forces rather than to mobilise against them. The eventual consequence was that the party was itself incorporated into the Scottish middle class, and resented as such.

Devolution: Scottish Labour Consensus

Scottish Labour channelled the energies of class and national resistance to Thatcherism into the project of a national parliament. However, by 1999, there was little talk of saving 'Scottish industry', the initial purpose behind the coalition for devolution. The damage had already been irreparable for over a decade, perhaps much longer. The parliament was constructed during the height of the 'borderless-world' and 'end-of-history' ideologies; and the devolution settlement gave Holyrood few economic levers. Meaningful control over immigration, monetary policy and the regulation of Scotland's core industries – energy and finance – were reserved to Westminster, while the UK parliament had itself surrendered key powers to the Bank of England and the European Union. The Holyrood parliament began with no direct power over varying rates of national taxation; Tony Blair had even sought (unsuccessfully) to curb all of its tax-raising powers. All of this should have raised doubts about the legitimising narrative of devolution – namely, that it would foreclose another 1980s experience in which outsiders imposed 'reforms' on an unwilling population.

Where Holyrood did develop an economic strategy, it explicitly broke with the campaigning legacy of the Thatcher era, warning: 'The takeover of Scottish enterprises is a natural process of corporate governance that is outwith the control of government.'[17] For New Labour, this was now simply the way of the world. Nation-states could no longer exercise meaningful controls on free-flowing capital. While devolution gave Scotland a limited policy palette, this was not substantially different from what now passed for 'national independence': states had already surrendered sovereignty to transnational trade rules. 'The legislation for the Parliament's powers set out to advance the wellbeing of Scottish people, not in the sheltered economies which gave rise to the old nation states of the past, but in the new global economy with its multilayered institutions', explained Gordon Brown and Douglas Alexander. 'The Devolution plan rightly places in the hands of the Scottish Parliament those key drivers of supply side policy training and education, business and regional development, Scottish enterprise itself that are so fundamental to jobs, and future economic success.'[18]

Yet, despite the globalising gloss, the cultural contradictions of the 1980s were still imprinted on Scottish consciousness. The orthodoxy of markets still had to be reconciled with a national project of anti-Thatcherism. Scotland's dominant centre-left, faced with no right-wing competitors of note, had to pay moral homage to the struggles of the past – and, for all the factional hatred between parties, they formulated this problem in terms strikingly similar to the Thatcherite orthodoxy they had displaced. 'We didn't mind the economic side so much', said Alex Salmond, referring to Thatcherism. 'But we didn't like the social side at all.'[19] Likewise, Brown and Alexander asserted that what Scotland had 'found unacceptable about Thatcherite Britain was not its commitment to enterprise ... but its lack of commitment to social justice'.[20] Rhetorically, Scotland had thus moved seamlessly from being an outlier into the ideological mainstream. In a global era dominated by the personalities of Clinton, Blair and Schröder, the centre-left gained electoral dominance by combining the core of Thatcherite economics with remedial social policies and an openness to liberal feminism, youth culture and globalisation. This was precisely the formulation praised across what passed for the Scottish left.

Yet a burgeoning open market was easier to praise in theory than to deliver in practice. Shattered by deindustrialisation and privatisation, and kept afloat by government spending, Scotland offered few outlets for capitalist renewal. The Scottish parliament had limited economic influence; in any case, even for the free market's devotees, there was little left to privatise. Alex Salmond's then-fashionable enthusiasm for the Celtic Tiger model – get independence, reduce taxes and regulation, experience take-off, spend the resulting windfall on social welfare – had the virtue of crude consistency; but he failed to explain, if his theory worked, how Europe could avoid a debilitating race to the bottom. Scotland's small right wing, grouped around think tanks, argued that further privatisations would spur an entrepreneurial renaissance. But their only practical proposal was an ultimately unsuccessful bid to privatise Scottish Water – and, far from spurring an indigenous entrepreneurial renaissance, such selloffs simply transferred control of Scottish assets overseas.

Within Labour itself, the neoliberal trend is best illustrated by Wendy Alexander, who would briefly take the helm as Scottish Labour leader. Like Salmond, Alexander was an enthusiast for Ireland's Celtic Tiger model. But while Salmond emphasised Irish sovereignty, Alexander stressed cultural influences, locating Irish success in a Riverdance generation that had dropped its nationalist 'victim' badge and embraced market globalisation. 'I see the recent rise in Irish self-confidence as linked to a retreat from the traditional "victim mentality" and moving beyond a preoccupation with relations with the UK', she argued. 'Ireland went from the self-pity satirised as "MOPE – most oppressed people on earth" syndrome to promoting the hibernisation of all cultures; across the world it became "cool" to be Irish.'[21]

This obsession with Ireland, which marked much of Scottish policy after devolution, is not an accident. As Fintan O'Toole, a leading Irish journalist, rightly observes, the Celtic Tiger was the global cultural stand-in for the dominant capitalist ideology of the 1990s and 2000s, proving that Alexander was correct to speak of the 'hibernisation of all cultures':

Between the late 1990s and 2008, other countries were told they must struggle to be like Ireland. What made Ireland interesting to people around the world was not so much its destination as its journey. Its story had a Hollywood-style narrative arc. It was a tale of misery, struggle, transformation and triumph. And it came with a ready-made moral: neo-liberal globalisation works ... Instead of being a small place with very specific circumstances, Ireland came to stand for a formula that could be applied anywhere from Armenia to Zambia.[22]

Devolution had been the cultural surrogate for Scotland's passive experience of economic losses in the 1980s. It was seen both as revenge against Thatcherism and as a renewal of Scottish agency, with a determination that Scottish Labour would never again be the 'feeble fifty' who stood by as Conservative governments wrecked jobs and industries. But by the time Holyrood assembled, one era of social democracy was decidedly over, and another had taken its place. Centre-left politicians now imagined economic renewal by looking to economies, like Ireland, that had gone even further than Thatcher in experimental neoliberalism. In place of political vision, they now offered enterprise: a promise to stop stifling ambition, get off the public's collective backs, and enable people to pursue their own life projects. Increasingly, all public service spending had to be justified in these entrepreneurial terms, regardless of whether there was any logical link between the service and the act of starting a business. It was not always clear that politicians really believed all their pro-business rhetoric. Sometimes, no doubt, it was merely a thing to say, to demonstrate their commitment to prevailing neoliberal norms. But it testified to a dearth of alternative collective projects. While market choice was endlessly championed, political choice was all but abolished.

The Crisis of Scotland's Neoliberal Society

In 2005, a Freedom of Information request revealed the social functions organised by Scotland's first minister, Jack McConnell, and his wife Bridget at their official residence of Bute House. 'The dinners start with a drinks reception in the upstairs drawing room, the 14 guests getting to know each other while musicians from the Royal Scottish Academy of Music and Drama play quietly in the background', reported the *Scotsman*. 'Then it is down to the candlelit dining room on the ground floor, where the large dining table is decorated with contemporary silver ornaments commissioned by Donald Dewar when he was the First Minister.'[23] At one fairly typical event, guests included the editor of the *Glasgow Herald*; the controller of BBC Scotland; the European Commission representative in Scotland; Campbell Christie, formerly general secretary of the STUC; and the chief executive of the Royal Bank of Scotland, Fred Goodwin.

Under New Labour, twenty senior bankers were handed official honours. Even by these standards, however, Goodwin's knighthood was remarkable, if only for the recipient's youth: he was still only forty-five when he became 'Sir Fred'. It was McConnell's proposal. A New Labour spokesman said that Goodwin had 'undertaken many projects to the benefit of his bank and the good of Scotland as a whole'. Goodwin, in fact, earned his nickname, 'Fred the Shred', after laying off 18,000 workers during the NatWest integration. In retrospect, perhaps this should have been a clue to the events that would lead to the biggest financial crisis since the Great Depression. But in the ideological climate of the 2000s, the nickname was more or less affectionate. Shredding might suggest efficiency, competitiveness, a thirst for change – out with the old, in with the new! – qualities that, according to the prevailing narrative, were absent in Scotland's risk-averse provincial elite.

Goodwin's ambition was never in doubt. He was a disruptor. He would ultimately make RBS the biggest bank in the world. When it crashed, taking much of the British economy with it, the same centre-left commentators who had complained of Scotland's low ambitions would indulge in endless handwringing, lamenting the qualities in Goodwin that had previously earned him that precocious knighthood. But blame equally – indeed, chiefly – lay with the politicians and the cheerleaders for an era of financial innovation. Goodwin had simply embodied the dominant capitalist ethic of his age and ours: move fast and break things. The more he broke, the more he was praised and rewarded. By contrast, the politicians had wanted to associate their parties and Scotland with success, and financial services was the only area that could be bent to New Labour's narrative of an ambitious Scotland enjoying the fruits of globalisation. If only Scotland could produce a buccaneering Fred Goodwin in every sector, the story went, then the country would be ready for the twenty-first century. Arriving just as devolution rolled round, Goodwin was presented as the man to save Scotland from its status as a provincial backwater.

Certainly, McConnell's judgement was correct on one front: Scotland's financial cluster had transformed the nation's economic structure. In the six years after devolution, financial services grew by an average annual 7.7 per cent, compared to 1.8 per cent across the economy as a whole.[24] Scotland's two largest banks were not simply the biggest companies in Scotland; by 2008 they were among the biggest in the world. Thanks to a series of aggressive takeovers, they held assets that dwarfed the Scottish economy itself. As Ian Fraser, Scotland's leading financial journalist, observes,

> At the height of the financial crisis in September 2008, the combined assets of Scotland's two big banks – Royal Bank of Scotland and HBOS – both of which narrowly avoided insolvency thanks to UK government intervention, were 21 times Scotland's GDP. In Iceland, a poster child of incompetent regulation and banker recklessness, the bank assets to GDP ratio reached 9.8 times in 2008, while in Ireland it was a mere 4.4 times.[25]

In parallel, following devolution the already-struggling Scottish manufacturing sector slumped further, from 17.4 per cent of total GVA in 1998 to 10.7 per cent in 2016.[26] The result was a transformation in Scottish society that contrasted starkly with its social-democratic parliament and national self-image. As New Labour's influence peaked and the Scottish banks boomed, it was revealed that two out of Britain's top three millionaire hotspots were in Edinburgh. Much of Scotland's new wealth was absorbed into the incomes of the richest 1 per cent. And while Scotland experienced a slightly lower increase in inequality than the UK average, this difference disappears when London and the south-east are excluded.

This culture did not lead to a reinvigoration of Scottish enterprise; the loss of ownership and control of top Scottish industry continued. When the financial boom became a crash, this also came to engulf Scotland's two top banks, which were fully absorbed by the City of London. Ultimately, for all the rhetoric, Scotland's centre-left parliament presided over an era of rising top incomes and diminished working-class influence without strengthening Scotland's international business reach.

The chief beneficiaries of Scotland's transformation were the financiers, corporate oil men and the transnational capitalist class. Their influence over Scotland's economic affairs was overwhelming. But a secondary feature of the neoliberal era was the transformation of politics, with the growth of 'cartel parties' feeding off the state's resources. A range of private, public and third-sector actors grew up to take advantage of the devolved parliament. Links to the Labour Party became a vehicle of preferment, and a secondary layer of intellectual fixers, professionals and various worthies came to symbolise their dominance in Scotland. Intellectually these were pro-business realists, but socially they were dependent on the state's resources. Resentment at their public role became a focus for class antagonism in devolved Scotland, shaping the public impression of Labour's role as its facilitator. Crucially, these networks of influencers had begun to seem like alternatives to building union branches and power in local communities.

A decade of Scottish Labour in power ended just as the financial crash began. In that period, the richest percentile of Scotland had done exceptionally well, its gains far exceeding those of any other demographic. The locus of the economy had shifted to financial services, with a corresponding rise in indebtedness. Inequality had risen. Trade union numbers and council house occupancy had slumped. In essence, Scotland, despite the political irrelevance of its right wing, was an atomised, neoliberal society. Many of the expected historical benefits of progressive voting had failed to materialise. Devolution itself was largely epiphenomenal to these changes, neither helping nor hindering Scotland's transition except on the margins. But this was the point. Loyalty to Labour's schemes seemed increasingly irrelevant to everyday life. When the crisis of neoliberalism hit in 2008, Labour's pragmatism – bank bailouts followed by austerity – confirmed that the overall legacy would be one of comparative failure. Any marginal gains from the long 1990s boom would be cancelled out, irrespective of how voters responded.

Better Together versus the Independence Movement

Given subsequent events, it is necessary to re-emphasise that New Labour, positioned at the centre of the anti-independence Better Together coalition, still possessed extraordinary institutional power. The crucial area of exception was control over the Scottish government. Nonetheless, in all other areas conditions were in its favour. In Westminster, the real centre of power, it controlled forty-one of fifty-nine Scottish seats, while the SNP held just six. Support for independence was running close to a historic low, at somewhere between 25 and 33 per cent. Mass media overwhelmingly backed the Union: only one newspaper, the *Sunday Herald*, belatedly backed the Yes campaign. Large-scale businesses likewise tilted overwhelmingly against independence. Academia was a similar story, especially in the strategically crucial economics departments. Beyond Salmond's government, elite support for independence was largely concentrated in Scotland's cultural avant-garde, with a smattering of small-to-medium businesses, plus the voluntary sector grouping SCVO. That aside, all evidence pointed to a humiliating defeat for the Yes campaign that would reinforce Scotland's unionist forces: this, as we have seen, was why Cameron agreed to the referendum.

The Yes vote, at 45 per cent, ultimately fell short of breaking up the UK state. However, given the unequal starting point, the movement for independence represented an epochal, radicalising shift in attitudes. The demographics of the vote gave crucial indications as to where and why that shift happened. By official occupational divisions of class, 53.6 per cent of working-class people voted for Scottish independence, significantly stronger than the official rate for middle-class voters (41.7 per cent). This, in truth, rather exaggerates the class divide, reflecting the inadequacies of mainstream definitions of the term. Looking at income divides shows the nuances: over 56 per cent of bottom-quartile income earners voted yes, but only about 42 per cent of the next-lowest quartile did so. Support was thus strongest among the very poor, those with 'little to lose', who were the biggest victims of austerity. Home ownership therefore proved a crucial variable, with a critical divide between owner-occupiers, who were strongly against independence, and social renters, who were fiercely in favour. From Labour's perspective, the generational shift was probably the most worrying factor. If the pensioner vote had been subtracted, Scotland would have supported independence.

Yes support was concentrated in communities once synonymous with Labour Scotland. Arguably the biggest blocs of support were among people in social rented accommodation and the Irish Catholic community: an extraordinary 61.9 per cent of the former and 57 per cent of the latter voted yes. The voting of trade unionists is unknown, and remains largely uninvestigated. What is known, however, is that the Labour-affiliated unions largely failed to endorse the Better Together campaign; indeed, very few signed up even for Labour-linked No campaigns. Anecdotally, three factors have been associated with this. Firstly, some Scottish union leaders were informal supporters of the Yes campaign, and even had close links to the SNP government in Scotland. Secondly, even those leaders who remained loyal to Labour had no wish to cause discontent among their declining memberships and activist bases, many of whom supported the Yes campaign. Thirdly, even the most unstintingly faithful, like future Scottish Labour leader Richard Leonard, then a GMB official, could not stomach Labour's alliance with a Conservative–Liberal administration that was imposing unprecedented austerity. The failure of those in the Scottish union machinery to do their duty and obediently swing behind Labour and Better Together was itself a kind of 'heartland rebellion'.

One obvious point about Scottish Labour's fading authority is that it overlapped with international trends. Around the world, traditional centre-left parties were trying and failing to discipline voters to the status quo. Labour's disintegration in Scotland, while disastrous, was arguably not the worst among its European sister-parties. In a similar timeframe, Dutch Labour's vote fell from nearly 25 per cent to just over 5 per cent, while the French Socialist vote fell from 29.4 per cent to 7.5 per cent, and Irish Labour's fell from 19.5 per cent to 6.6 per cent. Further east, in Hungary, the once-dominant Socialist Party vote fell from 43.2 per cent before the crisis to 11.9 per cent in its aftermath. Most famously of all, PASOK, once the dominant force in Greece, collapsed from 43.9 per cent support in 2009 to 4.8 per cent in 2015. The broader context was plunging faith in neoliberal globalisation: large numbers of voters had understood that 'open' economies would continually deliver rising living standards, or at least rising opportunities for debt-financed consumerism. While centre-right parties found they could reposition as anti-migrant authoritarian outfits, the likes of Labour had fewer options. Increasingly, they found they stood for little beyond a narrow scope of middle-class cosmopolitan consumer preferences.

But rather than examine their own political agency, Scottish Labour have tended to portray themselves as the hapless victims of an irrational wave of the 'virus of nationalism', in the words of former leader Johann Lamont. In truth, the case of Scotland's relationship with Labour suggests the potential crudity of explanations based on a supposed cultural backlash: after all, the Yes movement was pro-immigration, anti-nuclear and anti-war, with a substantial base in environmentalism; Labour, at the time, was none of those things. Moreover, Yes and the SNP received some of their strongest votes from Scotland's various underrepresented groups (although initially not from women). What unites Scottish Labour's collapse with other cases is simply that there are huge demographics of working-class voters who feel neglected, and that their political agency has been stolen by self-serving politicians. The extraordinary sight of Alistair Darling linking arms with Cameron and Clegg hardly helped to dispel these impressions. In that discomfiting context, many working-class voters preferred the risks of independence to the certainties of the status quo.

Leonardism: A Failed Experiment

Corbyn's shock successes in the 2017 general election allowed the British radical left to ground itself in the machinery of Westminster. Richard Leonard's election as leader of Scottish Labour came soon after, and grew out of these exceptional circumstances. Given his background (educated in an English private school), his lack of experience in parliament (a matter of months), and the total absence of leftist support among figures in Scottish Labour's parliamentary cohort (almost nothing beyond veterans like Neil Findlay and Elaine Smith), he would, in a normal contest, have been a classic paper candidate. But Labour had no other choice. Their parliamentary party had been discredited, whether by past associations with New Labour and Better Together, premature gloating over the 'chicken coup' against Corbyn, or, in Findlay's case, an unsuccessful previous bid for the leadership.

The theory stated that Leonard would inject some of Corbyn's 2017 electoral magic into the tired machinery of Scottish Labour. But the resurgence never came, and Labour's vote declined further under Leonard. His time as leader would be characterised by Labour's deepening irrelevance in Scottish politics. Rather than following Corbyn's 2017 roadmap to revival, Leonard's tenure foreshadowed the problem that would ultimately destroy Corbyn and one of the biggest ever left-wing experiments in British parliamentary politics.

Although Leonard was elected as Corbyn's man in Scotland, the contrasts between them are marked – at least, to anyone familiar with the fractious world of far-left politics. In many respects they represent opposite wings of the 'old left'. Whereas Corbyn was an activist, passionate about international causes, and an open dissident, Leonard learned his politics in trade-union officialdom. Leonard's interests were in labour movement history, interpreted in a partisan manner. His campaigning on Old Labour issues of poverty and regional policy, while laudable enough, was invariably skewed to serve a tribal narrative of Labour loyalism. Indeed, while Corbyn was ecumenical to a fault, Leonard belonged to a wing of Scottish Labour tradition that made tribalism the essence of class politics.

At any other time, these minutiae would have made for harmless far-left polemics. Yet, after decades in the wilderness, Labour's left wing suddenly found itself thrust into leadership just as the party was suffering an acute haemorrhage of working-class support. And the two were linked: as New Labour's strategies succumbed to their inner contradictions, party members turned in desperation to unknown leftist backbenchers in a desperate bid to reconnect with heartland voters. Corbyn and Leonard were expected to advance immediate explanations for Labour's losses and to devise immediate solutions by the next electoral cycle.

But Leonard's responses were from the outset built on a misdiagnosis. He was doubtless correct to assume that austerity had much to do with distrust of the Westminster mainstream. Equally, the question of class was a crucial contributor to the wider sense of democratic deficit. However, it was an error to assume that matters of cuts and class could be simply 'fixed' by offering injections of investment, welfare and government spending. This approach grew from a tendency, pronounced in the overlapping milieus of the Labour Party, academia and the NGO community, to reduce class to the question of material deprivation and to imagined geographies of poverty. Such caricatures were always better designed to appeal to middle-class moralists – partly because they have much to gain from an expanded government (more jobs for the professionally trained), and partly because they appeal to their altruism. The contemporary Labour left betrays a sense of embarrassment about working-class self-interest. This was best demonstrated during Corbyn's heavy defeat in 2019, when Britain's only left-leaning tabloid, the *Mirror*, led on the day of the election with a front page featuring photographs of various deprived groups, homeless people, and so on, with the headline: 'Vote for them'.

None of the above is meant to deny Labour's moral responsibility to confront poverty, or indeed its growing preponderance. The point, firstly, is that Labour was already speaking to working-class people from a standpoint of alienation. Endless talk of returning to bread-and-butter issues only served to highlight the growing ideological distance between Labour and its imagined community base. 'Listening' to the communities could quickly become its opposite, when voters asked questions about political accountability, remote government – or, for that matter, immigration, the EU and independence. At these points, Labour could only shake its head at the demands of the hapless victims of nationalist demagoguery. The fact that voters, or Labour itself, might have political agency was rarely considered. Winning voters to a political project had become unimaginable. Once the old formula of tribal loyalty in exchange for technocratically delivered material benefits had expired, so did the whole attendant notion of 'the communities' that informed the worldview of all of Scottish Labour's ideological factions.

Leonard assumed that community alienation was simply rooted in Labour's turn to the right under Blair (not New Labour as a whole: the Scottish Labour left tend to exempt Brown). A break

with austerity in favour of investment – highlighting the hypocrisies of Sturgeon, who Leonard continually compared to Margaret
Thatcher – would thus suffice to win Labour's voters back. But the
sense of collective economic failure, and of the withdrawal of
social rights, that surrounds British politics has also served to
reinforce distrust of authority and establishment politicians. In
that context, Scottish Labour's status as an unloved old guard, and
its proprietorial attitude to its former voters, has made it difficult
to secure the trust necessary to enthuse anyone with promises of
public spending. Under these circumstances, simply shifting to the
left might even have added to Labour's problems – and so it proved.
Darren McGarvey observes: 'While many on the cultural left . . .
appear capable only of blaming right-wing conservatives for everything, increasing numbers in communities like Castlemilk are just
as hacked off with the left as they are with everyone else.'[27]

Labour's status as the voice of Scotland's working-class communities was always built on a striking paradox. As the decades wore
on, rather than emerging from those communities, its representatives were engaged in worthy Fabian service-delivery within them:
they knew what was best for 'ordinary people'. Meanwhile, society
was shifting towards more pronounced individualism and, by
comparison with the 1970s, extraordinary economic inequality.
When the debt-based machinery of capitalist growth exploded,
Labour was engulfed in the flames. The backlash was most
pronounced where Labour had most lazily assumed itself to be
safe from democratic pressures. Rather than reckon with this,
much of the Labour left preferred to resort to the party-political
game of blaming failures on the SNP and the Tories – or, worse, on
the irrationalism of their traditional voters.

Liberal critiques of Scottish nationalism often focus on alleged
similarities to the type of Brexit preferred by Nigel Farage. The
comparison is more revealing of the accusers than of those accused.
The unpleasant features of Brexit, most notably the link to anti-
migrant attitudes, have no counterpart either in the SNP

leadership or in the wider movement. Compared to all sectors of established British politics, the SNP is significantly more liberal on questions of borders. Yet, for all its cosmopolitan gloss, the SNP's success does have obvious similarities to the Leave victory, in that both were beneficiaries of Labour's legitimacy crisis in non-metropolitan areas. The urge to pathologise tends to disguise the more pressing question of how Labour lost its 'heartlands'. While the latter concept has elements of mythology about it, the loss of these constituencies has left Labour dependent on a more deracinated, essentially postmodern appeal to liberal morality.

Labour has tended to reduce its failures to objective, external forces. Globalisation meant it could no longer cling to its heartlands; nationalism meant that voters were swamped by waves of irrational fervour. The party's political agency rarely figures in its electoral post-mortems. But the party made choices – and nowhere more so than on matters of social class. Indeed, the tactic of bypassing 'core constituencies' was actively celebrated under New Labour, as Blair's supporters sermonised on the need to reach 'swing voters' who were (according to the fashionable theory) newly affluent and upwardly mobile. 'It is the middle class that populates marginal seats up and down the country', noted Deborah Mattinson, a psephological advisor to Gordon Brown. 'So these votes have taken iconic status, becoming the battleground voters for any election.'[28] The electoral system thus enfranchised tiny sections of voters and disenfranchised the rest. 'The reason why every election is fought only on the issues that matter to Mondeo Man, Worcester Woman and the rest of the Pebbledash People is that they are the only electors whose votes really count', said Robin Cook after his resignation over the Iraq War. 'Increasingly, the campaigners hone their message to the one per cent of the electorate whose swing votes in the target constituencies decide which party is in government and which is in opposition.' But even the class-first left of Labour was actively hostile to tinkering with a system that crushed their electorate's agency, as Cook noted: 'It puzzles me that many of my colleagues who complain that Labour's core voters are ignored also stoutly defend the first-past-the-post system which is the reason why core voters are neglected.'[29]

New Labour's tactics proved seductive because, for decades, whole swathes of Britain really would vote Labour regardless of circumstances. Generations of collective loyalty and solidified class interest – essentially credit secured through post-war welfare reforms amplified by the impact of Thatcherism on industrial Britain – ensured an electorate stable enough to secure strong, predictable majorities. Labour won so comfortably in many Scottish, northern English and Welsh seats that campaigning barely seemed necessary; branch organisation shrivelled; increasingly, even voting became an afterthought, and many did not bother. The collapse in trade unionism that followed deindustrialisation and anti-union legislation removed a second source of collective power and political education in Britain's northern constituencies. Britain's elites now had no real reason to fear the agency of (post-)industrial workers. The latter had been reduced to a walk-on part in electoral dramas with south-east English and middle-class protagonists. This freed Labour strategists to focus on the smaller fractions who possessed real political autonomy.

It was no accident that this electoral scheme collapsed under the pressure of two referendums. By its nature, a referendum removes the biases of geographical constituencies: every vote counts equally, regardless of where it is cast. Insurgent campaigns against the status quo, whether 'Yes' or 'Leave', explicitly focused on these vulnerabilities, uncovering huge pockets of discontent previously disguised by the voting system. They convinced these isolated communities that the referendum was a once-in-a-lifetime chance for their vote to have meaning and power. In the Scottish referendum in 2014, it was common to find people in the most deprived housing schemes telling canvassers that nobody had knocked on their door for generations. A similar story was told about 2016 in English and Welsh constituencies. The two referendums offered empowerment to sections of voters who had felt politically superfluous for decades.

Characteristically, Labour's response was both eminently paternalistic, whether it was in demonising voters as nationalists and
racists – or their naive dupes – or in converting political disenchantment into a technocratic problem to be solved with injections of jobs, services and welfare. Both responses built on elements
of truth. But the overriding impression was of a party that saw a
surge in political agency among its traditional base of support, and
panicked. Having spent years competing with Liberals and
Conservatives to be 'tough on the deficit', Labour's sudden rever-
sion to economic leftism was bound to seem opportunistic. It also
reinforced a sense that only voting *against* Labour would make the
party listen, empowering renegades to repeat their act of disobedi-
ence. The underlying problem, clear from both referendums, is
that Labour can no longer play its time-honoured role of disciplin-
ing voters to the prevailing style of state power.

5

The Fault Line of SNP Hegemony

On 23 March 2020, as states worldwide imposed lockdowns to halt the spread of the coronavirus, Scotland's former first minister Alex Salmond walked free from Edinburgh's High Court, cleared of fourteen indictments ranging from breach of the peace to attempted rape. Diehard supporters thronged outside, braving the virus to yell 'Captain! My captain!' The press pack were out in numbers too: if not for the looming global pandemic, a trial of this magnitude would have saturated news agendas for months.

Salmond's prosecution was extraordinary by any standards. It had the melodrama and technicolour hues of politics in a far-distant country: squint and it could have been the trial of Silvio Berlusconi or the impeachment of Bill Clinton. Certainly, this sort of thing was not meant to happen in Edinburgh's Holyrood village, a governance community not prone to fireworks, whose greatest collective vanity has rested on emulating the beige tones of Scandinavian social democracy.

Quite apart from the serious charges levelled against him, Salmond's combination of shrewdness and bombast had always made him an unwelcome guest at the post-devolution feast. One of Scotland's most notorious faces, he was celebrated – and just as often reviled – for making the Scottish national question the most important fault line in UK politics. It is no insult to say that he ranks with Nigel Farage as one of two great disruptors who defined a decade of British identity crisis; but unlike Farage, whose success was a product of carping from the fringes, Salmond had the gravity that comes with having held the burden of national leadership. To supporters, he had turned the Scottish parliament from a jumped-up regional authority into a true government with aspirations to state power.

For all the focus on Salmond, the trial's newsworthiness was just as much about the accusers as the accused. His successors in the SNP leadership had staked much of their political capital on securing his conviction. All the allegations originated from staff who had been employed either in the SNP apparatus or by the Scottish government. Some of Salmond's allies hinted at an establishment plot – not by MI5 or Westminster, but by forces aligned with his protégée and anointed successor as first minister, Nicola Sturgeon.

Before the trial, Sturgeon's government had been forced to pay Salmond legal costs of over £500,000 after procedural bungling during the initial probe into the accusations. As had become standard practice in the Sturgeon era, there were no resignations. For Dani Garavelli, the trial was 'a referendum on the #MeToo movement; a litmus test for contemporary attitudes on sexual offending in the workplace'.[1] If this was what was at stake, the trial was damaging by any measure. Women watching the outcome could have been forgiven for seeing either feminist agendas weaponised for a faction fight or a Scottish legal system that protected powerful workplace predators. Neither verdict was liable to increase confidence in Scottish law as a beacon of women's rights; and neither verdict was a glowing endorsement of the SNP. The affair was marked by extraordinary errors in decision-making and an absence of accountability that brought the half-baked institutions of devolution to breaking point.

Nor was Salmond's impropriety – which was real, even if the jury found him not guilty of criminal acts – an isolated incident.

Scandals are a routine part of politics (Conservative Westminster is certainly no exception); but the interesting feature was how many accusations appeared to originate from within the bitterly factional SNP itself. It thus became increasingly harder to dismiss tabloid stories as a unionist vendetta. They testified to battles for power that were variously ideological and personal. Success at the polls did not insulate Sturgeon and her husband, party chief executive Peter Murrell, from grievances on issues ranging from internal democracy to Scotland's Gender Recognition Reform bill (GRR) and the government's neoliberal economic package for Scottish independence, the Sustainable Growth Commission. But Sturgeon and Murrell were in no mood for compromise. With opposition forces posing no threat, the struggle for power had turned inward. Discipline, for the SNP leadership, was less a matter of maintaining a façade of party unity than of crushing internal rivals.

The upshot of the whole affair was a crisis within a party that had become the country's natural governing class. It goes without saying that this type of collective hubris often portends electoral collapse, as with the sleaze scandals that preceded the end of Conservative rule in 1997. Yet, to the contrary, a week after the trial Sturgeon was scoring near-record net favourability ratings.[2] And that support remained solid despite a host of damaging revelations following the trial.

Part of this story is a fluke of historic proportions. The trial and its aftermath coincided with the coronavirus upheaval, which led to a further dwindling in public faith in an incompetent Westminster leadership, and a rallying to the flag – the Saltire – in a national crisis unprecedented since World War II. Normal political rules were suspended. There was thus an element of luck to Sturgeon's political survival, and an apparent lucky streak has been a feature of the party's recent history: even before the pandemic, it benefited enormously from the bungling of the British political class during the referendum period of 2014–19.

Nonetheless, to attribute the party's resilience to luck alone would do it a disservice. In truth, the SNP has proved spectacularly well adapted to the historical environment that followed the financial crash of 2008. This has been reflected in election results, membership numbers, and (until recently) an unusual aura of being free of factional squabbling.

If anything, the SNP has been over-adapted to its environment. Enjoying a life of comfort with no natural predators, the party apparatus has had little extrinsic motivation to push for its substantive purpose: Scottish independence. Unionist critics may pretend to believe that Sturgeon is 'obsessed with independence' and 'not interested in the day job'. But there is every possibility that the greatest peacetime crisis of the British state will pass without constitutional incident, Sturgeon never betraying her managerial calm by risking outright conflict with London. To critics within the independence movement, Sturgeon has been leading Scotland towards 'neo-autonomism': as an imagined community, entirely sovereign; as a legal and financial entity, enjoying borrowed legitimacy from Westminster.

Salmond's effort to launch an electoral rival, the Alba Party, fell decidedly flat. But it did attract thousands of former nationalist branch activists dejected by Sturgeon's apparently elastic enthusiasm for the SNP's central purpose. At the time of writing, mobilisation around independence has stalled, only recently having been counted as Scotland's largest ever political movement. Protests that attracted tens of thousands only a few years ago have dwindled to the small hundreds of diehards. The pandemic was the proximate cause, but the deeper problem is a growing recognition that Sturgeon, having captured the independence movement within what passes for the Scottish state, lacks the political will to risk outright confrontation with Westminster or to solve the gaping intellectual holes in the nationalist case for 'independence in Europe'. Nor does anyone else have the agency to challenge Sturgeon – least of all Salmond. This insight has generated rage and recrimination: the true believers know they have lost the faction fight. But the deeper truth is that Sturgeon herself cannot afford to ditch the party's cause for the home comforts of mere governance: to stay in power, Sturgeon needs independence just as much as the movement needs her.

Ideological and Class Foundations

The SNP's absolute domination of Scottish politics dates, at the earliest, to 2011, but can more plausibly be located in the period between 2014 and 2019, during the acute crises of the British state occasioned by the mixture of constitutional referendums and austerity. Scotland's emergent political establishment thus has, at one level, shallow historical foundations: it is a creature of the post-2008 crisis of capitalist democracy. Nonetheless, the prehistory of outright Scottish nationalism, as a protest movement consisting first of determined outsiders, then as outriders of devolution, laid down social and ideological foundations that continue to act as a lure to new recruits and a limit on Sturgeon and Murrell's power.

The party's status as electorally significant is also historically shallow, dating back a mere half-century. To the extent that Scottish nationalist energies surfaced before the late 1960s, they were channelled through Scotland's dominant parties of social class – the Conservatives/Unionists and Labour. The SNP's impact barely registered: electorally, it was often eclipsed by the Communist Party. These wilderness years were nonetheless formative for the party. From the start, with the merger of the centre-left National Party of Scotland (NPS) and the pro-Empire Scottish Party during the depths of the 1930s Depression, the SNP represented a coalition characterised by acute social tension. It was composed of factions deriving from two political parties that represented two titanic social classes. Symbolically, the party began with the dual presidency of the Duke of Montrose and Robert Cunninghame Graham, who, with Keir Hardie, had been a founder of the Scottish Labour Party.

To make the alliance palatable to Scotland's upper class, NPS leader John MacCormick purged radical (and especially pro–Irish republican) influences from their ranks. But the alliance never escaped the symptoms of political marginalisation, factionalism and wild ideological oscillation. Some early leaders even flirted with fascism – a story gleefully recounted by unionist critics of the SNP, who perhaps forget that fascistic sympathies were rife across the UK ruling class, in Labour, and even the old Liberal Party. More commonly, the SNP recruited Toryish elements – petty bourgeois or part of the crumbling aristocracy dismayed at Scotland's declining status within the British Empire. A third element, probably the biggest, saw the SNP as a force to pressure the Labour Party: Douglas Young, the party's wartime leader, possessed dual membership. All of this merely reinforces the point that the SNP was orbiting the parties of mass representation, rather than coalescing into a distinct political force.

Under the post-war Attlee government, 2 million signed the Scottish Covenant calling for Home Rule; but this mass mobilisation merely served to expose the SNP's isolation from popular sentiment. Prominent members resigned to pursue a less sectarian path, including Young and MacCormick. National consciousness remained part of the landscape, but the welfare state and the secular decline of heavy industry shifted Scottish opinion in a broadly unionist direction, towards regional policies to tackle the national decline symbolised by unemployment and emigration. In the view of many historians, most recently David Edgerton, this was the high point of British nationalism, with an abandonment of imperial cosmopolitanism in favour of managed economic borders.[3] The SNP's position within this landscape was confused. It became known for the production of implausible pamphlets detailing how Scotland was being robbed blind for its taxes by the British state – claims that flew in the face of what everyone knew about the realities of Scottish decline and the post-war regime.

For all the SNP's early wandering in the wilderness, the difficult inter-war and post-war periods shaped its ideological makeup. It was established, at the cost of many leading members, that the SNP would be more than merely a pressure group for Home Rule:

independence as such would be its goal. This prevented the party from being assimilated into other larger formations. But it also left a lasting strategic tension between so-called gradualists and fundamentalists that has haunted the party down to the Brexit era. Would further devolution of powers serve as a bridge to full autonomy? Or would this simply cause confusion and lead to the further incorporation of Scotland into the institutions of the British state?

Moreover, having established itself as a separate entity, the party still had to find its place in Scotland's social landscape. The problem of political sociology, which dates from the SNP's origins, has never entirely disappeared. Some sought to supplant Labour as the party of the urban working class, a programme most famously articulated by Stephen Maxwell; others sought respectability, aiming at rural, petty-bourgeois and business voting blocs.[4]

Finally, the collapse of the British Empire brought an end to the old notion of Scotland as a sovereign partner in managing the Commonwealth. But British geopolitical decline left doubts about Scotland's role in wider spaces of trade and influence. The party's break with coalition-building and its preference for full self-rule opened it to radical critiques of state power and hegemonic power blocs. As a result, the party has historically been hostile to Nato, nuclear weapons and even – a matter it prefers to forget – the European project. By contrast, since the late 1980s, the SNP has repositioned itself as a 'modernising' force, with full globalising credentials. This led it to embrace first the EU, then the single currency (which was quietly dropped when the depths of the Eurozone crisis became clear), and then Nato (noisily adopted in a bid for respectability). Nonetheless, autonomist, self-rule traditions remain part of its cellular structure, and form the basis of the only real internal battles of any seriousness in the modern era – over Nato in 2012 and over the currency question in 2019.

Oil and the Seventies Crisis

After decades of disappointment, the SNP's breakthrough into
mainstream recognition came in two stages. In 1967, Winnifred
Ewing, the standard-bearer of the party's right wing, shocked the
British establishment with her victory in a Hamilton by-election.
Technically, she was not the SNP's first MP: that honour goes to
Robert McIntyre, who was elected in Motherwell for three brief
months in 1945. However, Ewing's victory was less easily dismissed
as a fluke. In tapping into the new energies of an emerging capitalist order – feminism, commercialism, the decline of social class
affiliation – it hinted at future electoral realignments.

Still, it might have been easily forgotten but for a moment of
rupture that would redefine Scottish history. In the early seventies,
decades-old received wisdom about Scotland's economic development was overturned by the discovery of oil in the North Sea. The
rude intrusion of advanced capitalist modernity, in its most brash,
monumental and American form, created a jarring effect, contrasting with a national identity accustomed to thinking of itself
through the lens of decline and underdevelopment. For Tom
Nairn, such counterpoints of backwardness and modernity were
central to producing an entirely original form of nationalist mobilisation: 'The impact of the oil industry on Scotland and of the US
multinationals on the French midi is provoking a new Scottish and
Occitanian separatism; but, to a greater extent than is realised, this
is a sui generis phenomenon which should not be assimilated to
classical European or Third World "nationalism" at all.'[5]

Oil provoked, in the true sense, a crisis – a moment that forced
a reassessment of established alliances in Scottish culture, society
and politics. While any large oil discovery acts as a catalyst for
political change, the North Sea discovery coincided with a crisis of
oil imperialism (the Arab–Israeli War and the OPEC crisis), and
with the wider 1970s crisis of stagflation. The immediate effect was
a qualitative shift in Scotland's expectations. From being one of the
most technologically backward parts of the UK, it was suddenly

positioned at the cutting edge of scientific development and geopolitical tensions.

All of Scotland's existing parties and blocs, to varying degrees, were forced to reassess their roles. Gordon Brown, then a student leftist, observed: 'For the first time since the Union, oil and the political response to it has swung the balance of influence within Great Britain in favour of Scotland, giving the Scottish Labour Movement in particular a new bargaining power.'[6] Jimmy Reid's famous 1972 rectorial address focused on alienation, which he defined as 'the cry of men who feel themselves the victims of blind economic forces beyond their control.'[7] Yet Reid, a pragmatic idealist, was also forced to accept that the shaping of Scotland's industrial future by external ownership and control was already a *fait accompli*. Symbolically, the Upper Clyde Shipbuilders' work-in, led by Reid, ended when the Clydebank yard was sold to an American multinational to construct North Sea oil rigs.

At the other extreme, oil reinforced the self-conscious insecurities of the old Scottish bourgeoisie, which was already, in schemes like 'Oceanspan', touting for massive state investment in infrastructure to save itself from redundancy, without ever abandoning its longstanding hostility to trade unions and collectivism. The prospect of vast new oil revenues provided one potential mechanism for bankrolling substantial renewal, yet business suspicion of Labour dominance in Scotland ultimately killed off bourgeois support for devolution, despite Edward Heath's earlier concessions to the idea.

In party-political terms, the SNP was the early beneficiary of this upheaval. In the second election of 1974, running on the slogan 'It's Scotland's oil', it won eleven seats and almost a third of the vote – its highest share in a Westminster election until 2015. However, the effect of Scottish nationalism extended beyond the SNP into unionist institutions. Nationalist narratives – and myths – began to influence Labour intellectuals, including those who were most adamantly opposed to the SNP. Many Labourists thus claimed that Scottish independence was impossible *precisely because Scotland was becoming a colony of England* (and international capitalism more broadly). Brown observed that 'with American and British multinationals increasingly dominant in Scotland, and with the aims of public policy being to respond rather than lead, the Scottish economy is perhaps more subject to the influence of multinationals than any other similar industrial country'.[8] Culturally, the most iconic text was John McGrath's play, *The Cheviot, the Stag and the Black, Black Oil*:

> In other parts of the world – Bolivia, Panama, Guatemala, Venezuela, Brazil, Angola, Mozambique, Nigeria, Biafra, Muscat and Oman and many other countries – the same corporations have torn out the mineral wealth from the land. The same people always suffer.
> Then it was the Great Sheep.
> Now it is the black black oil.
> Then it was done by outside capital, with the connivance of the local ruling class and central government –
> And the people had no control over what was happening to them.
> Now it is being done by outside capital, with the connivance of the local ruling class and central government.[9]

The McCrone Report, a civil service memo explaining that an independent Scotland stood to gain substantially from oil revenues, has been portrayed as a British state conspiracy. This is disputed by McCrone himself, who notes that key findings had already been reported (albeit perhaps without receiving the attention they deserved) in the mainstream press. What McCrone did represent, however, was an emerging technocratic bloc in Scotland pushing for state-led capitalist renewal funded by oil. The Scottish bourgeoisie ultimately lacked the leadership and agency to push through its Oceanspan vision. But various factions and class alliances were pushing plans for massive investment in a complete recasting of Scotland's economy.

Yet, for all the SNP's parliamentary success and wider influence on mainstream politics, its progress depended on turning a cultural moment into unalterable institutional change. Such hopes evaporated in 1979. On 1 March, the referendum for a devolved parliament failed despite a narrow majority in favour. In protest, the SNP withdrew its support from the minority Labour government, hastening the famous general election that was won emphatically by Margaret Thatcher. The nationalists lost nearly half their votes, and nine out of eleven constituencies – seven of them to Thatcher's Conservatives.

The effect was to reinforce all the old questions about Scottish nationalism. Politically, gradualism had suffered an extraordinary setback, inviting new openings for fundamentalists who claimed there was no route through UK politics. Sociologically, the party was stranded once again: electoral success had been concentrated in rural, respectable 'Tartan Tory' constituencies; by contrast, support for devolution was strongest among the Labour-supporting urban proletariat. The party's more strait-laced parliamentarians thus ran up against the modernising instincts of nationalist intellectuals like Stephen Maxwell. Finally, the question of Scotland's place in the world was defined by contradictory instincts. Faced with American techno-capitalism in the North Sea, some turned to anticolonial metaphors, while others, including Nairn, imagined a cosmopolitan future in which the continent's small nations would radicalise the European project.

Salmond Emerges

Alex Salmond's career was formed simultaneously by the optimism of oil and the demoralising defeat of devolution – a defeat followed in short order by Thatcherism and the sudden jolt of economic collapse, which Christopher Harvie has dubbed 'instant post-industrialisation'. From the outset, Salmond developed an interest in the material, productive forces that might sustain national independence, spending seven years at the Royal Bank of Scotland, mostly as an oil economist, which informed his belief in Scotland's fiscal solvency while also establishing a lifelong familiarity (or perhaps chumminess) with the corporate world.

Politically, by contrast, Salmond spent much of the early 1980s engaging in factional warfare in the SNP as part of the '79 Group, which sought to capture Labour heartlands by embracing a militant working-class aesthetic and ethos. Throughout the decade, he continued to excoriate the 'feebleness' of Scottish Labour in the language of class war: 'Scottish Tories may have betrayed their country, but Labour have betrayed their class.'[10] Political combat did not stop with other parties. Indeed, members of the faction, including Salmond and future cabinet minister Kenny MacAskill, were briefly expelled by the SNP after the '79 Group was proscribed from the party.

Salmond's origins form the basis of subsequent controversies about his true political identity. Even much later in his career, during the height of the neoliberal boom, he never entirely disowned his youthful radicalism. 'I thought that the work the '79 Group [did] in supporting workers' occupations, in Bathgate for example, was absolutely fundamental', he said.[11] However, the much-deliberated question of whether Salmond was a mere opportunist or truly a creature of 'the left' misses the point. Salmond's support for militant tactics was ultimately defensive and nationalist in inclination, designed to defend the Scottish economy from its seemingly irreversible breakdown amid Thatcherism and globalisation. This was true, equally, of much of the response of civil society – still, on aggregate, at that time, within the camp of Labour hegemony – to deindustrialisation. What the episode reveals of Salmond is a characteristic adventurism and indifference to respectability, and an opportunistic instinct for Labour's vulnerability in its heartlands. These political traits would form the basis for subsequent SNP success.

Certainly, after his election as SNP leader in 1990, any lingering traces of socialist dogma disappeared. Instead, following the herd of European centre-left parties, the SNP quickly embraced the 1990s culture of competitive globalisation. Salmond's glossy, populist message centred on reframing the SNP as the party of economic openness, and enthusiasm for the European Union and the Irish Celtic Tiger. Inspired by the latter, the specific offer of corporate tax cuts became the centrepiece of the economic promise of independence.

Any traces of the republicanism of the '79 Group were also abandoned: while most SNP politicians disguise their anti-Windsor sympathies to avoid unionist attacks, there is a suspicion that Salmond, alone among nationalists, revels in royalism. Undogmatic in its pursuit of wider influence, the party took advantage of Labour's squeamishness to court social conservatives, including Brian Souter, a millionaire beneficiary of bus privatisation who battled against LGBTQI+ rights, and Cardinal Winning, a crusader against abortion rights.

However, it is symptomatic of the wider political era that, in most matters of policy, Salmond's SNP stood recognisably to New Labour's left. This included marking out some controversial territory that once again demonstrated Salmond's cavalier attitude to respectable middle-class opinion. As Labour embraced crusading American military power, Salmond took sizeable risks to stake out an anti-imperialist position, famously condemning Nato airstrikes on Yugoslavia as an 'act of unpardonable folly' – words that drew fury from liberal interventionists across Europe.

There was thus a peculiarity to the SNP. The nationalist left followed much of the 1980s left in embracing post-Thatcherite approaches to markets. Yet whereas many former Trotskyists and Stalinists embraced imperial adventurism in New Labour, Salmond remained distinctly sceptical about the virtues of unharnessed American power. As George Kerevan explains, his generation of left nationalists pictured globalisation as a mechanism for disrupting traditional world power:

> For a while, some on the radical left – I include myself in this admonishment – thought the answer lay in a dash for global growth stimulated by the cornucopia of new and 'democratic' technologies that emerged in the 1980s. The Internet would break the economic power of the old capitalist monopolies while the re-entry of the former Communist states into the world market offered a chance to subvert the dominance of US imperialism. In this new economic and political space, a host of small states would emerge to political freedom, including Scotland . . . A new Europe of the Nations, influenced by these smaller member states, would replace the EU of the big bully states and their multinational investors. Seductive as this 'pragmatic' approach appeared at the time, we should have known better.[12]

It is thus an irony of history that, when anti-war sentiment emerged from the fringes to dominate British politics after Iraq, it never benefited the SNP. By 2003, Salmond was long out of power, after unexpectedly quitting the leadership over issues that always remained mysterious. John Swinney, his successor, represented the party's right wing, and cut an anaemic presence. The SNP vote fell markedly in the 2003 Scottish elections, as left-wing voters embraced the more radical messages of the Greens, the Scottish Socialist Party and, to a lesser extent, the Liberal Democrats in the era of Charles Kennedy. While Labour, as expected, lost six seats, the SNP lost eight, and won just 20.9 per cent of the regional vote. It was small consolation that the night's main victors, the SSP and the Greens, were pro-independence, meaning that the actual weight of pro-independence forces in the parliament increased despite the SNP's miserable performance.

Salmond's leadership defined the modern SNP, but the success of his opportunism reflected world-historical shifts. In an earlier era, outright Scottish nationalist energies were either crowded out or incorporated into class-based parties of representation centred on securing advantages from the British state. Insofar as meaningful boundaries existed between Labour and the Conservatives, the

SNP's cross-class alliances were spread too thinly to matter. Salmond's iconoclastic populism, with its brash commercialism, anti-imperialism, everyman jocularity and openness to social conservatism, thrived in an atmosphere where traditional alliances and loyalties were breaking down.

Salmond in Government

In the 2007 election, Salmond returned triumphantly to lead the SNP to victory. By one seat, the SNP emerged as the largest party in Holyrood, and formed a minority government. This result marked Scotland's first conclusive break with decades of Labour hegemony. However, at this stage the SNP benefited less from a surge of nationalism than from waning enthusiasm for the leftist parties of independence. The SSP had split acrimoniously in 2006 after its spokesperson, Tommy Sheridan, became embroiled in a tabloid sex scandal; under the tired leadership of Robin Harper, the Green vote also fell markedly. There is a strong likelihood that these lost voters migrated into the nationalist fold, which, under Salmond, at least possessed a chance of unseating New Labour.

It is a hallmark of Salmond's big-tent style that his leftist appeal never stopped him seeking new allies from big business and the right wing. He formed an abiding alliance with Rupert Murdoch and a short-lived bond with Donald Trump – which soured only when Scotland's wind turbine roll-out made an unlovely backdrop to Trump's golf courses. As Hassan observed, 'Salmond's style seems to involve "big beast politics", of deal making, attracting controversial, charismatic alpha-males and being impatient or oblivious to the downside of such actions.'[13] His anti-establishment posturing simultaneously appealed to leftists seeking a break with New Labour's servility to American power and to business disrupters who found Labour guileless, sullen and feeble.

In the 2011 election, where the SNP formed its first majority government, Salmond's boardroom base expanded further. He gained a shock endorsement from Sir David Murray, who, as former chairman of Glasgow Rangers, was a cultural pillar of Scottish unionism. Murray stopped short of supporting the SNP, and was actively hostile to independence, but testified that Salmond made 'a fine first minister' and led a 'competent' government. Yet Murray's testimonial, far from illustrating nationalist hegemony, actually showed how little big business leaders worried about the prospect of independence. Sections of the Scottish bourgeoisie happily endorsed Salmond precisely because they saw no prospect of Scotland moving in that direction. Independence ranked among voters' lowest priorities, and was widely considered the SNP's chief electoral weakness. Confident that independence was a paper tiger, and that Salmond was in no position to push the question, sections of corporate Scotland rallied to him as a charismatic evangelist for 'jobs' and modernisation. Murray, a forthright British nationalist, was more alarmed by the listlessness of Scottish Labour leader Iain Gray than by the SNP's seriousness about independence.

Salmond's enthusiasm for raw boardroom power dominates the cruder leftist accounts of his office. Yet it is a sign of New Labour's success in Scotland – or of the weakness of the Labour left – that Salmond shifted Holyrood to the left. In many respects the SNP built a bonfire of Scottish Labour's neoliberal 'modernisation' programme, scrapping prescription charges, reversing accident-and-emergency closures, ending private-finance initiatives and Thatcher's 'right to buy'. In 2011, it would go further, resisting moves to establish university tuition fees. On wider cultural and political issues, including immigration, nuclear weapons and war, it remained solidly to Labour's left. This background is crucial in explaining why subsequent moralising critiques from socialists within Scottish Labour failed to find an audience. For all that Salmond aggressively courted corporate power, the period has largely been remembered as a break with the era of New Labour centrism. The SNP's ranks were swelled, albeit modestly at first, while dejected socialists sought a more winnable historical cause.

Scottish Labour's critiques of the Salmond era demonstrated ongoing ideological confusion. Under Johann Lamont, it concentrated its fire on the SNP's commitment to universalism: policies such as free bus travel for the elderly and free prescriptions were singled out as representing a 'something-for-nothing culture'. Scottish Labour's conceit, reflected in Gordon Brown's barrage of means-testing, was to present itself as defender of the 'working-class interest' against the middle-class beneficiaries of universalism. Leaving aside the problems with means-testing, the symptomatic feature is how badly her critique landed. The hostile reaction that greeted Lamont's comments testified to the passing of an era when Scottish Labour could credibly speak for class and 'the communities', their traditional heartlands. In another era she might have been celebrated as a tough-minded pragmatist; instead, her moralising demonstrated her emotional distance from her supposed electorate, prefiguring the deluge of 2015.

The Global Context of SNP Power

During Salmond's first term of office, the world underwent a colossal crisis of capitalism, the biggest crash since 1929. The 2008 crisis raised existential doubts about the combination of deregulation and debt-based growth that had dominated Western economies since the nineties. Across Europe and America, the subsequent rise and fall of parties would be based on their ability to leverage these circumstances to their advantage. The victims, as a rule, were the traditional parties of social democracy who had embraced neoliberal globalisation in the uncritical mode of 'modernisation'. Scottish Labour's failure was in keeping with this pattern.

However, the SNP had potential weaknesses of its own. It was also a centre-left party that had drunk the 'Third Way' cocktail of market boosterism and communitarian rhetoric. Theoretically, the crisis did more damage to the SNP's economic narrative than to Labour's: the collapse of Scotland's two flagship corporations, RBS and HBOS, had required a UK taxpayer bailout that an independent nation simply could not have paid for. The crisis also dismantled 'economic miracles' that Salmond was trumpeting as part of Northern Europe's 'Arc of Prosperity'. Nor was the SNP benefiting from a surge in Scottish nationalism. By many measures, support for outright independence was falling to near-historic lows; quietly, the SNP was shifting to agendas such as so-called devo max – the transfer of all fiscal powers to Scotland; a move designed to maximise public backing and, just as importantly, secure the support of corporate boardrooms.[14]

Relative to Labour, the SNP's chief advantage was its absence of historical baggage. Under Neil Kinnock, John Smith and Tony Blair, Labour had engaged in wrenching internal warfare to 'modernise' the party. Bad blood from the purge of the Labour left complicated efforts to come to terms with neoliberalism's economic, moral and ideological collapse. A generation of party insiders had been reared on scare stories about the disasters that befell anyone who sought to break with American power or the discipline of the market. At the same time, the party also had to drag along the unions and the British left, further weighing it down. The result was paralysis. A characteristic post-2008 Labour move was to abstain on the Conservative welfare bill, neither taking responsibility for austerity nor embracing opposition to it. Such half-hearted moves were guaranteed to stoke public contempt (a problem redoubled in the later Brexit debate).

On top of this, Labour had more than a decade of injudicious government decisions to defend. In Scotland, this included a series of market-friendly policies, most notably private-finance initiatives, that aimed to capture the pragmatic, consumerist ethos of the noughties. These legacies also weighed them down. Scottish Labour's critiques of the SNP came across as carping, and was always trumped by pointing to Labour's record of policies that were, in historical retrospect, both unpopular and unprincipled, such as their failure to abolish the Thatcherite right to buy. Equally, the party's fetish for 'solidarity' with Westminster Labour governments meant it carried the can for every mistake made by Blair, Brown and their successors – including the disaster in Iraq.

By contrast, the SNP was new to government. It was not heavily encumbered by historical traditions (with the obvious exception of the commitment to independence, which opponents always sought to exploit), and it was entirely footloose with respect to Westminster governments. Internally, there were no organised social forces to manage, whether unions or business groups – the only possible exception being eccentric backers like Souter. This allowed the SNP to approach the crisis of neoliberalism in entirely opportunistic terms, in stark contrast to a Labour Party sagging under a long legacy of feuds, ideological schisms and competing interests. These were characteristics of many of the new formations that thrived in European politics after 2008. The chief Scottish exception is that, whereas many so-called 'populists' stressed their commitment to illiberal democracy, the SNP, like all six Holyrood parties, was fully signed up to economic and social liberalism.

The Referendum and the Rise of Sturgeon

This era of capitalist crisis and austerity conditioned the rise of Salmond's deputy, Nicola Sturgeon, as Scotland's hegemonic politician. Like Salmond, she was nurtured far away from Scotland's urbane metropolitan core. Sturgeon was a product of the periphery: Dreghorn, the North Ayrshire coalmining town where she grew up and where her parents live to this day, epitomises much of 'flyover' Scotland, politically as well as socially. Dreghorn, like all such towns, was once a Labour heartland, but is now safe territory for Scottish Nationalists. Sturgeon can thus claim to hail from 'a fairly standard, normal, working-class family' who lived with the fear of unemployment during the Thatcher era.[15]

Ideologically, Salmond and Sturgeon are both exponents of 'centrism' – the blend of social and economic liberalism that dominated all politics in the nineties. But unlike Salmond, the archetypal disruptor, Sturgeon's ultimate triumph would be as an insider, a representative of continuity. Stylistically, they would drift ever further apart as she emerged from his shadow. This largely accounts for their contrasting public images. Salmond's modest origins contributed to his reputation in governing circles as a perverse, ill-mannered upstart. Sturgeon's story, by contrast, brings to Holyrood a sense of 'meritocracy' that flatters the governing class, and lends credence to interlocking governing myths.

Naturally, it helps preserve the Scottish myth of the 'lad (or lass) o' pairts' – the notion of a peculiarly Scottish culture of providing 'equality of opportunity' to the underprivileged. Many nations have these myths, but Scotland's social mobility myth has endured (despite evidence to the contrary) because the English 'class system' was so notorious as a fossilised order of manners and inherited snobbery. The rise of a Bullingdon elite in Westminster gave these tropes new popular currency. National stereotypes have thus made it easier for Scotland to pose as a bastion of meritocracy. For Scotland's governing elite, the myth is doubly flattering for being so closely aligned with the dominant ideology of high-ranking global professionals.

Historically, centrist parties are most electorally successful when they represent the status quo with a populist supplement. As Chris Bickerton argues, 'techno-populism'– the mixture of claims to govern by expertise with claims to represent the people, of being an insider and an outsider – has been a feature of successful political management since the nineties.[16] The quintessential Third Way leaders (Blair aside) often had a rags-to-riches tale and a claim to represent the national heartland, like Bill Clinton or Gerhard Schröder. Narratives of hard work and personal accomplishment, for these leaders, made for contrasts between earned and unearned privilege. Sturgeon's rise is much of a piece with this. It is no accident that Sturgeon trained as a lawyer, the necessary professional qualification for almost every Third Way centrist leader, including Clinton and Schröder, but also Blair and Keir Starmer. Like all of these figures, Sturgeon flirted with anti-establishment politics (as a member of CND) before emerging as a paid-up member of the state nobility.

Sturgeon's trajectory was nonetheless distinctive, in that her status as an outsider lasted longer. This was partly because Scottish nationalism itself was regarded as a fringe cause until roughly 2007, making it harder to become absorbed into the governing class without friction. But there was also a personal component: unlike Clinton, Blair or Schröder, the dominant politicians during Sturgeon's political genesis, the young Sturgeon was no 'smooth' operator. Her early public image was as a fanatic, a capable but irritable protégée of the – even then – much-demonised Salmond. This was the source of her (demeaning and undoubtedly sexist) nickname, 'nippy sweetie', a Scottish term, largely aimed at women, referring to someone who is congenitally cheerless. In less enlightened times, a Scottish journalist encouraged Sturgeon to take 'lessons on how to smile so she can stop being outraged all of the time'.[17] Colleagues reported that she became highly conscious of this reputation. 'It had got to the stage that it had become the dominant narrative about her and I got the impression that a) she felt the nippy sweetie tag was unfair, and b) she had to convey something else in order to combat it.'[18]

Subsequently, as the Clinton–Blair–Schröder era collapsed, Sturgeon would emerge as one of the world's last centrist leaders with a popular base. But her metamorphosis into a centre-ground figure meant little while she was in Salmond's shadow, only emerging as politically significant during the 2014 referendum. In the early part of the campaign, when Yes was heading for a humiliating defeat, Salmond was portrayed as a divisive liability whose presence was a frequent topic of complaint on the doorsteps. Unusually, given his reputation for bombast, his appearances during the campaign often appeared timid or faltering. This allowed Sturgeon to take the stage as the SNP's more relatable face just as the Yes campaign was abandoning its Tartan Tiger origins and rebranding itself a dissenting vote against David Cameron's austerity programme – all of which added a gloss of populism to

Sturgeon's reputation. Stylistically, like her Third Way predecessors, the Sturgeon that emerged was a hybrid: managerial enough to look the part in the corridors of power; sufficiently demotic to retain anti-establishment credibility; autonomous enough from Westminster to give Scotland a flattering aura of moral autonomy; sufficiently professional to enjoy the confidence of the nation's elites in holding off 'fundamentalists'.

Yet this only adds to the mystery of Sturgeon's success: she has thrived in an era in which her ideological cohort failed. On the surface, she shares many of their shortcomings. She is a creature entirely of professional politics, having little adult experience of a world beyond Holyrood. Her successful presentational transformation has only reinforced the potential to appear as a focus-grouped, managerial figure. Her delivery may be practised and polished, but it is also composed of stock phrases that would be mocked in a figure who did not enjoy the cushion of mass credibility, which Sturgeon has inherited from the anti-establishment upheavals of 2014. If not for the latter, Sturgeon could thus easily appear as a creature of the isolation of the administrative state from 'ordinary' voters – the problem that makes her ideological bedfellows, figures like Hillary Clinton, Gordon Brown and Keir Starmer, electoral liabilities.

In other circumstances, Sturgeon could seem a quintessential insider, a career politician with few accomplishments to show for a near-decade running the country. But that would be to ignore the historical trajectory of mass politics and anti-establishment feeling in Scotland. Sturgeon's success is thus rooted in something more than competence, or even style. It is really a function of what she inherited: a party with a missionary cause that gained credit for unseating a hated establishment and restoring to Scotland a national *amour propre* as leader of the anti-Westminster opposition. Much of working-class and peripheral Scotland feels bound to stand by the moment of 2014–15, and independence has offered Sturgeon something lacking in a Starmer or a Clinton: the legitimacy of a disruptive project of popular democracy.

Equally, Sturgeon's manner has been disarming to those social forces most worried by 2014, the Scottish state apparatus and professional elites (although she has had less success in winning over business). They trust that Sturgeon will preserve the status quo and discipline what they see as the dangerous, demotic and demagogic elements of the independence movement. The legacy of 2014 thus doubly contributes to Sturgeon's legitimacy: she appears both as servant of that movement and protector from it.

The importance of 2014 is covered elsewhere in this book.[19] Its relevance to the SNP should be obvious: the referendum, above all, prefigured the intellectual and moral collapse of its only viable opponent, Scottish Labour. However, the importance of 2014 to the SNP as a party machinery and a party of government needs particular emphasis. Most mainstream accounts fixate on the personal qualities of individual leaders (often as a moral tale of goodies and baddies), while paying little heed to the historic role of the agency of peripheral activists and voters. This tendency is exacerbated by a sense of contempt for the political activities of ordinary people – visible in talk of Yes voters representing, variously, the 'death of enlightenment' or 'cybernats'.[20]

More often, the story is less of scorn than of condescension, or just obliviousness to mass politics. Thus, the Yes campaign in the 2014 referendum, a grassroots movement of extraordinary importance, functions in both academic and journalistic accounts of Scotland as mere historical colour, window-dressing for the rise of Sturgeon. The convenience of this narrative becomes more glaring when one considers the class interests represented by Sturgeon, who lacks Salmond's curiosity about the workers and capitalists of the private economy, and whose hegemony rests on the state and satellites of lawyers, journalists, academics and grant-funded entities.

Naturally, leadership matters in history, and Sturgeon brought qualities as a communicator that were often lacking in her predecessor. But historical processes conspired to leave her with a providential inheritance. Events beyond her control – the Yes campaign of 2014 was highly spontaneous – had cleared the ground of Scottish Labourism, delivering hundreds of thousands of new recruits and mobilised communities of voters to the SNP. Those events happened irrespective of leadership, partly due to accumulating pressures on post–social-democratic parties, partly due to the blundering of British state managers from Iraq to David Cameron's succession of referendums. Sturgeon's role was to take this turbulent momentum – a product of the 'populist moment' sweeping post-2008 Europe – and package it as stability.

Salmond–Sturgeon: A Misleading Divide

If these circumstances are about mass legitimacy, there is also the puzzle of her legitimacy on the left. Beyond the fact of being a woman and not being Salmond or Boris Johnson, Sturgeon has accomplished little to explain the easy ride she gets from 'progressives', including the Greens, who not only entered a formal pact with the SNP following the Scottish elections in 2021 but also offer Sturgeon cover even where there is no formal requirement to do so.

Part of the answer to this puzzle lies in the tendency to attach culture-war categories to the interpersonal battles of career politicians. Defending Sturgeon against Salmond – even though the latter poses almost zero electoral threat – thus acts as a proxy for a wider battle between liberalism and 'social conservatism'. As Foley has argued elsewhere, much of activist and professional-managerial Scotland has developed a 'parasocial' bond with Sturgeon, seeing her 'struggles' as their own, and wishing to defend her from being 'victimised' by criticism.[21] This illustrates a much wider transformation in the public's role in political representation: far from holding politicians to account, the politically invested minority treat certain politicians (regarded as different from run-of-the-mill careerists) as friends requiring moral support. Similar fandoms emerged around Ed Miliband, Jeremy Corbyn and

Alexandria Ocasio-Cortez on the left, and Boris Johnson and Donald Trump on the right.

These personalised, emotionally charged investments are usually impervious to facts; the true political record will always paint a more nuanced picture. As a career politician whose legitimacy emerged under the umbrella of Salmond's rise to power, Sturgeon has a chequered history that defies easy categorisation as 'woke'. For instance, despite her conceit of being a champion of LGBTQI+ rights – and for all the socially conservative critiques of Sturgeon as a queer theory fanatic – her public stance on the central battle against Scotland's traditionally homophobic culture, the repeal of Section 28, was decidedly ambivalent. 'We believe that the value of marriage should be clearly referred to in the guidelines, without denigrating other relationships or children brought up in other kinds of relationship', she said.[22] Since making this remark in 2000, Sturgeon has followed other centrist politicians who have mirrored liberalising shifts in public attitudes (gay marriage, for instance, was introduced under David Cameron). Thus, while Sturgeon has taken progressive stances, she has rarely taken the sort of *brave* stance that carries political costs. Instead, her progressive postures reflect shifts in prevailing attitudes, of which Sturgeon (contrary to what supporters and critics imagine) is more of a follower than a leader.

Indeed, matters are even more subtle than this would suggest. Sturgeon's side has often been rather ambiguous about identity causes in practice, making use of them when convenient and non-costly, only to drop them when they become burdens. Alyn Smith MP, one of Sturgeon's key allies, tried to throw equalities groups off the SNP's National Executive Committee, claiming that their influence was disrupting party management. 'Broadening the NEC to bring in a wider range of voices, while a laudable aim, has to my mind diluted discussion of the interests of the whole of Scotland and building the case for independence', he asserted in a leaked internal email. 'We are the Scottish National Party – we must reflect and work upon the priorities of the people of Scotland, not our own projects.'[23] Smith went on to suggest that the SNP risked being portrayed rather like Labour's 'loony left'. Equally, while Sturgeon did sign up for gender-recognition reform, the assumption was that it would pass quietly, with little resistance other than from religious zealots. Faced with an unexpectedly diverse coalition of opponents, she performed the established Scottish government manoeuvre of locking thorny issues into a scrimmage of consultations – or, even more conveniently, postponing them until after an imminent election. Sturgeon is in general more conservative than her cheerleaders would suggest, while Salmond, reflecting the times, is more liberal than his critics would allow – even if his personal behaviour has been inexcusable.

Culture-war attitudes are often overdetermined by considerations of foreign policy. On this topic, there is a more marked contrast between what Kenny MacAskill calls 'Old SNP' and 'New SNP'. Certainly, compared to Sturgeon, Salmond led as a cavalier outsider, and was more pronounced in taking anti-imperialist (or at least anti-American) stances. Out of office, this division has reached the point of caricature, with Salmond presenting a show on the Kremlin-sponsored Russia Today channel. Meanwhile, figures close to Sturgeon have embraced New Cold War rhetoric.[24] These Atlanticist efforts have been led by Angus Robertson, a rumoured leadership successor, and Stewart McDonald MP, who, while claiming to be a Palestine activist, has sponsored a pro-Israel front group and spoken in glowing terms of the 'inspiration for Scotland [Winnie Ewing] saw in Israel [when] meeting then Prime Minister Menachem Begin and travelling to see tourist sites in his limousine' – an anecdote that would be darkly humorous if recounted with any hint of irony.[25] Sturgeon herself has used her Twitter platform to praise hawkish American politicians ranging, from Hillary Clinton and Madeleine Albright to Henry Kissinger and John McCain.

But even here, such shifts are more nuanced than Salmond's supporters would allow. A section of Sturgeon's younger cadres evidently has an uncritical attachment to the idea of Nato and

American foreign policy as shields of liberal civilisation against Russia. Some of them doubtless share the cringe-worthy aesthetic sensibility of young politicos worldwide, who tend to inhabit a psychic world formed out of clichés from President Bartlet and the fast-talking gossip of Aaron Sorkin's *The West Wing*. That said, the New SNP has made little concrete progress in moving the party's foreign policy to the right, and the first move to embrace Nato – a nuclear-armed anti-Russian alliance – emerged under Salmond's leadership. Since then, the SNP has conducted an internal cold war over foreign policy, but differences have rarely emerged in public. Formally, the SNP remains committed to unilateral disarmament. There are legitimate doubts about how that squares with seeking Nato membership – but these anxieties are an inheritance from the Salmond era.

With that in mind, the differences between Salmond and Sturgeon are comically exaggerated. They are interrelated actors in a broadly liberal cultural and economic hegemony – a drama whose players have all worked in tandem for decades. Murrell began his political career working in Salmond's office; Sturgeon spent many years as Salmond's deputy, and was happy to describe him as her 'mentor'. Famously, when Salmond returned from exile, they struck an agreement rather like the infamous Blair–Brown pact, whereby Sturgeon would be chosen as the anointed successor. At that stage, any disagreements between the two of them were hidden from public view.

Eventually, Salmond's combination of anti-establishment posturing, saturnine charisma and unprofessional conduct made him a barrier to 'modernising' the party's image – particularly when he refused to leave the stage conclusively after the referendum defeat and the loss of his parliamentary seat. This was superficially a question of style. But it arguably bears on a more important articulation of class politics in liberal-centrist coalitions. Salmond's appeal was to outsiders who were sceptical of politics, to whom he promised a shake-up, a break with conformity. He deliberately went after both the boardrooms and Labour-voting, perhaps socially conservative layers of the peripheral working-class – two groups that are suspicious of official power – while being openly confrontational towards governing cliques and the professional-managerial class. By contrast, Sturgeon has built her hegemony on insiders, and on orchestrating patronage networks: the same centrist message, but organised on a different class basis. On the other hand, this group is too small to constitute a true political base, and Sturgeon continues to borrow credibility from the disruptions of 2014.

Brexit and Sturgeonism

Sturgeon has often appeared uncomfortable with the independence movement. Symbolically, she refused to attend the 'All Under One Banner' (AUOB) marches, which were arguably some of the largest mobilisations in Scottish political history. It was equally symbolic that she provocatively *did* attend the 'People's Vote' marches in London, and chose to pose for selfies with figures like Blair's spin-doctor Alastair Campbell.

To pro-Sturgeon leftists, the difference was that the AUOB marches were organised by figures with unsavoury backgrounds. But this rationale appears less clear-cut in light of the fact that the People's Vote demonstrations were organised by the intellectual architects of the War on Terror and the extraordinary attacks on British Muslim civil liberties that issued from it. Leftist moralising thus does a poor job of explaining the discrepancy. In truth, the difference between the People's Vote and AUOB is not inherently moral, or even crudely ideological. The difference is between a movement led by insiders and one led by outsiders. AUOB was a populist revolt against the status quo massing from flyover Scotland; the People's Vote was an anti-populist assemblage of middle-class liberalism centred on restoring the status quo. This represents a truth about Sturgeon's political character: that she 'found herself' during the post-2016 crisis surrounding Brexit. It was here that she emerged as the darling of liberal Britain and a fixture of supposedly progressive American chat shows.

Not by accident, this period saw a major shift in the class composition of support for independence. According to one estimate drawn from Scottish Social Attitudes data, prior to Brexit, Yes support among Scotland's 'elite managers' ranked as low as 11 per cent; by 2019, it stood at 59 per cent, this group now representing the biggest enthusiasts for independence, having been its biggest pessimists in 2014. Working-class support has largely remained static, and some polls have shown a downward trend, following Brexit – although it should be noted that it has largely remained solidly behind the SNP.

Perhaps the more significant factor is that the 'populist moment' in 2014, for all its talk of class politics and 'changing Scotland forever', failed to correct imbalances of political representation from the neoliberal era. Under Sturgeon, the SNP has bolstered professional-managerial hegemony. Michael Keating's research suggests that most Scottish parliamentarians now emerge from 'politics-facilitating' professions:

> In the post-war decades, Scottish Labour recruited more MPs from the old blue-collar working-class occupations and the Conservatives more from aristocrats and landowners than their counterparts in England. Amongst MSPs, this has been reversed, with a common middle class background predominating. Many such occupations – such as in law or education – were once described as 'politics facilitating' because they offered the skills or connections conducive to seeking election. Now, the main focus is on the occupations that may be used as a stepping stone towards elected office, such as MP and party assistants, members of think tanks or interest groups sympathetic to particular parties, and work in public relations or the media, close to the political centre.[26]

Some, Keating included, question whether these trends are a problem: Are credentialed professionals not just as focused on the
'common good' as others? And if the focus is merely on citizens as
consumers who experience the delivery of services, perhaps there
is no problem – although it could be said that 'delivery' has stalled
under this emergent class coalition, given rates of disenchantment
with services like health and education.[27] Equally, if the focus is on
politicians as avatars for value preferences and objects of our parasocial investments, then class may be less significant. But, insofar
as we see political representation standing for social conflict over
wealth and power, these trends are signifiers of decay – doubly so
for those who value the idea of democracy in its deeper sense, as
not just representing a divided society but providing the platform
for alternative projects in the use of political authority to reorgan-
ise society.

In Scotland, conflict over independence, real or imagined,
serves to distract from the absence of other serious disagreements,
and thus the absence of electoral choice. By mobilising peripheral
and 'left behind' voters, 2014 represented a potential rupture with
this social consensus. However, the 2016 referendum and its aftermath served as a moment for the restoration of order around new
national myths. Most especially, there was the myth of a cosmopolitan Scotland whose will had been crushed by callous
Westminster leaders. This myth has proliferated because it is port-
able and useful to diverse political factions, from European
bureaucrats wishing to strengthen their negotiating hand against
London, defeated London liberals looking to disparage the credibility of the 2016 vote or point to Brexit's self-harming nature, and
national populists in Scotland itself, to Scotland's governing elite,
which has nurtured a politics of grievance and victimhood to
burnish its credibility as representative of mass opinion.

All myths have some foundation in fact, and the most sober
researchers have noted that Scotland's new European fixation is a
myth precisely in the sense that social scientists take seriously. 'We
are in the realm of "myth", in the anthropological sense, truths held

to be self-evident, which are stimuli for social and political action, regardless almost of their truth-status', notes David McCrone. 'Scots are "European" after the events of 23 June 2016 because they voted to Remain in the EU . . . This "fact" is another brick in the wall of Scottish identity, whether we like it or not.'[28] But McCrone also observes that 'facts are chiels that winna ding'. Prior to the 2016 vote, recorded Euroscepticism in Scotland stood at 60 per cent – just 5 points below the English figure. Less than 5 per cent of Scots give their identity as 'European' when forced to choose.[29] And anyone familiar with Scottish political history will know that, historically, Scottish people were more Eurosceptic than their English counterparts, just as the left was more Eurosceptic than the right.

The tributary myths of this grand narrative are also questionable and morally dubious in their implications. Thus, the notion of Scotland being 'open to immigration' has been questioned by generations of social scientists, and critics claim it contributes to a 'no problem here' narrative that helps the Scottish national community to avoid its historic culpability for imperialism and its contemporary culpability for racism.[30]

This aside, as McCrone suggests, the 'European Scotland' narrative should be treated as a national myth in the proper social-scientific sense. The point is less its intrinsic truth value than its mobilising function: it survives and prospers because it proves useful in the pursuit of inconsistent and often divergent political agendas. Populist nationalists use the myth to inflame a sense of grievance against Tory Westminster; Sturgeon's cohort use it to present the SNP and Scottish governance as credible components of a liberal consensus.

However, those two forces are invested for reasons that can come into conflict. The populist part of nationalism, represented by AUOB, jumped on the anti-Brexit bandwagon believing that it would hasten moves towards independence. By contrast, the most active critics of Brexit – the professional-managerial class represented by the People's Vote movement – objected to the 2016 vote precisely because it spelled constitutional disruption. The 2016 referendum served to move many of this cohort – temporarily, at least – into the pro-independence camp; but their loyalty to that cause has never been seriously tested. Sturgeon has no choice but to reckon with and manage these contradictions.

In historical retrospect, it has been the populist or 'fundamentalist' wing that has lost out from its over-investment in Brexit. SNP leaders gained numerous mandates for an independence referendum, and were notorious for promising that referendums were months from going ahead. In practice, though, the cause was always relegated to the prosecution of the wider (and ultimately, in England, electorally disastrous) People's Vote campaign for a UK-wide referendum on cancelling Brexit. Subsequently it has been placed behind coronavirus recovery, and may struggle to garner once again the popular currency it enjoyed during the peak 2016–19 crisis of the state – at least in the near future. Beneath many recent grievances lies the sense that Scotland's moment was missed.

In all of this, Sturgeon was a better mirror of passive public opinion than her more mobilised counterparts in the independence movement. Nonetheless, she runs the risk of leaving office with few accomplishments to her name, having figured largely as a crisis manager rather than a leader or mobiliser towards the cause of independence, or any other cause. A unique historical moment has passed without a substantive breakthrough – and, whether on health, education, the environment or poverty, the domestic front has offered no fall-back option. Sturgeon's reputation has rested on her being neither Boris Johnson nor Alex Salmond, and on her (effectively global) role as the avatar of anti-Brexit resistance. But as Brexit has become a settled fact, it has exposed major holes in the party's intellectual prospectus for independence – all of which gives reason to doubt both her seriousness about the cause and her self-image as a professional, detail-oriented politician.

The Salmond–Sturgeon War

The trial of Alex Salmond began with complaints made by two female civil servants, both of whom showed real bravery in reporting an authority figure. What emerged subsequently was a confusion between these starting points and internal politicking within the SNP, which culminated in Salmond successfully suing the government – and, in the subsequent trial, the prosecution losing all elements of its case against Salmond. This debacle would expose both the weakness and the lack of accountability of what passes for political authority in Scotland. Having, by the government's own admission, failed the women concerned, it has produced neither meaningful reforms nor resignations. Much of civic Scotland determined that its parasocial investment in Sturgeon's clash with Salmond mattered more than any questions of accountability, and thus the buck had nowhere to stop. In earlier eras, the public was, as a rule, cynical about politicians, and sceptical that they could ever improve their lives. Many retain that cynicism. But there are many others who over-invest in political personalities, seeing them not as representatives of the public interest in a divided society, but rather as 'goodies' or 'baddies' requiring applause or jeering from the sidelines. In many respects, this mode of politics has been more incapacitating than the earlier apathy. Sturgeon's supporters increasingly have no expectation that she will improve anything; or rather, delivering on policies has ceased to matter (naturally, the same goes for many of Salmond's supporters). For these new politicos, rather than politicians functioning as arbiters of public interests, the public functions to provide politicians who are 'goodies' with moral support.

An intellectually autonomous left, being subservient neither to Salmond nor to Sturgeon, would have taken a more nuanced view of proceedings. The great irony of the conflict was that, in humiliating the two doyens of contemporary Scottish nationalism, it may have reinforced the case for independence. If the struggle demonstrated nothing else, it was the half-baked nature of devolved authority and the resulting vacuum of accountability in crisis scenarios. Holyrood was designed for New Labour hegemony, and has nothing like the resilience to withstand twin poles of nationalism in Edinburgh and London. There is no hope of moving backwards to the old unionism. Neither is there hope of further reform, as too many interest groups have coalesced to exploit the nationalist moment. Only independence offers the prospect of meaningful curbs on politico-judicial authority. Instead, however, the narrative was either of Salmond as boy scout, or Sturgeon as victimised woman in a man's world; neither interpretation gives much credit to the public's capacity to appreciate nuance.

Scotland's subaltern unionist bloc did try to hold Sturgeon, her husband and the SNP leadership to account. But many penetrating individual points failed to cohere into an overall critique. It is difficult to avoid the conclusion that Sturgeon, intentionally or not, misled parliament; that women were poorly served by a process that sometimes jumbled factional fighting with justice; and that the lines between prosecution services and political power had been badly warped. To put it mildly, these points posed serious questions about the limits of power. But the question would ultimately boil down to whether the public preferred Sturgeon, on one hand, or Salmond or Boris Johnson, on the other. That false dilemma expresses far broader failings in media, academia and civic leadership.

Sturgeon's unionist critics were doubtless correct in saying that Salmond's behaviour had allowed her to pose as the victim while the administration she presided over failed women. Yet, ensconced in their political agendas, many felt secure in ignoring these grains of truth. Conservative critiques, no matter how lawyerly their construction, would always seem like faux outrage while their own party was led by Johnson, and while it overlooked their own breaches of the ministerial code in Westminster. Labour and the Liberals suffered from overlapping problems. Certainly, someone in Sturgeon's midst should have been held accountable; the absence of any resignations did Scotland's governance community no credit. That said, this culture of slippery accountability was a product of the crumbling Lib–Lab devolved state, to which their only solution was further rounds of devolution. Equally, in their own way they were also damned by the behaviour of Conservative ministers who broke ministerial codes with impunity – or else by the legacy of New Labour, which bent rules to breaking point to justify the invasion of a sovereign country and suffered no consequences.

In a polarised culture, it has become almost impossible to state the most ironic outcome of the Salmond–Sturgeon trial. The truth is uncomfortable for all sides. Yet it seems obvious, in retrospect, that, by centring himself, Salmond's ultimate role was to save Sturgeon from a yawning crisis of purpose. Following the trial, with Salmond temporarily in hiding, Sturgeon had been experiencing an extraordinary rebellion inside her own ranks. Internal SNP elections were a story of bruising setbacks for the leadership amid the first signs of open factionalism in decades. Just prior to Salmond's reappearance, the SNP Common Weal Group (CWG) inflicted defeats on a succession of leadership darlings, including Alyn Smith – the figurehead of ostentatious (and uncritical) pro-EU sentiment. In total, the anti-leadership faction won a third of seats on the party executive. Committed to internal party democracy, opposed to the Growth Commission and favouring a 'Green New Deal', the faction was by most historical standards to Sturgeon's left – the only exception to that rule being its proximity to 'gender critical' feminists.

Nonetheless, efforts to paint the CWG vote as unambiguously leftist, or (even more absurdly) 'alt right', ascribe to it too much coherence. Neither left-leaning economics nor the culture war was the decisive factor in giving wide support to the faction's challenge to Sturgeon. The common denominator of what CWG did represent was a growing bloc of disaffection about stalled progress towards independence: anxiety that an unprecedented crisis of the British state would pass without any decisive constitutional breakthrough. This sentiment was so pervasive that it made room for other factions of dissent. But that should not disguise the underlying cause: hundreds of thousands joined the SNP seeing it entirely as a vehicle for independence; but many saw the prospect slipping away, with the moment of maximum opportunity already passed.

Much of the SNP's historic left would side with Salmond during the subsequent parliamentary investigation, the evidence against her (and especially her husband) being regarded as so intrinsically damning as to make resignation inevitable. But despite much damaging testimony, and evidence from Murrell that was widely panned as 'shifty', nothing conclusive emerged to suggest direct wrongdoing on Sturgeon's part, and independent investigations exonerated her of breaching the ministerial code. Sturgeon emerged from Salmond's testimony not just unscathed, but with her authority enhanced.

Salmond's decision to re-enter politics, with the launch of the Alba Party, only compounded these problems, serving to flush out leadership critics from the SNP. As many jumped to Salmond's side, others faced the choice of staying to represent a diminished rump of dissenters or opting for safety in numbers. Those who stayed, such as Joanna Cherry, experienced dejection and exclusion. Those who jumped, including much of the historic left wing of the SNP, experienced a bruising election defeat. Having promised to revolutionise Scottish politics, Salmond's new party got nowhere near the threshold to elect a single MSP. Since then, the Scottish Greens – a party representing much of the nation's progressive attitudes – has rallied to Sturgeon's side in coalition, despite the SNP's long list of policy failures and the leadership's neoliberal programme for independence. Having only recently been under ferocious attack, Salmond's re-entry into politics has served to give Sturgeon considerable (and arguably unearned) cover from the left.

Sturgeon's supporters may have felt vindicated by the result. To them, it demonstrated that Scotland was not ready for overnight moves towards separation from the UK; their gradualism had been justified at the ballot box. There is doubtless a certain truth in this interpretation: for all that forming new electoral parties has a high likelihood of failure, the fact remains that the public knew of Salmond's Alba Party and its more radical constitutional offer, and chose, for whatever reason, not to vote for it. Sturgeon's promise of moral autonomy and practical continuity doubtless better represented Scotland's hopes and fears in aggregate.

But this may represent little more than a self-fulfilling prophecy. Nationalism is highly dependent on mobilisation and leadership – and while there was much spontaneous protest from the bottom, the leaders refused to inject agency from the top. More broadly, political parties, nationalist or not, exist not just to mirror public attitudes passively (a notion that emerges from the Blair era of focus-grouping), but to mobilise, marshal and lead coalitions behind programmes that accomplish change – especially at moments of historic crisis. Indeed, this surely represents the real test of parties and party leaderships.

While Britain's instability leaves open the possibility of new ruptures, the suspicion remains that Sturgeon missed the SNP's historic moment, when public sympathy peaked with the crisis of the British state, for fear of a breach with her post-2016 supporters in metropolitan Britain. The result, for now, is a disfiguring, intellectually stultifying deadlock.

Assessing Sturgeon's contribution is therefore not straightforward. Insofar as she appears, for some of the left, as a culture-war avatar against Salmond's 'social conservatism', she has achieved mixed success, epitomised in the long and circuitous route to passing the GRR legislation which is so central to Sturgeon's moral legitimation, despite a clear parliamentary majority in its favour. Insofar as Sturgeon seems to represent the aggregate of public and commentariat preferences – the desire for moral autonomy from Westminster without the risks of separation – she has been an unqualified success. But the question remains whether any Scottish government can fulfil even modest public expectations within that political climate. For now, robust crisis management has proved effective in staving off accountability for a litany of failures, from drug deaths to the poverty-related attainment gap. A devolved settlement with rival nationalists facing off in Edinburgh and London appears to be the ideal arrangement for keeping domestic policy off the agenda.

Insofar as Sturgeon was meant to be an agent of the SNP's historic mission of independence, matters have arguably regressed. Support for Yes may have grown slightly after Brexit, but the ultimate result has made the British state more resilient. It has gained confidence that it can absorb any SNP challenge led by Sturgeon. The latter's intransigent attacks on Jeremy Corbyn, and willingness to deal with the New Labour leadership of the People's Vote (PV) movement in the spirit of undermining Corbyn, has left Scottish nationalism in longer-term disarray. If Britain had plumped for a 'soft' Brexit and remained in the Single Market, as seemed inevitable before PV took command over Labour, Sturgeon's mild vision of independence would be more viable. Instead, PV hysteria polarised Britain into warring camps, resulting in the collapse of Labour's English heartlands. The outcome has posed intellectual challenges surrounding borders, fiscal policy and currency that seem beyond the grasp of the current leadership. This is before even considering the end of the oil era. The strongest evidence that the SNP leadership is not imminently planning a battle over independence is its failure to address these doubts head-on.

One question, then, is whether Sturgeon could move Scotland into a post-independence scenario that we have called 'neo-autono-mism' – a phrase we have borrowed from the Catalan left. In essence, this would involve a permanent nationalist framing of regional political alliances, without a corresponding movement towards statehood. Certainly, there is much to recommend this view. It seems guaranteed to maximise support without risks, which fits with much of the party's recent behaviour. In terms of class analysis, neo-autonomism seems ideally suited to perpetuat-ing the lifestyles of the professional-managerial class, who orbit

Holyrood and form the social base of Sturgeonism. It guarantees those Scottish professionals who depend on the state a sinecure without all of the attendant risks of establishing a state.

But we would also stress the limitations on a neo-autonomist trajectory. Firstly, the SNP remains a nationalist party with a mass base. The routine business of party management, such as financing and election canvassing, depends on mobilising enthusiasm behind a cause. This is rather different, for instance, from Labour or the Conservatives, who may have broken from their origins as parties of social class, but who, for reasons of habit if nothing else, still depend respectively on labour (the unions) and capital to finance their operations. The SNP's opponents will say in private that their biggest fear is less Sturgeon's aura than the party's ferocious political machine: they are skilled experts at mobilising and getting out a vote. Such machinery will not work on patronage networks alone. There are growing signs of how this might be a problem. Despite overwhelming dominance in Holyrood, the party struggles to finance elections, and routinely resorts to desperate fundraising drives centred on the imminence of independence. With many who understand the party's inner workings having defected, to Alba or elsewhere, these risks are heightened. The party was even investigated for fraud, having spent money raised for an independence campaign on running routine party operations. All moralising aside, the point is that the SNP literally cannot afford total demoralisation. It depends on the enthusiasm of a largely older generation who will part with money to see independence in their lifetime. Outright demobilisation is thus impossible. The halfway house, to critics, has looked more like the Grand Old Duke of York: 'march them up to the top of the hill then march them down again'. Hopes are raised, then dashed, in successive, never-ending rounds.

A second limitation is the weakness of the SNP's domestic record. Sturgeon's reputation for competence has largely centred on comparisons with Boris Johnson, but her time as leader is short on outright achievements. Most of the SNP's triumphs were products of the Salmond era, a fact which says less about the two leaders' respective qualities than about the passage of time, since Sturgeon inherited a party that, while basking in the populist upsurge of 2014, was already running out of ideas on policy. Sturgeon's time has seen worthy rhetoric on poverty, 'fair work', attainment gaps and green jobs that has amounted to rather little. As we have seen, even the domain of gender politics is far from an unqualified success story, and shocks like drug deaths should have done far more to scandalise Scottish civil society than they have.

Since the crisis of 2008, voting publics have been unkind to those who have remained expectant of re-election while delivering little. Indeed, the SNP's triumph over Scottish Labour was a spectacular illustration of that trend. Clearly, though, the party risks succumbing to the same force, and might have done so already but for the promise of independence. The latter continues to dominate Scottish elections in practice, if only because of the absence of other meaningful differences between Holyrood parties. By surrendering the question, without substantive breakthroughs elsewhere, the party risks the type of meltdown into cynicism that befell so many centre-left parties in Europe.

Another problem emerges from the over-centralisation of the party in the hands of Sturgeon and Murrell – a problem only exacerbated by parasocial investment in her victory over Salmond. Since 2014, when the SNP gained 100,000 new members, the couple has run a highly centralised operation with extreme expectations of loyalty to the leadership. All morality aside, the problem is that the party has promoted uncritical loyalists who equate discipline with conformity, who lack intellectual autonomy – and thus the independence of spirit to build on the Salmond–Sturgeon era. Unlike her predecessor, Sturgeon has no protégé. The tabloid takedown of Derek MacKay, her rumoured heir apparent, only served to expose the miserably low level of her court of flatterers. This suggests a further limitation on a neo-autonomist solution for Scotland. Nobody can play this game like Sturgeon – and eventually she may grow tired of it. The organised hypocrisies of Holyrood governance would crumble under a weaker leader, and Sturgeon has neurotically promoted a cohort barely capable of reproducing the status quo.

Finally, beyond the question of whether neo-autonomism might work, there is the question of how the left should approach it. Many leftists, especially those wedded to a communitarian or culture-war perspective, have grown tired of independence dominating all agendas. They may conclude, not incorrectly, that important questions like poverty have become lost amid the constitutional wrangling between London and England. They rather like the prospect of Scotland retaining its moral autonomy without the attendant risks: after all, if the SNP's independence prospectus were ever to be delivered, it would ultimately mean austerity. They may prefer a future of negotiated constitutional reforms and a prospective 'progressive alliance' in Westminster, composed of Scottish nationalists, Greens and Labour.

But this is a fantasy future. In truth, an inconclusive end to the national question is unlikely to end the SNP's status as Scotland's largest party, even if Sturgeon resigns. Nor will it end the habit of elections being fought between unionist and nationalist camps, as was so evidently the case in 2021. The bigger risk is complete political demobilisation, especially in working-class communities. Unresolved questions of accountability will fester, and the gap between politics and the people will grow once again. Neo-autonomism is the name we give to the drift into organised hypocrisy represented by Sturgeon's government. There are real limits on it, but it remains Scotland's most likely trajectory – and a left in full command of its senses would see it as the most dangerous and cunning enemy.

6

Progressive Neoliberalism
Confronts the Pandemic

The previous chapters primarily addressed the years between 2008 and 2019 – a long decade of global financial crisis, unprecedented austerity and political turmoil for liberal democracies. Quite against nationalist predictions, prospects for Scottish independence emerged not from booming market globalisation, but from this era of economic slowdown and political alienation. As if to emphasise this point, as the book was being finalised, a new and perhaps deeper crisis struck the capitalist system. The 2020 coronavirus pandemic shattered any remaining ideological credibility attached to neoliberal economics, as governments worldwide injected extraordinary doses of state support to prop up businesses.

In Scotland, reactions to the pandemic confirmed the shift in elite attitudes to the nationalist government in Holyrood. The SNP's earlier reputation as separatist saboteurs had all but disappeared. As one of Europe's last managerial 'centrist' leaders to command a popular base, Sturgeon drew effusive praise for her handling of the pandemic, most especially in the liberal press. 'It has been painful to watch the steadiness and sombre dignity of the first ministers of the devolved parliaments – notably Nicola Sturgeon', wrote Ferdinand Mount in the *London Review of Books*, 'and then to turn to the slapdash boosterism of [Boris] Johnson and his associates.'[1]

In this narrative, the successes of devolution serve as counterpoints to the libertarian populist bungling of Johnson and Trump. With scientific experts enjoying renewed authority, liberal anti-populists felt vindicated and ready to retake the reins of power: for many, it came as some relief to announce that playtime was over, and that it was time for the adults to take charge again. Holyrood served as an illustration of what they might achieve, but for the intrusion of Brexiteer saboteurs in Westminster. There was, of course, the obvious irony that Scottish nationalists now served as exemplars of technocratic stability. But, more importantly, stock contrasts between Johnson and Sturgeon illustrate just how much culture-war polarisation now fixates on questions of style. An examination of actual decision-making tells a different story: rhetorical graces have absurdly little counterpart in everyday reality.

Indeed, given Sturgeon's Scottish nationalist starting point, the real surprise is how little her Edinburgh government deviated from her much-maligned counterpart in London. In the crucial early days of coronavirus, when the real damage was done, Sturgeon's administration followed Johnson's in lockstep. When Johnson embraced 'herd immunity', so did the Scottish government; when Johnson reversed that decision and imposed a lockdown, Holyrood followed. As the *Financial Times* observed in a rare critical article, 'Sturgeon . . . made no attempt to challenge the UK's relatively late implementation of lockdown, which is widely seen as the main reason why the death rate has been higher than other nations.'[2]

In those early weeks, the Scottish government also made its own calamitous errors, quite separately from any bungling at Westminster. By far the biggest was the decision to discharge elderly patients from hospitals into care homes without testing them for coronavirus. Within three months, an astonishing one in twenty care-home residents had died from Covid-19. The care-home crisis was described in one report as 'possibly . . . the single greatest failure of devolved government ... since the creation of the Scottish Parliament'.[3]

Mistakes, it can be argued, are inevitable in an emergency. But a consideration of the wider structural background to the pandemic crisis highlights systemic failures. The deadly care-home crisis was itself a symptom of decades of privatisation and underinvestment in the wider architecture of public health. This story involves three dangerous and interlocking processes – deregulation, privatisation and financialisation – that are both symptoms and causes of decades of economic failure. Far from slowing commodification, two decades of devolution, under various incarnations of centre-left rule, served if anything to exacerbate these underlying problems.

Social Care: A Financialisation Story

Care-home privatisation, according to Professor Allyson Pollock, was 'one of the most under-reported sell-offs of the Thatcher and Major years'.[4] That it went unnoticed was partly a question of timing: coming in 1996, during the dying months of Conservative rule, it merely added to the litany of earlier divestments. Nobody had much incentive to politicise the question. Given the incoming New Labour administration's reluctance to reverse even the most detested Thatcherite policies, such as rail privatisation, it was unlikely to stake political capital on a question that had attracted so little controversy.

This was the political background to Four Seasons Care, a firm that epitomises the scandalous mismanagement of the 2020 pandemic. From humble origins, starting with just one care home in Kirkcaldy, Four Seasons boomed in the Blair years, expanding from seven homes in 1997 to 101 by the millennium, making it, at one stage, the UK's biggest provider. Four Seasons epitomised Britain's emerging enterprise culture, which is to say it grew in proportion with the state's withdrawal from direct provision of public services.

It was also during this time that Scotland's new parliament introduced free personal care for the elderly – a justly celebrated piece of progressive legislation. However, socialisation of risk was accompanied by an acceleration in the privatisation of underlying assets: home care delivered directly by Scottish local authorities fell from 82 per cent in 2000 to 44 per cent just over a decade later. Commodification continued apace, in apparent pursuit of social justice.

Private care homes, meanwhile, were being buffeted by arcane revolutions in financialisation, which transformed all types of asset management. Global private equity firms colonised a sector that had only recently consisted of humble local-authority operations. Four Seasons was bought out twice by these entities, leveraged by huge amounts of debt. These revolutions in business management imposed a regime of economies of scale and cost savings in matters of training and staff remuneration. In a sector already notorious for a toxic mix of maltreatment and poverty pay, costs were hammered down and down. One 2017 study found the big private providers could expect to make profits of 21 per cent, one of the highest margins in any sector.[5]

For all that, the outcomes were financially disastrous, and in 2019 Four Seasons had entered administration, £500 million in debt and burdened by £50 million in annual servicing costs. Beneath this peculiar failure was the esoteric complexity of contemporary capitalist business models. A *Financial Times* analysis found that 'tracing the finances at Four Seasons is all but impossible; the company's sprawling structure consists of 200 companies arranged in 12 layers in at least five jurisdictions, including several offshore territories'.[6]

Squeezed from one side by capitalism's competitive dynamics, care homes also suffered politically from local government austerity. When the SNP first came to power in 2007, they promised to replace the (regressive and much criticised) Council Tax with a new progressive form of local taxation. But this never materialised. Instead, as a minority government, the party made an informal agreement with the Scottish Tories that froze Council Tax for the entirety of their first administration. Subsequently, when the Tory–Liberal coalition took the reins at Westminster, austerity measures would eat further chunks of funding. Local authorities suffered the brunt of cuts to Scotland's block grant. Yet the SNP also wanted to preserve universal entitlement to care – a centrepiece of Scotland's progressive credentials under devolution.

The outcome was to push councils towards further rounds of outsourcing and privatisation. From 2007 to 2017, the number of local authority care homes fell by 31 per cent. Today, councils are effectively funding privately run care in Scotland: despite 67 per cent of care homes being mainly or wholly local-authority funded, 75 per cent of residents are in private care homes. As private equity firms seized the rewards of the outsourcing of care, public money was being channelled into private profits: one UK study has found that, for small care providers, £7 out of every £100 spent on social care goes towards profits and executive pay, compared to £15 out of every £100 for the big private providers.[7]

Privatisation, arcane business models and austerity were necessary, if not sufficient, causes of the 2020 tragedy. Unsurprisingly, a Four Seasons home in Cranhill, Glasgow, was the site of Scotland's first major eruption of Covid-19. Thirteen people died in that one outbreak.

Class and Care Homes

These are the underlying developments lying behind the 2020 disaster. It is a complex story in which all of Scotland's major parties share complicity: New Labour building on Tory-era privatisation and outsourcing; the Conservative–Liberal austerity regime; SNP budgets that squeezed local government, leading to further rounds of commodification. However, to understand the sheer scale of the 2020 catastrophe, we must examine the dynamics of emergency management and response.

Seeking to free up hospital beds as the pandemic approached, Scottish officials discharged thousands of elderly patients into care homes without stopping to test them for Covid-19. This flow of lethally infectious people lasted a full two months before officials introduced mandatory testing. It was a home-grown error with stark consequences. By the start of June, Covid-19 had killed more people in care homes than in hospitals: indeed, an extraordinary 5 per cent of Scotland's care-home population fell victim. A study of twenty-six developed countries found that only Spain had a higher rate of Covid-19 mortality in care homes than Scotland.[8]

The circumstances of this very Scottish disaster are well known. A sense of panic gripped government as forecasts spoke of over-flowing hospitals; NHS managers were under pressure to avoid hospital 'bed blocking'. But if these were the proximate causes, relationships of social power were embedded in the fabric of the problem. In emergency situations, voices clamour to be heard: some are centred, others overlooked. It was not as if care-home managers, workers and residents were silent. Indeed, anxieties about the absence of personal protective equipment (PPE) in care homes were well reported, particularly in the trade-union movement. The problem was that nobody was paying enough attention to trigger government action. A critical analysis must establish why nobody noticed that care homes were the weak link in the chain of disaster management.

Given that all of society was mobilising to prevent Covid-19 deaths, why was so little attention devoted to care homes? A clue lies in the social background of the likely protagonists. The majority of elderly people in Scotland's care homes are supported by local-authority funding, which means that the assets accumulated in their lifetimes total less than £26,500 – just a little below the average annual salary. In plainer terms, they come from working-class backgrounds. By contrast, wealthier retired people tend to make other arrangements: most commonly, they avoid care homes entirely and buy in care at their private homes.

Those elderly people with the most clout and influence were thus protected from the system's risks and hardships. There can be little doubt that there would be greater alarm if thousands of deaths had afflicted retired bankers, academics and museum directors rather than cleaners, factory workers and security guards. But care-home residents belong on the most unfashionable rungs of the working class, and thus they and their families struggled to make their voices heard in the media and policy process. Lacking cultural and social capital, they could effectively be ignored until they became a grim statistic.

Workers in the sector were victims of low pay, low status and union busting. They were thus equally easy to ignore. Staff not only went untested; many also had to do without PPE. Just as worryingly, those who did have masks were issued official Scottish government guidance warning them only to wear them if residents were displaying clear symptoms. As the risks became more obvious and the first Scottish social carer, Catherine Sweeney, died from Covid-19, a letter emerged signed by hundreds of social carers that blamed Sturgeon directly. 'We do not feel safe at work', it read. 'You have lost our confidence by publishing guidance without consultation with front line workers and by forcing us to work with insufficient PPE.'[9] By the time the Scottish government responded, unrelenting staff sickness had produced labour shortages. Elsewhere, there were reports that workers were continuing to work in care homes while sick, as they could not survive for two weeks on statutory sick pay. Through little fault of their own, they accelerated the risk to vulnerable elderly people.

Covid-19 ran rampant through the interstices of a radically capitalist system of exploitation. To illustrate the problems this caused, consider the case of Home Farm care home in Portree, on the Isle of Skye. The scenic island, like much of the Scottish Highlands, remained all but free of the coronavirus. But the care home was a deadly exception: thirty out of thirty-four residents and the majority of staff were infected. How the virus entered and spread in an otherwise disease-free environment has never been fully resolved, but one explanation is that it stemmed from staff shortages, which forced the home to recruit emergency agency staff from across the UK, including as far as Kent in south-east England, who likely brought the virus with them.

Home Farm's shortcomings also illustrate the deeper, systemic roots of this crisis. Managed by the monolithic HC-One, the largest UK provider and owner of fifty-six care homes in Scotland, Home Farm had failed four inspections going back to December 2018. The Care Inspectorate raised regular concerns about its performance and risk-management procedures. The Inspectorate was forced to hand out first, second, third and fourth warnings – although without imposing serious sanctions. The putative authorities, in the words of Nick Kempe, a former care homes commissioner in Scotland, 'effectively have no power'. Kempe describes the Inspectorate as having a 'culture that puts partnership working before standards', a 'regulatory framework which treats private ownership and private financial interests as absolute', and resources that are 'hopelessly inadequate'.

After a further failed inspection in May, Home Farm's licence was revoked. NHS Highland was forced to step in and clear up the mess, ultimately paying £900,000 in Scottish government cash to HC-One to take control of the home. It was a familiar story, in which the public sector provided the backstop when privatisation failed. But to lay the blame on private contractors is to miss the point. As private enterprises are designed to do, they pursued maximum exploitation of profit-making opportunities. And HC-One can legitimately claim that they broke no rules by bringing untested agency staff from across the UK into their workforces. The Scottish government was just as culpable; but unlike the privateers, they are insulated by layers of left-wing cover in Scottish civil society.

The Care Inspectorate's report on Home Farm was damning. Management was unprepared for an outbreak, was not transparent, did not put infection controls in place; residents had been left lying in urine and faeces due to neglect. Yet no further action was taken against the company, and it continues to run fifty-five care homes in Scotland, many of which suffered further outbreaks.

The Shallow Piety of Scottish Progressives

Despite all of this, the pandemic in fact boosted Scotland's already healthy national self-image and standing among liberal elites. All signs thus point to the production of a mutually convenient ideology: the notion of 'good devolution' serves interests in Scotland and beyond, in a manner that has little to do with the unionist–nationalist binary. While Conservative Westminster depends on national populist rhetoric, Scotland, though ruled by a formally nationalist government, in fact serves as an outpost of what Nancy Fraser calls 'progressive neoliberalism', which she defines as an alliance of liberal social movements (feminist, anti-racist, LGBTQI+) with liberal, globalising business interests, negotiated through networks of professional preferment. As Fraser notes, this alliance is essentially the displaced *ancien régime*, a rear-guard rump of the 1990s consensus. But it also explains why Sturgeon has a worldwide popular following: she is among only a handful of cases of consistent electoral success for a formula that fails everywhere else.

Unsurprisingly, Scotland also illustrates the limits of this old guard's programme. Rhetorical graces are rarely matched by actual advances. This applies even to supposed staples such as 'equalities'. Formally speaking, Scotland's parliament champions all manner of progressive causes: Sturgeon's government has hailed Scotland as a 'feminist place to be', a mongrel nation that welcomes immigrants, a safe haven for LGBTQI+ people, a beacon of climate justice. However, this proliferation of liberal talking points is rarely matched by substantive progress. Indeed, on some basic measures Scotland is outperformed by England. Scotland, for instance, has only ever elected eight ethnic-minority representatives during the entirety of the parliament's history, despite the overwhelming liberal hegemony within it. By contrast, at the time of writing, there are four people from an ethnic-minority background in Boris Johnson's cabinet.

The underlying causes are complex, but consider the SNP's totemic Hate Crime Bill, the centrepiece of the government-mandated equalities agenda. Authored by the privately educated Humza Yousaf MSP, it focuses on acts 'motivated by prejudice based on race, religion, disability, sexual orientation, and transgender identity'. As Darren McGarvey has observed, the symptomatic missing piece in that puzzle is social class.[10] This not only misses the fact that class hatred – from above – remains arguably the most vicious of all Scotland's ancestral prejudices. It equally misses how liberal cultural policy commitments add up to little – and can even be actively counterproductive – when they ignore underlying economic injustices.

Or take the issue of gender, which dominates much of the discussion on the internal politics of independence. Here, endlessly lauded progress at the elite level (for example, fifty–fifty quotas on electoral lists) masks brutal continuity at the everyday level of exploitation. The above-mentioned social carers, more than four in five of whom are women, having endured the brunt of the crisis as 'essential workers', are among Scotland's lowest paid. Close to half take home an annual salary under £20,000; 10 per cent are estimated to be on zero-hours contracts. Far from protesting, Sturgeon's government has actively collaborated in reproducing this structure. Indeed, at the height of the pandemic, amid the clapping for carers, the SNP teamed up with the Conservatives to defeat a parliamentary motion that proposed allowing trade unions to enter care homes.

Ethnic minorities, meanwhile, make up less than 2 per cent of MSPs, but comprise about 10 per cent of the ultra-exploited field of social care. If social care workers experience the sharp end of labour-market policy, Scotland's ethnic minorities experience the sharp end of social care employment. A poll by Unison found that they were more fearful of Covid-19 infection at work, less likely to

receive full pay while absent, more likely to be in lower-paid, insecure roles, and more worried about losing their job than other
workers.[11] Nonetheless, Sturgeon, in a pitch-perfect illustration of
'progressive neoliberalism', cites social care as a key argument for
further immigration: without influxes of easily exploited workers
from abroad, Scotland will be 'critically short of staff' in the social
care sector.

Consider any field of injustice, and a parallel story emerges.
'Progressive' Holyrood has created a little room at the top for an
elite of women and minorities, though not nearly as much as it
likes to pretend. The beneficiaries are largely the well-heeled and
the well-connected among those identity groups. Holyrood
governance allows campaign groups and progressive NGOs room
at the top table – and even offers them small tranches of funding
– to author policy documents, provided they issue recommenda-
tions that do not impose serious political or economic costs. But
underneath, the system reproduces injustice with greater ferocity
than ever.

Where progress occurs, exploitation is ramped up somewhere
else. Universal free personal care – a praiseworthy ambition –
was matched by privatisation and poverty wages. Universalism
in public services, where not funded through progressive taxation, primarily provides savings for middle-class service users
(witness the university system). Consequent 'efficiency savings'
in public service delivery end up bolstering the exploitation of
cleaners, carers and gardeners. Theoretically, the Scottish government has been right to commit to universalism in public service
delivery: evidence shows that, unless the middle classes use
services, they become afflicted by problems of stigma. However,
where universalism is not backed by equality in workplaces and
progressive taxation, Scottish Labour, for all their characteristic
tone-deafness, are correct to point to the risk of 'middle-class
perks'.

During the pandemic, one now largely forgotten scandal illustrated how Scotland's emergent elite sees the world. Catherine

Calderwood, Scotland's highly remunerated chief medical officer, who had fronted the government PR campaign telling Scots to 'stay home', was caught visiting her scenic second home on two occasions, in clear contravention of her own rules. Progressive Scotland's immediate instinct was to rally to Calderwood's defence. SNP MP Stewart McDonald said it 'must be personally mortifying' for Calderwood, and that she should not have to resign; Toni Giugliano, SNP activist and Mental Health Foundation Scotland policy manager, said it was a 'sad day', as Calderwood was being 'thrown under a bus'; Andrew Wilson thought it a 'very human error of judgement', and called on 'armchair politicos' to 'please focus energies positively'. When mass public outrage eventually forced Calderwood out, much against Sturgeon's initial instincts, Wilson lamented 'a shocking and dispiriting day'.

None of the above stopped the demonisation of working-class and young people who ventured into public parks to catch a suntan. Nor, it should be added, did it stop the same individuals calling for harsh reprisals against former Tory spin-doctor Dominic Cummings for a similar offence, illustrating again the contradictions of Scotland's emergent elite of politics, policy and punditry. Rather often, easily monstered figures like Cummings allow Scotland's own ruling bloc to protect its own from serious scrutiny. Meanwhile, the system reproduces the everyday injuries of social class; and insofar as class tends to reproduce layers of injustice, it deepens all other inequalities.

Social Class Redux: The Exams Fiasco

The coronavirus had an uneven impact on Scotland's pretensions around social class. In the pandemic's opening weeks, societies worldwide belatedly discovered the labour theory of value, as few could deny that 'essential workers' – checkout operators, cleaners, nurses, porters – were keeping society functioning while chief executive officers (private or public sector) experienced the pandemic passively from their lawns. Quickly, however, the dominant paternalistic idea of social class – what McGarvey calls the 'poverty industry' – reasserted itself. Workers' newfound status as everyday heroes was revoked; the poor were reduced again to pitiable victims. But the passions of class anger soon re-emerged and briefly threatened to engulf Holyrood governance when working-class pupils received their examination results.

Coronavirus restrictions led to the first cancellation of Scottish exams since 1888. In the absence of formal assessment, pupils were awarded their grades based on teachers' assessments of their expected performance. This much was uncontentious. What was contentious was an extra layer of 'moderation' imposed on these assessments by Scotland's examination quango, the Scottish Qualifications Agency (SQA). The organisation's algorithm, intended to 'balance' teacher assessments, had the almost uniform effect of downgrading pupil performance based on social class: it baked inequality back into the system. Pupils from Scotland's most deprived schools were 'moderated' down by 15.2 per cent, the least deprived by a mere 6.9 per cent. A school in Scotland's poorest local authority, Inverclyde, was downgraded by an astonishing 39 per cent.

Such results were especially embarrassing given that Sturgeon, as we saw in earlier chapters, had specifically asked to be judged on her performance in reducing the 'poverty-related attainment gap'. Tellingly, her instinct was to back the quango, its algorithm and the education secretary who had signed off on the system.

But the issue would not disappear, and the Scottish government suffered major publicity damage thanks to a pupil-led campaign organised amid the pandemic. The Greens, the SNP's informal coalition partners, would come to Sturgeon's rescue by defeating a No Confidence vote in the parliament on education secretary John Swinney; but even that came at the cost of being forced to scrap the SQA system and essentially revert grades to align with teachers' judgements, despite the government having previously claimed that such an about-face could never have 'credibility'.

Most importantly, however, these events would end up strengthening the inbuilt defence mechanisms of the Scottish establishment. They would *reinforce* the idea of Scotland as a progressive beacon, thanks to a depressingly familiar pattern.

A week later, the English examination system was hit by a similar algorithm-related disaster. Predictably, the Westminster government bungled the crisis one increment worse than its Holyrood counterpart. Scottish liberals could thus retell the fiasco in their favoured narrative of *West Wing* or *Borgen*-style enlightened compromise, in contrast to the sinister Tory elitism in London, when really this should have been a story of the Scottish establishment colluding to protect its own. From having served to expose Scotland's home-grown injustices of social class, the incident somehow served to reinforce the establishment's home-grown myths of educational equality – at least insofar as Scotland continued to judge its own social order by the yardstick of Westminster.

Don't Grow Up in Inverclyde

There was an element of poetic injustice in the fact that Inverclyde suffered the brunt of Scotland's exams fiasco. The region's fate illustrates the problem with Sturgeon's entire philosophy – namely, that divorcing school-based injustice from the surrounding injuries of class is effectively impossible. In 2020 Inverclyde recorded Scotland's largest drop in life expectancy. Baby girls now have a life expectancy 1.7 years shorter than those born five years ago. It should hardly be surprising, then, that Inverclyde also earned the grim distinction of having Scotland's highest rate of Covid-19 infections in the first months of the crisis. For all the suggestions that coronavirus does not discriminate on grounds of class, residents of Scotland's most deprived constituencies were twice as likely to catch it as those in the richest.

Areas like Inverclyde had endured a bruising transition from an industrial to a post-industrial capitalist economy. Shipbuilding and other manufacturing industries were already declining long before Thatcherism. For a while, it seemed possible that the area might turn its fortunes around. Inverclyde had plenty of unfashionable people willing to work for less, and electronics firms had come since the fifties in search of low-cost labour, government grants and access to the European market. With a little help from Scottish Enterprise, Inverclyde might even have illustrated the Thatcherite notion of 'creative destruction'. Here was a struggling Scottish region rising from the ashes of industrial decline to assemble cutting-edge products for the global market. But any renaissance was short-lived. Greenock's low wages were simply not low enough to compete in the global economy, and the likes of IBM and Lenovo moved on, searching for new horizons of exploitation in eastern Europe and China. Today, Greenock Town Centre is officially classified as Scotland's most deprived area.

The movement for Scottish devolution grew out of the post-Thatcher distresses of peripheral Scotland. Certainly, Scotland's miseries were linked to an outdated industrial structure in an era of capitalist globalisation; but they also reflected weaknesses of political agency. Workers in these Labour-voting areas struggled heroically to impose their will on the historical process. In Greenock itself, during Thatcher's first government, women textile workers at the Lee Jeans factory barricaded themselves in the factory for seven months to protest its closure.[12] The energies of these struggles were ultimately channelled into a Scottish parliament to solve the nation's 'democratic deficit'.

Yet devolution itself made little impression on these injustices. Indeed, since 1999 wealth inequalities have grown within and between Scottish regions. The finance boom and lashings of well-paid public administration jobs made Edinburgh one of the UK's private property hotspots. In the capitalist boom of the nineties and noughties, house prices and the debt economy were replacing wages and incomes as the key determinants of personal economic security. Areas like Inverclyde were, to use the common phrase, 'left behind'. Since devolution, property wealth has had an ever-greater impact on life chances in Scotland. Wealth grew from five to seven times Scottish GDP between 2008 and 2018, while taxes on wealth remained static. One study has found that inheritance will soon outweigh earnings in determining standards of living.[13]

Devolved structures have issued a feeble response. Scotland's mechanism for taxing wealth, the Council Tax, is founded on notorious injustices. Governments have repeatedly promised and failed to reform what is essentially an institutional prop of middle-class dominance, rooted in Conservative compromises that followed the end of the Poll Tax. Of all the absurdities behind Scotland's local tax system, consider the following. Firstly, its valu-ations of properties reflect assessments made in 1991. The subse-quent three decades of unprecedented shifts in house prices have been overlooked. Secondly, Council Tax is levied on rent-payers rather than landlords. Thirdly, it is a regressive tax: those in the best areas pay an average 1.6 per cent of their income, compared to 4.6 per cent for those in the poorest neighbourhoods. It follows that many are in Council Tax debt: Citizens Advice Scotland calls it the single biggest source of problem household debt.

While Council Tax entrenches individual penury, the parallel truth is that local councils are impoverished themselves. If the UK government stands at the top of the heap, councils are decidedly at the bottom, suffering the brunt of austerity and much of everyday public anger. The Scottish government occupies the relatively priv-ileged position of the middle, allowing it to blame the country's problems on Westminster while pushing cuts down the chain to councils. In truth, Scotland's parliament has allowed local service funding to remain unreformed for the same reason Scottish Conservatives wanted to trial the Poll Tax north of the border: they fear the wrath of upper-middle-class Council Tax payers. Any serious review of property valuations would, to put matters mildly, be to the disadvantage of key 'swing voting' cohorts targeted by all parties. Devolution has thus reproduced the underlying class basis of the 'democratic deficit' of the Thatcher era. Working-class voters (who now vote predominantly for the SNP rather than Labour) are punished for their loyalty. As before, real political agency belongs to a small upper layer of middle-class Council Tax payers – only they now vote for various respectable 'left' parties rather than for the Conservatives, which merely disciplines 'the left' into accepting the status quo.

Under this settlement, areas like Inverclyde lack both economic and political agency. Their desperation to attract footloose investors means they are liable to accept the worst of conditions. Much-trumpeted achievements include bringing Amazon warehouses to the region by doling out millions in Scottish Enterprise grants. This race to the bottom between councils vests all power with Amazon, which thus refuses to pay the real living wage, allow unionisation or even provide basic workplace conditions. There have been reports of workers sleeping in tents next to a Dunfermline warehouse to save on transport costs.

Faced with these facts, economic fatalism is often the answer. In this narrative, areas like Inverclyde were doomed by the transition to globalisation and post-industrial capitalism. These are the unfortunate by-products of living in a cosmopolitan world of endless consumer choice. Seekers of opportunity will simply move to a university town, or to Glasgow or Edinburgh, or to London, just as Polish workers migrate to Scotland or Ireland. This is simply the way of the world, and populists who complain of it are simply postponing the inevitability of creative destruction.

What these narratives ignore is the link between politics and economics. The impact of neoliberalism was not simply the destruction of regional economies and the growing gap between rich and poor. It was also a transformation in political allegiances, as the parties representing working-class voters became what Peter Mair calls 'cartel parties', servicing middle-class constituencies ranging from businesses and corporate lobbyists to workers for trendy NGO 'causes' and academics. Working-class disorganisation at the economic level (the collapse of private-sector trade unionism) was accompanied by political disorganisation. Workers lacked industrial leverage in the new business environment dominated by services. But they also lacked political leverage. Social democrats had no reason to take them seriously. Middle-class voters learned to use their political versatility to punish politicians who failed to adhere to their interests; until recently, working-class voters had no options. Thus, politicians had little incentive to make economic interventions on their behalf.

The old Scottish joke had it that areas like Inverclyde would vote for a 'monkey in a red rosette'. The same could be said of Northern England. Nowadays, these constituencies vote for the SNP and the Conservatives, which has only bred further condescension: the voters must be mindless morons who do not understand their own interests. Truly critical accounts should instead understand these as desperate bids for political independence – efforts to rescue areas that have been shattered despite a generation of centre-left rule. As we have demonstrated elsewhere, credible analyses show that Labour-voting constituencies fared the worst under New Labour domination. There are thus perfectly rational reasons to lend votes elsewhere to try and gain political purchase, as middle-class 'swing voters' have always done. Nonetheless, the SNP leadership has proved enormously effective at channelling grievances against Westminster while persisting with the status quo (a trick invented by Scottish Labour in the devolution campaign). How else to explain the essential Sturgeon paradox – that her popularity has risen while satisfaction with Scotland's public services has declined?[14]

Governance by Charlotte Street Partners

The maddening truth is that the condescension shown to working-class SNP voters is partly founded on fact. It would be misleading to say that the SNP has moved Scotland to the right, compared to the earlier phase of Labour dominance; in its first term the SNP even introduced some genuinely progressive measures. Nonetheless, as it has grown more powerful, so it has replicated the New Labour mode of social and political management: it has itself become a cartel party, and, thanks to its mass membership, a powerful one to boot. Symptomatic of that trend is the outsourcing of policy thinking to shadowy lobbying groups led by Charlotte Street Partners, a firm headed by the ubiquitous Andrew Wilson.

Wilson has come to represent what passes for thinking in the SNP leadership. Much of Scottish civil society has been won over, including elite sources of progressive opinion formation. Notably, Wilson was given a column in the *National*, supposedly a centre-left newspaper, to replace socialist campaigner Cat Boyd, as the emergent power bloc shed its radical skin in favour of progressive neoliberal pieties. As if to underline Wilson's emerging hegemony, Scotland's award-winning left-wing columnist Neil MacKay wrote a puff piece describing Wilson as the 'man who has done the hard thinking for the Yes movement'.[15]

How little 'hard thinking' Wilson had done should have been clear from the experience with coronavirus. Having authored the key economic paper on the future of Scottish independence, proclaiming that only a decade of hard austerity would win the confidence of the boardrooms and financial markets, Wilson was forced to change tack as governments worldwide unceremoniously booted aside the old neoliberal framework in favour of debts and deficits. With big business no longer willing to brook the old rules, Wilson had to concede that his old plans were in tatters. 'Everyone's world view will have to change now', he wrote in a company blog. Nonetheless, he remained true to a few core principles. 'Taxing the rich rhetoric will see us through maybe one election, a satisfying, reckless, and ironic self-indulgence', he wrote. 'The truth is that this is a burden all will have to bear. The state will be larger, but it must also be better.'[16]

Wilson's role in Scotland's more extreme neoliberal experiments has never been a secret. Ian Fraser's justly acclaimed history of the RBS scandal shows Wilson at his finest, as a public relations agent for the Fred Goodwin regime, where he was deputy head of communications. In 2007, not long before the bank's spectacular collapse, Wilson penned what Fraser called an 'extraordinarily hubristic and bombastic document' proclaiming the bank's strength. 'It was one of the few times Fred [Goodwin] ever congratulated anyone in media relations for anything', an insider told Fraser. 'He was delighted with that document. [Wilson] got a lot of kudos.'[17] Latterly, Wilson reinvented himself through Charlotte Street Partners, and took a key role in devising the currency policy of sterlingisation – a proposal that more than rivals Goodwin's takeover of ABN Amro as a high-stakes neoliberal experiment that will surely explode upon contact with reality.

The peculiarity of Scottish civil society consists in having a formal commitment to leftist values supplemented by the subcontracting of economic dirty work to the likes of Wilson, who is only too happy to oblige. Few have complained as Wilson has taken the commanding role in media, communications and economic policy. Indeed, for much of Scotland's left-leaning establishment, complaints about Wilson are regarded as the height of bad form and marginal thinking.

The outsourcing of economic policy to Scotland's corporate elite was in fact accelerated by the coronavirus. For all the hullabaloo about 'essential workers', the Scottish government handed the task of devising Scotland's economic recovery to former Tesco Bank CEO Benny Higgins, who now chairs Buccleuch Estates – one of the biggest landowners in Europe. Other members included Anton Muscatelli, the University of Glasgow principal who earns an annual salary of £342,000; Lord Kelvin, a land and property developer who owns a private island; and Dame Sue Bruce, former chief executive of Edinburgh City Council and board member of energy giant SSE. As the world was breaking all the rules of neoliberalism, Sturgeon had announced that the old elites were back in charge. Clientelism, revolving-door government and all the rest was here to stay.

It is less clear what Scotland's left receives in exchange for these compromises. Rather than concrete achievements, Sturgeon's popularity with the commentariat effectively rests on a mixture of tone – simultaneously feminist and managerial – and an emphasis on studiously marginal differences from Westminster. For these conscience-salving gains, the dirty business of economic policy has been contracted out to those who would surely have been considered 'class enemies' in earlier generations.

The Saudi Arabia of Green Energy?

The coronavirus crisis, reflects the sociologist Bruno Latour, is likely just a first test for the ecological disasters that will follow from climate change.[18] Indeed, Covid-19 has served as a stark demonstration that mankind's metabolic relationship with nature remains central to our economic wellbeing. Here, again, Scotland has stolen the headlines. Sturgeon has declared a 'climate emergency' and positioned the Scottish government as a 'world leader', alongside Jacinda Ardern of New Zealand, in establishing a set of high-level 'wellbeing' principles that broadly account for social and environmental factors in economic terms. This builds on longstanding commitments to rebuild the Scottish economy around green jobs. The Scottish parliament, meanwhile, has set an interim target of a 75 per cent reduction in CO_2 emissions by 2030 – an aim that is among the most ambitious in the world.

However, in conformity with Scotland's usual pattern, conscience-salving rhetoric collides with the corporate capture of economic policy – the only relevant arena for ensuring that Scotland makes meaningful environmental progress. Notably, the Sturgeon-sponsored Sustainable Growth Commission (the 'Sustainable' part of its name was tagged on belatedly, following criticism), aimed at establishing Scotland's economic future under independence, makes barely a mention of the environmental 'externalities' of the current growth regime. Where climate is mentioned at all, it is in the context of 'market opportunities'. The SGC dismisses the natural world as 'a broader debate' which it hopes 'the foundations provided by the work of the Commission can provide a basis for'. This, again, illustrates the contortions of progressive neoliberalism: climate change is a priority in every area of government policy except where it might have a serious impact.

What trade unions call Scotland's 'green jobs crisis' illustrates how these problems interact with social class. In 2010, Salmond promised 28,000 new green jobs over the decade, to turn Scotland into the 'Saudi Arabia of renewables'; as of February 2020, official estimates put the number at just 1,700 full-time jobs – about 6 per cent of the promised figure. Insofar as Scotland is making a transition to a low-carbon economy, there is nothing 'just' about it. Indeed, the skills, infrastructure and businesses needed to deliver Scotland's low-carbon revolution are disappearing from the country as multinationals win procurement contracts and outsource the supply-chain work. As a result, the nation's strategic low-carbon manufacturers are collapsing. The year 2020 alone saw the collapse of Campbeltown's CS Wind, Britain's only manufacturing facility for offshore and onshore wind towers, and mass layoffs at Alexander Dennis, a leading manufacturer of green buses.

But these tragedies pale in comparison to the symbolism of BiFab, a Fife-based manufacturer of steel 'jackets' for wind turbines. Theoretically, BiFab's business should be booming. It is in prime position to exploit Scotland's emerging economic model. However, despite years of government money and union collaboration, the firm has now finally expired – the Scottish government, inevitably, blaming EU state-aid rules.

BiFab's workers had fought heroically to keep their yards open: in 2017 they saved the firm by staging an occupation of their premises and marching on the Scottish parliament. This forced the hand of the Scottish government, which took on part-ownership of the firm. Soon thereafter the company's luck seemed to turn, with the announcement of a massive new wind farm off the Fife coast, Neart na Gaoithe (NnG). Geographically, BiFab was ideally placed. But the government contract for NnG went to French giant

EDF Renewables, who staked their bid on being 'price competitive', not on providing supply-chain work to local manufacturers.
For EDF, cost-reduction was the name of the game.

Rather than source the work in Fife, EDF subcontracted the
bulk of it to Indonesia-based Saipem, a company benefiting from a
state-sponsored 'enterprise zone' offering special tax, regulation
and infrastructure incentives – or, in other words, from a lax and
oppressive regime for Indonesian workers. Given that such
constructions are geared to environmental goals, it should be
considered that the cost alone of shipping these jackets from
Indonesia to Scotland was equivalent, by STUC estimates, to the
carbon footprint of 35,000 new cars on the road. BiFab was fed the
scraps – a total of eight jackets. Eventually, after missing out on
further contracts, the Scottish government pulled the funding
plug, citing EU regulations. The owners immediately moved to
liquidation.

If unions were understandably angered, the wider point was that,
given the Scottish government's declaration of a 'climate emergency',
progressive Scotland is stuck on the horns of a dilemma. Either the
Scottish government is correct, and EU state-aid laws genuinely did
cause this sorry crisis: in which case, there is a clear conflict between
EU membership and rhetorical commitments to a 'just transition'.
Or, alternatively, the Scottish government, having determined the
project too economically or politically costly, used a smokescreen of
EU law to mislead the people of Fife at the expense of livelihoods
and carbon emissions. Neither interpretation suggests a government committed to fighting an emergency.

In truth, EU law might have been circumvented in this case by
a government more determined to assert its sovereignty (this
controversy happened prior to the UK's formal departure from the
EU). However, given the centrality of 'Europeanness' to Scottish
nationalist rhetoric, the government was unwilling to risk serious
conflict with Brussels, which could have served to remind voters
of the drawbacks of EU membership while souring EU institutions
on future Scottish entry. Equally, the Scottish government is not

entirely disingenuous in saying that EU rules prevent it from undertaking serious 'green' measures. Certainly, EU rules have proved enormously effective in helping governments stave off serious campaigns for reform. When Thatcher insisted 'there is no alternative' to market globalisation, she meant in part that the public, given the choice, would demand nothing less than economic freedom. Today, as the public demands an alternative, a raft of impersonal laws and regulations agreed in closed intergovernmental meetings work to enforce the same principle.

As academic specialists increasingly recognise, the imagined conflict between super-state and plucky national governments is misplaced. EU regulation is more a function of the need to shield national governments from the democratic demands of their population: the idea of sovereignty, for all its faults, always contains the germs of popular revolt against governments that fail to enact the popular will.

Governments were held captive by such democratic demands in the sixties and seventies. The EU works to foreclose them, and thus to shield governments from accountability. The laid-off workers of BiFab, faced with a substantively irrational decision, confront an inscrutable wall of law and bureaucracy. Political leaders throw up their hands and say, 'We don't like it – but what's the alternative?' EDF, majority-owned by the French state but with a mandate to maximise profitability (especially when operating beyond France's borders), has no scruples about popular accountability.

Scottish Independence after the Pandemic

Faced with the pandemic, many have resorted to Scotland's tried and tested formula: focus on Westminster's failings. Naturally, much of that critique will be justified, and Westminster remains the sovereign authority with ultimate, fundamental culpability. The trick, however, is to end the habit of seeing Westminster and Scotland's progressive neoliberal parliament as separate problems. Our claim is that they are interdependent: both the SNP and the Tories benefit from Scotland's current state of constitutional deadlock.

To implement unpopular measures like austerity, Westminster relies on letting shit flow downhill, from central government to devolved parliaments to local councils, and then down to individual schools and health boards. This process of 'devolving the axe' disperses the general mood of anti-political protest, which becomes fragmented against various micro-targets, from council bureaucrats and hospital administrators to disgruntled nationalists in devolved parliaments. Effectively, the SNP do the same from the opposite direction: protests are channelled back towards Westminster; politically costly decisions are deferred downwards to council offices or to local schools or hospitals. The apparent polarisation of Scottish politics is thus rooted in two elite factions that both depend on similar brinksmanship, facilitated by the structures of devolved power. This illustrates our theoretical claim: the various legal fictions of pooled or fragmented sovereignty tend to divide democratising forces and disperse democratic accountability. This is the root failing that connects capitalist globalisation to a pervasive sense of political alienation and 'democratic deficit'.

The SNP has been a major beneficiary of public protest against elites. It is patronising to dismiss this, in the habit of Labourist intellectuals, as an 'irrational nationalist wave'. Indeed, there is an underlying rationality to this behaviour: these are efforts to assert meaningful political choice, to make votes count for something after decades of their being rendered meaningless. However, the deeper problem is that parliamentary politics, especially under a devolved administration, has found ways to shield itself against popular impulses. Sturgeon faces a problem of incentive structures: she is rewarded when she protects the elite groups who have real power to cause her government harm. Thus, whenever class conflict arises, her instincts are understandably to play safe and back the establishment, whether over herd immunity, the SQA or state-aid rules. The same incentive structure would apply to any likely devolved government; the earlier phase of combined Scottish Labour and Liberal rule should be evidence enough for this.

The above analysis also illustrates why Labourist solutions are wrongheaded. It is difficult to foresee a renewal of working-class leverage in politics without a revolt against the fragmentation of sovereignty, based on an understanding of how divided accountability reproduces elite power. Labour is demanding further rounds of the same system that sustains Sturgeon and the Conservatives in power. Far from resolving the question of independence, the most likely beneficiaries will be those who already benefit from the current system: British nationalists in Westminster and Scottish nationalists in Holyrood.

The pandemic has reinforced all the paradoxes of Sturgeon's rule. Public anger at the coronavirus response has been intense. Scotland's public health response has been identical to Westminster's, give or take the mildest of incremental differentiation, and this is reflected in the data about infections and deaths. Yet Sturgeon's reputation has grown markedly, both at home and abroad, at the expense of that of Johnson, who often serves as the stock comparison.

Independence will go some way to resolving these problems, but much depends on defining its nature. Independence for whom, and *from* whom (just Westminster?), and to do what (further rounds of Andrew Wilson–inspired neoliberalism, the post-pandemic state-led capitalist consensus, or real changes in the ownership and control of resources?). Equally, it depends on a clearer statement of purpose. In our alternative account, independence is about maximising the conditions under which politics can channel the state authority towards collective goals.

Conclusion: The Two Souls of Independence

These new middle classes, awakening to the grim dilemmas of backwardness, are confronted by a double challenge. They have (usually) to get rid of an anachronistic *ancien régime* as well as to beat 'progress' into a shape that suits their own needs and class ambitions. They can only attempt this by radical social and political mobilization, by arousing and harnessing the latent energies of their own societies. But this means, by mobilizing people. People is all they have got.

Tom Nairn, 'Scotland and Europe'

Exploring the weaknesses in Scottish nationalism need not mean abandoning an unapologetically expansive idea of national independence. Indeed, knowledge of the former is the necessary foundation of the latter. Contradictions, we argue, inevitably follow from the tension of being both a social movement and a party of power. That is why we speak of independence having 'two souls'. This is not the same as saying that Scotland's national psyche is uniquely contorted, or even 'schizophrenic', as the country's popular sociology has sometimes implied. Scotland's problems of cultural polarisation and electoral fragmentation are real enough, but hardly exceptional. Indeed, far from seeing the national question as an irrational expression of Scottish particularity, it is rather what unites Scotland to other European societies, all of them riven with social conflicts which, in the absence of institutional channels, erupt in unexpected bursts of chaotic political energy. Davidson was thus fond of quoting the French theorist Daniel Bensaïd: 'If one of the outlets is blocked with particular care, then the contagion will find another, sometimes the most unexpected.'[1]

In seeking to reclaim a certain idea of independence, the 'two souls' concept is a conscious reference to the American Marxist theorist Hal Draper. His ideas were drawn from very different historical circumstances. Nonetheless, there is a real analogy with his defence of 'socialism from below' against the encroachment of 'socialism from above', represented not just by Stalinism but by European social democracy, the labour movement bureaucracy, and even many forms of anarchism. Draper wrote:

> What unites the many different forms of Socialism-from-Above is the conception that socialism (or a reasonable facsimile thereof) must be handed down to the grateful masses in one form or another, by a ruling elite which is not subject to their control in fact. The heart of Socialism-from-Below is its view that socialism can be realised only through the self-emancipation of activised masses in motion, reaching out for freedom with their own hands, mobilised 'from below' in a struggle to take charge of their own destiny, as actors (not merely subjects) on the stage of history.[2]

Of course, the Scottish independence movement is not socialist as such (although it does largely encompass that tradition); but Draper observes that the dualism is 'not peculiar to socialism' but a feature of all class-based societies. 'The yearning for emancipation-from-above is the all-pervading principle through centuries of class society and political oppression', he observes. 'It is the permanent promise held out by every ruling power to keep the people looking upward for protection, instead of to themselves for liberation from the need for protection . . . Instead of the bold way of mass action from below, it is always safer and more prudent to find the "good" ruler who will Do the People Good.' Sturgeonism has represented a post-neoliberal rule of 'doing good from above'. Its popularity, including with much of the actually existing Scottish left, is standing testament to the absence of an agenda for independence from below.

There are thus strong affinities between Draper's distinction and the strategic dilemmas of the independence movement, as we illustrate in the table below.

	Independence from below	Independence from above
Relationship to global system	Rupture	Continuity
Constitutional vision	Self-rule	Extended devolution
Indyref strategy	Movement pressure	Official channels
Political-economic philosophy	Socialist/social democratic	Progressive neoliberal meritocracy
Movement relationship	Bottom-up	Top-down

In applying this to the real world, the same caution must be exercised as with any abstract dichotomy drawn from political science. These concepts are ideal-types, and are not neatly separated within the independence movement. The spirit animating Scotland's mass movement is not always one thing or the other, but rather overwhelmingly pragmatic. Nonetheless, while the two souls may be difficult to separate in real cases, and may even be at war within one individual, they do represent distinct poles of attraction – rival meanings, competing class interests and conflicting relationships to state power.

Since 2014, the balance between these competing forces has swung back and forth. However, for all the extraordinary vigour of the street protests, the intellectual momentum has been with independence from above. This factor deserves deeper consideration than it often receives from liberal critics, who often complain of the wayward thinking and absence of serious intellectual calibre within the idealistic movement, relative to the 'credibility' of SNP figureheads like Sturgeon and Wilson. In turn, this narrative forms the basis of stock contrasts between 'utopianism' and 'pragmatism'. Certainly, independence from above has a programme – the Sustainable Growth Commission – while the other pole, for all the efforts of grassroots groups like Common Weal, remains fuzzy and inconclusive.

Nonetheless, we would caution that the utopianism-versus-pragmatism framing risks eliding crucial nuances. Firstly, there is a risk of missing the strongly utopian character to the SNP leadership's centrist programme. Wilson draws on the energy of nostalgia for a return for the booming, liberal nineties economy, but his vision of open markets is riddled with inconsistencies and unresolved conflicts: for example, between sterlingisation and membership of the EU Single Market. His programme has been rendered incoherent precisely because the historical conditions for neoliberal globalisation have passed. While it may be possible to persist with the old solutions, it would almost certainly come at the cost of substantive economic, environmental and social progress. In other words, what passes for a mainstream vision of independence would depend on a mixture of dogmatism and utopian nostalgia: it is 'pragmatic' only insofar as it is easier to sell to Scotland's boardrooms.

Secondly, there is arguably an exaggerated pragmatic streak to much of the street movement. Indeed, it is the movement's sheer pragmatism – anything to get over the line to independence – that leads it to flail between implacable trust in the leadership and bursts of rage when Sturgeon flouts the movement's desires because she dares not disturb the settled devolved order that reproduces the SNP's position in power. Dogmatic 'pragmatism' ensures that the street movement, just as much as Sturgeon, fails to confront the big challenges that all states face after the 2008 crisis: climate breakdown and the coronavirus pandemic.

Throughout the book, we have stressed the weaknesses of independence from above – its mixture of utopianism ('normality' will be restored simply by joining the 'mainstream of Europe') and cynicism (manipulating the national divide to secure constant re-election while minimising scrutiny of state power). We recognise the incoherence at the pole of independence from below. However, we do not make these criticisms from the standpoint of bad faith and passivity. Our goal throughout the book has been to face with honesty the challenges facing Scotland as a European society undergoing extreme restructuring and economic failure. In this spirit, we will attempt to outline the concepts that could define a coherent movement. This is not the same as a comprehensive programme for socialism, if only because the radical left is some way from winning the consent of the majority for a real challenge to capitalism. However, we believe that reimagining the state around the themes of popular sovereignty may remove some of the barriers to addressing climate breakdown, extreme inequality and corporate oligarchy. Given these challenges, the left's goal should be to maximise the space for democratic authority over economic decision-making, and to minimise constitutional limits to the latter.

Popular Sovereignty as Strategy and Idea

Far from revelling in visions of a fantasy future Scotland, the independence movement tends to exert diligent discipline over its imagination. It matches Sturgeon in adhering to a strict divide between manual labour (pounding the streets, handing out leaflets – the role of the mobiliser) and mental labour (imagining the state – the role of professional elites, Charlotte Street Partners and the government). This is regarded as a temporary surrender, as it expects that, having won a future referendum, the design of a post-independence state will be immediately open to citizen initiative and democratic scrutiny. Leftist critiques of the Growth Commission, Nato, poverty, and so on are thus met with cries of 'Wait until independence!' or, in the Scottish vernacular, 'Wheesht

for indy': citizens can begin their role in reimagining the new
Scottish state on Independence Day, but no sooner. Until then,
'pragmatism' must prevail.

This is the precise sense in which All Under One Banner and
the street movement has been apolitical: there is a strong tendency
to imagine that states begin on day one, and, from then on, are
defined in a spirit of full democratic openness. It almost feels
callous to reflect that, in most real history, the social coalitions that
produce states emerge long before that 'one fine day'. The moment
of achieving independence is likely to involve demobilisation, as,
when the mission has been accomplished, political leaders negoti-
ate with elites from Scotland and around the world, bypassing
those who knocked on doors and pounded the streets, who will be
effectively sidelined in the spirit of realism. By contrast, those
mobilisers for independence are at their most potentially powerful
prior to independence itself. That is when democratic impulses
can shape the future, before the state has to congeal around various elite groups agitating for their slice. By trading on the fiction
that independence will be entirely open to full democratic control,
the real imaginative work of state production has thus been handed
to Sturgeon's coalition: Andrew Wilson, Angus Grossart, Benny
Higgins and other figures of corporate Scotland. The movement
openly dislikes this reality, but effectively surrenders to it by disa-
vowing its own political agency in the spirit of pragmatic unity.

There is an even more glaring inconsistency with the movement's disciplined pragmatism. Handing the brainwork to
Sturgeon's team effectively ensures that they will pursue the path of
least resistance – which is to say, a strategy of non-confrontation
with the British state. Or, if recent history is any judge, a strategy of
proxy wars of position that help re-elect the SNP but never break
into a concluding manoeuvre towards independence. As will be
clear to anyone familiar with Scotland's political culture, this is not
some doom-mongering projection, but the prevailing reality.
Under Sturgeon's leadership, the SNP inches one step away from
Westminster, maintaining a small but studious rhetorical distance,

while avoiding outright confrontations. The commentariat cele-
brates the formal and stylistic accomplishment of Sturgeonism,
but rarely reflects on whether this type of management will achieve
any type of substantive breakthrough.

Real breakthroughs always imply a more dynamic relationship
between political movements and mainstream leaders, one that
goes beyond the inhibiting mental–manual divide. Herbert H.
Haines, in his acclaimed history of America's Civil Rights movement, attributes success to a 'radical flank effect'. In this account,
the mobilised part of the movement serves not only to keep
mainstream leaders honest, but also to frighten the state into
negotiating with the movement's mainstream elements. Andreas
Malm has argued for the necessity of a radical flank to emerge in
the climate movement, but the theory can equally be applied to
the Scottish independence movement.[3] Indeed, the need for a
radical, intellectually autonomous flank is doubly clear in
Scotland's case. Since Sturgeon's team has centralised control of
the movement while also administering the bureaucracy of a
devolved government, it experiences extraordinary pulls towards
compliance and intellectual complacency. These problems are
not rooted in personal failings, but rather in institutions.
Ultimately, Sturgeon herself has been a victim of the movement's
embrace of Sturgeonism after 2014. The intellectual and political
failings of independence are unintended consequences of the
SNP leadership's capture of the national question for their own
electoral purposes.

This offers another illustration of one of this book's central
arguments: that sovereignty, fundamentally, is about the tension
not between Holyrood and Westminster, but rather between the
citizen and the state. Having the capacity for initiative independently of the Scottish government is thus about developing autonomous citizen agency over history in a time of turbulence and
confusion. Parties are necessary to mobilise and unify around
programmes. But when parties become servants of administration
or mere mirrors of passive public attitudes, they contribute to the

weakening of democracy, and only exacerbate the void between the public and power.

Once the question of sovereignty is understood as a dynamic between citizen and state, further questions emerge about how the Yes movement relates to the SNP. State managers and para-governmental insiders like Wilson have engaged in pre-emptively parcelling up Scotland's sovereignty for external powers: for Nato and the EU, but most especially for markets. Control of monetary policy – one of the major sources of economic power for the state – will thus be handed to the external Bank of England, purportedly to win the confidence of external bondholders. Examples here could be listed indefinitely. The crucial point is that political operators are handing control to forces that exist beyond any realm of democratic control or accountability. This is happening long before Independence Day, and could easily prove irreversible. Wilson's neoliberal views are as deserving of consideration as a socialist prospectus. But the danger is that they are locked in from day one, precluding democratic oversight and the public's capacity to bend public authority to other types of economic renewal.

A defence of popular sovereignty is thus not the same as delusional economic nationalism. There has been a history on parts of the broadly defined Scottish left of imagining that indigenous capitalists are nicer people than our current ruling bloc, with its national and transnational elements. Some have also implied that Scotland will be uniquely capable of resisting the pressures of globalisation that have so limited democracy in other states. Our position, by contrast, is that the most democratic state will be one that maximises the possibility for citizen initiative to bend economic institutions to the collective political will. Whether that takes the form of individualist-libertarian or collective-socialist answers, or something in between, should be a matter for party-political competition. But the prospect of either should not be foreclosed.

By contrast, the more institutions are inscrutable and shielded by external rules, competing prerogatives and layers of shadowy accountability, the more we are reverting to all of the old problems that disfigured politics in the neoliberal era. External control, or the perception of external control, shields state managers from accountability for Scotland's political and economic failings.

Wilson and his cohort are thus committing, under the banner of expertise, acts that violate an implicit social contract. They are handing powers that could belong to a Scottish citizenry to external forces that shield the state from real public scrutiny. They are doing so while promoting, through the independence movement, the convenient, face-saving fiction of full democracy from day one. In recognising this, the independence movement should have, as a strategic priority, the goal of maximising the realm of public control and accountability in a future Scottish state. This agitation would need to begin long before independence, and indeed starts with pressuring the Scottish government to move to a stance of greater confrontation with Westminster.

Components of Popular Sovereignty

Thus, the problem with the SNP's vision for the 'softest possible form of independence' is not that it is less Scottish than a fuller vision, but that it is less open to democratic impulses.[4] Of course, having imbibed the post-1989 consensus, the SNP leadership is fully convinced that there is no alternative, and no amount of evidence after 2008 has persuaded it otherwise. Its vision of a tightly curtailed, externally controlled Scottish state is fully summarised in the Sustainable Growth Commission. It is easy to see the flaws in that approach, but it is equally imperative that the movement begins to articulate its alternative. Here we outline some features of a radically sovereign Scottish state, not as a full list of progressive policies, but as the broad principles that the left should pursue in the state-making process.

Internationalism from below

In Scotland, internationalism has taken on an increasingly top-down meaning, amounting to little more than membership of (and uncritical enthusiasm for) institutions like the European Union and Nato. Our point is not simply that another, more democratic tradition of internationalism is possible. We would go a step further. The two souls of internationalism are mutually contradictory: while one seeks to maximise the prospects for democratic control of a shared project of state power, the other seeks to minimise democratic impulses, to shield elite power from scrutiny behind a complex layer of rules, external market forces and inscrutable bureaucracy.

The EU's role in sheltering elites from democratic pressures has been well established and was illustrated, albeit at its most extreme level, by the dismantling of Greek sovereignty in pursuit of a sadistic experiment in austerity. That case also shows two divergent meanings of international solidarity. For the German government and the 'Troika', solidarity meant European states standing together to face down Syriza and the Greek 'Oxi' referendum, to prevent their democratic contagion spreading to Portugal and Italy. By contrast, a truly internationalist left would have realised that, faced with austerity, the fate of Europe rested on uniting to defend Greek sovereignty against the prerogatives of Merkel, Brussels and the IMF. The European left, in allowing the EU to trample over Athens, effectively condemned anti-cuts movements across the continent to defeat. One mode of international solidarity thus triumphed at the expense of another. The two were entirely incompatible.

An even clearer example from our perspective is Catalonia, where the EU colluded to support extraordinary repression by the Spanish state in 2017. This case established that, for all the endless talk of 'regional Europe', the EU exists fundamentally to defend state power in its established form. Again, the two senses of international solidarity are clear from this case. Much of the

Scottish independence movement spontaneously mobilised behind Catalonia, its flags appearing across the demonstrations and even at SNP conferences. At the other extreme, Lisa Nandy, who has subsequently had a spell as Labour's shadow secretary of state for foreign affairs, said the British state should 'look to Catalonia' to learn lessons on how to beat breakaway independence movements – a neat encapsulation of internationalism from above, the collusion of high-handed state elites against citizen initiative.[5] Between these two extremes stands the SNP leadership, which, faced with the repression and criminalisation of their sister movement, confined their responses to half-hearted euphemisms, conscious of needing Madrid's support if Scotland should ever apply for EU membership. Leaked briefings from a disgraced former Spanish diplomat in the Edinburgh consulate, Miguel Ángel Vecino, show Sturgeon reassuring him that she does 'not wish to meddle in any kind of way with Spain's business'; Vecino added that he was 'completely sure that she will start to put aside her support of Catalan independence'.[6] In brutal summary, this illustrates where Britain's competing political forces stand in relation to state power and democracy.

Solidarity between state leaderships, then, must be distinguished from popular solidarity. In pursuit of the latter, Scotland's independence movement should target those aspects of the British state that limit the choices of democratic movements worldwide, understanding that the UK has forever been the enemy of anyone, anywhere pursuing radical, popular economic change. Trident should be dismantled in this spirit: in strong states like Britain, nuclear weapons exist as a last resort to discipline governments in Eurasia to adhere to the status quo. They are, moreover, the type of military power least open to citizen control: armies and navies can revolt, but nuclear warheads are always under the command of the state and big science. Nato membership likewise should be opposed on many grounds, but one is that it will likely force Scotland to make concessions over nuclear sovereignty, subordinating the popular will to the international balance of forces.

It should be added that pursuing popular solidarity is not, in every case, inconsistent with membership of elite groups of states. If the Scottish people decide to join the EU democratically, rather than in a prearranged stitch-up, that should be their right. If sovereignty is to be democratic it must include the right to parcel it away. However, this should be based on the principle of maximising popular control, including the right to withdraw: membership of the Eurozone currency, in that respect, is a violation of sovereignty, since it imposes bankruptcy on any state that seeks to restore a national currency. As we have argued throughout, EU membership must be based on an informed, hard-headed assessment. Most importantly, a democratic culture depends on parties openly contesting the consensus. Scotland's existing institutions fail in this regard: polarisation on the national question paradoxically serves to achieve consensus on all other fronts. A bland cosmopolitanism reigns across Holyrood, rooted neither in public attitudes nor in a socialist vision of internationalism, but rather in the intellectual complacency of professional-elite liberals.

Whether from within the EU or not, the truly internationalist goal is to maximise, across Europe, the prospects for democratic power in spite of the EU. Scottish independence, much against the will of SNP leaders, would likely open questions of international solidarity that actively undermine the EU's idea of internationalism. EU leaders may collude with the SNP to paint Scottish independence as merely a revolt for the status quo, against Brexit and Brexit alone. Nonetheless, movements in Ireland, Catalonia and the Basque Country, to name only a few, will have witnessed the first modern precedent for separatist success in western Europe. This will electrify questions of democratic power and accountability in their national contexts. States across Europe will be open to new questions of popular consent and control that did not exist before.

Radical republicanism

Another question relates to an independent Scotland's internal constitution. Here we must consider what Dan Hind calls the 'substance of popular sovereignty' – namely, 'what it means for a people to be self-governing, what it means for a people to be effectually free'.[7] With due caution, he calls this *republicanism*. As defined by Hind, a republic means 'shared ownership of the state', the 'public organisation of knowledge' being a necessary step to genuine political equality.[8]

Republicanism should be distinguished from what it usually means in the British context – namely, anti-monarchism. There is no doubting that the Windsor family are symptomatic of British imperial and democratic decay. There is equally no doubting that they remain, absurdly or not, the most popular artefact of British national tradition, albeit to a slightly lesser extent in Scotland than elsewhere. Confusing republicanism with anti-monarchism thus carries two major risks. The first is that the form of the state and other 'merely constitutional' issues are regarded as frivolous side issues, irrelevant to 'real peoples' lives', as Labourists have argued. The second risk is that republicanism becomes synonymous with its least popular proposition, limiting its appeal beyond leftist hobbyism. This is a problem because the people who need a republican perspective the most – those furthest from influence on political power – are often deprived of it by a problem of presentation. Popular elements of the republican programme, such as the answerability of the political class to the citizen electorate, have largely been lost in the frivolities of the crown.

It should be emphasised, therefore, that it would be theoretically possible for a self-governing republic to choose a monarch as its head of state. The problem is not simply that nobody has ever made an affirmative democratic choice for the Windsors, but that shared ownership of the state also assumes informed, critical knowledge about its operations. In Britain, by contrast, the entire popular media, including the BBC, simply assumes support for the monarchy as given. This supposed consensus is largely reflected in party politics, which further limit the space for rational discussion. Critical stances on the Windsors, or on any aspect of state power, are almost entirely absent outside the comment pages of the overwhelmingly middle-class *Guardian* (or occasionally, in Scotland, the *Herald*). Such critiques as do emerge focus on internal faction fights *within* the monarchy – between Charles and Diana or Meghan and Kate – with one side standing for tradition and the other for 'change'. Taking stances on these micro-political battles only serves to reinforce the overall strength of the institution. A republican perspective, by contrast, assumes a maximally informed citizenry capable of understanding rival arguments and rationally choosing the state's arrangements.

What implications does this have for Scotland? The process of state creation could, theoretically, involve a thorough review of all the arrangements linking the governors to the governed. As usual, the biggest barrier to those democratic arrangements would be the leftovers of the consensus of neoliberal globalisation: the European Single Market and Nato are barriers to republican government just as much as are the Windsors. Insofar as control over Scottish state power has already been pre-emptively handed to these organisations, the prospects of citizen control of a shared state have been curtailed without democratic scrutiny. Again, a fully informed public could sacrifice its sovereignty to a body of transnational political brokers, just as it could delegate head-of-state functions to a monarch. But it should do so under maximally informed conditions, and the ideological biases of the Scottish media and political class form a limit on the free exchange of critical information on state power.

In establishing a republican constitution, certain core policy principles must be assumed. Firstly, maximising citizen involvement in the construction of the state, perhaps through a democratic constitutional convention. In so doing, the case should be made for public institutions that are accountable to democratic impulses, not 'independent' from scrutiny and accountability.

Secondly, referendums on anything that transfers sovereignty from the people, including to the crown. This should be based on the principle that no transfer of power is ever final, and all institutions that borrow Scottish sovereignty, from the EU to the Windsors, should be open to further citizen referendums. Thirdly, strict limits on big money's control over politics. This could include, for example, equal citizen allocation of party funding; strict lobbying restrictions and participative citizens' forums for consultation; and a workers' wage for MSPs. Fourthly, the reduction of state and private moneyed control over media channels, university research and the wider public sphere. Openness, free speech and political diversity should be encouraged in all those fields, even if that disadvantages 'leftist' perspectives, as it might in academia. Lastly, the principle of maximising the capacity of citizen initiative to influence parliament and of parliament to shape public authority and intervene in the economy. A republican should minimise constitutional limits on democratic agency; questions around the monarchy are secondary to that broader principle.

Popular economic sovereignty

Of all the limits to popular republican government, the biggest is the perpetuation of capitalism and the persistence of wide economic inequalities. Hind thus emphasises that Republicanism 'must oppose capitalism insofar as it must oppose anything that threatens popular sovereignty'.[9] Consequently, even if all the above proposals were implemented, there remains every chance that the existing oligarchic class structure would re-emerge to dominate Scotland's state and economy. Our perspective is that the capitalist mode of production and exchange has emerged as the greatest barrier to human flourishing, particularly – though not exclusively – given climate breakdown. Equally, we also emphasise the importance of politics: the left must win the democratic consent of the public to use the state in transforming the economic system. That rules out the sad, self-defeating practice of writing off voters as deluded by their false consciousness. The left must seriously address the public's existing attitudes and values in a spirit of critical engagement.

Rather than proposing the abolition of capitalism in one country, our more narrow concern here is how to reimagine state power so as to prevent the reproduction of a closed caste structure around the state. Here, the left's values *should* – there are dishonourable exceptions – overlap with those of the public. The modern republican tradition has always aimed at curbing the state nobility. For Abbé Sieyès, writing on the eve of the French Revolution, the nobility had become 'a nation within a nation', because 'its private rights' made it into 'a separate people'.[10] In our own times, the same applies to the corporate elite and the higher ranks of managerialism and the professions. The risk is not simply that such groups overwhelmingly dominate the economy, but that their predominance in the private sector overwhelms public power, social institutions and the media. Far from there being a conflict between the market and the state, as neoliberals used to imagine, the truth is that the neoliberal era has burdened society with a doubly parasitic layer, leveraged by 'cartel parties' that no longer serve a social base but instead service networks of oligarchic privilege.

One reason the UK can never be truly democratic is the overwhelming coercive influence of the City of London. Proposals for 'federalism' tend to run aground on the nation's dependence on the capital and the capital's dependence on a single, parasitical industry, in marked contrast to the diversified federal states that often serve as models, such as Germany and the United States. The risk of federalism in a UK context is that, far from politicising this economic problem, it aims to depoliticise and demobilise, placating the regions by enhancing the power and opportunities of their elites, or else paying them off from London's revenues. The fact that federalism has been hinted at by Gordon Brown, who ranks with Nigel Lawson as the chancellor who did most to empower the City in the UK economy, should be sufficient cause for alarm.

Finance capitalism, as epitomised by London, has become almost entirely separated from the wages and prices which drive the living standards of the vast majority of workers. This was neatly illustrated by the coronavirus pandemic, in which, as low-paid essential workers traipsed to work, and taxi drivers, small shops and hospitality workers suffered bankruptcy, Britain officially recorded its sharpest recession on historical record on 12 August 2020 – while on the same day the FTSE100 rose. By December 2021, incomes of Britain's richest 5 per cent had grown by £3,300 on average since the pandemic had begun, while the bottom 50 per cent of income-earners were on average £110 worse off.[11] If we remain dependent on this growth model, there is no prospect of addressing the deep problems that have tethered us to an unjust, failing economic structure. In revealing the precarity of global capitalism, the twin crises of 2008 and 2020 also present an opportunity to rethink our twin dependence on parasitic finance and parasitic growth that uses the planet's resources at the expense of future generations.

By popular economic sovereignty, we mean maximum democratic accountability of political and business elites in the Scottish economy. This means ending the practice, for instance, of transferring sole liability for climate change to consumers. Equally, it means fighting against external rules that, contrary to their stated purpose, curtail free and democratic economic decision-making, such as EU state-aid rules. Some specific aspects of economic sovereignty might include:

- **Democratic control of natural resources**: Scotland's rich list is made up of owners of its land, water and whisky. Natural resources should compose part of the commons, their use carefully regulated to ensure sustainability and public value are maximised.
- **De-financialisation**: Scotland should have a publicly run financial system that ends predatory practices that generate

debt peonage and instead issue loans based on democratically defined criteria of social purpose. This would almost
certainly have to involve the creation of new public banks,
with the intention of undermining the City of London's grip
on the Scottish economy and unwinding the asset bubble in
land and housing.

- **De-globalisation**: Domestic production for domestic
  consumption should be expanded through support for the
  development of worker cooperatives (which are by their
  nature anchored in the national economy), using quotas and
  tariffs to limit imports, and capital controls to prevent financial outflows.

- **Rebalancing workplace power**: To reverse the worst effect of
  post-Thatcherite orthodoxy, government should encourage
  workers' agency and control within the workplace. Trade-
  union-friendly employment laws, wage ratios restricting
  inequality within companies, and a reform of company laws
  to prevent subcontracting and the use of companies as finan-
  cialised instruments through vehicles like private equity
  firms would be a starting point in rebalancing workplace
  power away from capital and towards labour.

- **Technological sovereignty**: Collective control of data is
  essential to economic and political sovereignty in the twenty-
  first century. Data should be made transparent and accessible, and consumers and workers given control over their own
  data, how it is used, and whether it can be sold on to third
  parties. Public data control could empower citizens to make
  informed democratic decisions on everything from the
  design of urban spaces to the best way to facilitate democratic
  participation.

- **Mission-orientated industrial policy**: The public should
  have a democratic say over public investment, which must be
  scaled up massively to rapidly decarbonise the economy. This
  has been called 'mission-orientated industrial policy'.[12] One
  of its key missions could be a Green New Deal and a locally

organised jobs-and-training guarantee scheme, which would deliver public-sector, socially necessary jobs for everyone who applied.

- **A care revolution**: In place of progressive neoliberalism, a 'feminism for the 99%', to use Cinzia Arruzza, Tithi Bhattacharya and Nancy Fraser's term, would transform the conditions of social reproduction.[13] This must start with a transformation of Scotland's care system. A national care service (NCS) must be publicly owned, with private care homes nationalised. To attract workers to the sector and reflect the skilled nature of the job, social carers should have training, pay and conditions which match those of the NHS. The NCS should be from cradle to grave, universally accessible and free at the point of use. And it must address all of Scotland's care needs: mental health, disability, drug and alcohol prevention and rehabilitation. Those caring for a dependent family member should also be part of the NCS, paid a living income and assured a right to a service for their loved ones if they decide to take time off from full- or part-time caring, or if they decide to take a different job.

The Politics of Popular Sovereignty

Are constitutional concerns too obscure to relate to ordinary life? We would challenge that assumption. Indeed, much to the left's surprise, the dominant 'populist' response to the crisis of 2008 and austerity was not a turn to bread-and-butter economic issues, but rather to emphasise public control over politicians accused (rightly or wrongly) of being unaccountable. In other words, it was those leftists who ignored questions of sovereignty who should really stand accused of remaining aloof from working-class concerns on the doorstep. The Yes campaign of 2014 emphasised 'Scotland's future in Scotland's hands'. Spain's protest movement emphasised 'real democracy', and Podemos organised its propaganda against *la casta* ('the caste'). On the other side, the Brexit campaign spoke of 'taking back control', and Trump called for 'draining the swamp'. In other words, all successful recent political insurgencies have tapped into national popular themes of democratic control and accountability.

Where the left has gained mass and especially working-class support for radical economic programmes, it has emphasised themes of popular sovereignty. Conversely, where the left has collapsed from a position of strength, it has been when it abandons those themes in favour of internationalism from above. Syriza's capitulation to the Troika saw them unceremoniously dumped from office. Podemos, meanwhile, has blunted its republican edges and gravitated towards traditional centre-left politics. Symptomatic of this trend was its weakness on Catalan self-determination. Labour's failures under Corbyn were a reflection of this context. Failing to address public distrust of the capture of state power by politicians and moneyed interests, Labour put all of its energies into an economic programme as compensation for working-class voters aggrieved over the Scottish national question or Brexit. All survey evidence showed that Labour's economic policies, by themselves, commanded strong public support.[14] Corbyn's team failed insofar as it tried to divorce these findings from their national-popular context.

Separatist parties have tended to be the most consistently successful of all leftist parties in Europe since 2008. Even when leaving aside the case of the SNP (which is more centrist than left-ist), Sinn Féin in Ireland, the Galician Nationalist Bloc in Galicia, EH Bildu in the Basque Country, and the ERC and CUP in Catalonia have all made substantial progress. Contrary to the Labourist imagination, this is less because these parties have deluded the electorate with toxic 'nationalism' than because their republican, separatist politics means they never entirely soften their critique of mainstream politics and state power. By contrast, most European Green parties and the likes of Podemos have a natural cycle of using anti-establishment credibility to gain a platform for coalition government, only to become sucked into the establishment and lose their credibility.

In Scotland, the potential constituency for popular sovereignty is large, going far beyond the immediate independence movement. Recent data on attitudes about inequality found that 72 per cent of Scots thought income distribution is either unfair or very unfair, while 75 per cent thought high earners should pay a larger or much larger share of tax. In the same survey, 42 per cent believed it was very or somewhat wrong that people on higher incomes could buy better healthcare, and 45 per cent believed the same about buying better education; 38 per cent believed society was like 'a pyramid with a small elite at the top, more people in the middle, and most at the bottom', while 24 per cent would go even further, agreeing that society was 'a small elite at the top, very few people in the middle and the great mass of people at the bottom'. Finally, 53 per cent believed it was the responsibility of government to reduce inequalities.[15] The point is not that such attitudes are markedly different from those in England – they are not – but that, where opportunities exist to escape the deadening split between Holyrood and Westminster, there are constituencies for radical democratic mobilisation.

Despite decades of propaganda, there is substantial evidence that people do not see the economy as a collection of isolated consumers. Instinctively, people incline to a form of national collectivism. A study by the New Economics Foundation, based on detailed focus-group data, found that people think of the economy as a container, where people either contribute to or drain from national wealth. They think the nation should aim to meet its own basic needs without relying on other countries. Despite cynicism about elites, people think the government is essential in fixing economic problems and regulating the economy.[16] This public imagination of the economy is far from being straightforwardly socialist, but it involves a radical break from the type of post-political globalisation trumpeted by both leftists and neoliberals for the past three decades.

There is a vast constituency for the ideas we have expressed that finds no consistent representation in mainstream Scottish politics, with its five liberal parties. Perhaps the closest Scotland has come was the Scottish Socialist Party before its split – for all of that project's flaws, it had genuine roots in (at least) the Glasgow working class. Efforts at revival on the basis of left unity, such as through the RISE project, ran aground by failing to build a coherent anti-establishment politics.[17] By contrast, where explicitly socialist parties do achieve even limited breakthroughs, like the Workers Party of Belgium and the Red Party in Norway, they have a disciplined focus on restoring the agency of the peripheral working class.[18]

An Agenda for Movement Renewal

The independence movement of 2012–14 helped re-engage the radical left with mainstream politics. But the consequences of that success have been demobilising for popular movements. Scotland's leftist milieu has been increasingly tied to the imperatives of SNP machine politics. The sense of autonomous agency that emerged around the referendum has been incorporated or driven back to the margins.

There is nothing particularly Scottish about this problem: in Europe and beyond, the post-2008 breakdown of global capitalism has led to a graveyard of leftist failures. Indeed, independence served to shield the Scottish left from the hostile forces that destroyed Syriza, Corbynism, and a wide array of other left-populist failures. By comparison, activists in Scotland are fortunate in having retained a radical-democratic framework for action that might still serve as the basis for a majoritarian class politics. Nonetheless, it is crucial to learn lessons from failures, and thus to embrace the task of rebuilding, rather than succumbing to the temptations of resignation or routine activism.

The wider independence movement, firstly, must consider

alternatives to its habit of orbiting the governing party. To take one example, the Catalan National Assembly is an autonomous body that openly rejects subordination to the pro-independence Catalan government. The Assembly builds independent organisational capacity, and is pointedly critical when mainstream leaders are absorbed into careerism and governance. In other words, this is a model in which the movement emphasises its distinction from state power: crucially, the Assembly recognises that superficial, polarising conflicts with the metropolis can be demobilising, and seeks explicitly to challenge this behaviour. The contrast with Scotland is clear. In Scotland, the government secures political cover almost regardless of whether ministers are progressing towards independence – or anything else.

But organisational autonomy alone is not enough. It must be matched by intellectual self-assertion. Movements may profess not to care about the form of a future independence, but other forces do care. Corporate Scotland and the wider transnational capitalist class have readymade proposals for how new states should be formed – which, in the absence of alternatives, will prevail either on the grounds of elite self-interest or (just as worryingly) from decades of habitual neoliberal dominance. The fact that such proposals are often riddled with inconsistencies – like the Growth Commission – should not disguise the strength of simply having something on paper. Until the radical flank coalesces around its own vision, the ideas of Wilson and Co. remain the default prospectus.

Finally, the independence movement must seek to build alliances and broaden its scope. The more the movement appears to be narrowly interested in the agenda of the Scottish government and its acolytes, the more it will be regarded with cynicism and suspicion. Its energies must be directed towards supporting strike action, campaigning against cuts – whether by the Scottish or British government – and giving political direction to the fragmented ecosystem of campaigns.

There is also the inescapable question of party organisation.

Movements cannot substitute for the democratic function of
parties in mobilising citizens, organising around programmes and
concretising alternatives in the public mind. Importantly, many of
today's parties are also failing to provide this function. All represent a similar social composition, which is neither working class
nor capitalist but formed of professional elites. All ultimately
conform to a capitalist realism that has prevailed since 1989, which
today neither represents the truth of public attitudes nor provides
valid answers to the big challenges that lie ahead. And all, in their
different ways, trade on a polarised electorate to ensure easy
re-election.

This only reinforces the discomfort that many feel about the
question of parties. Four parties in Holyrood claim to stand for the
left, as that term has been broadly defined in recent decades.
Despite the manifest failings of capitalism, Scotland (and England,
and Europe more broadly) is littered with the corpses of failed
efforts to establish more coherently leftist parties. Such projects, as
we have said, routinely run aground on a mixture of public suspicion, incompetent leadership and the hobbyist tendencies of activists, who have come to see politics as an outlet for subcultural
expression rather than a vehicle for the disciplined pursuit of
collective goals. Equally, as Jeremy Corbyn's allies discovered, such
problems do not disappear simply by virtue of leftists trying to
pursue their aims through mainstream parties. And the crucial
point is that the radical left must eventually pursue party organisation not out of self-interest, but out of respect for democracy –
even if that carries the real risk of failure.

Bertolt Brecht wrote of the suicidally ambitious tailor of Ulm,
who, having become convinced he had invented a flying machine,
climbs to the top of the church roof, spreads his false wings and
shouts to the bishop, 'Believe me, I can fly!' When the tailor inevitably falls to the ground in a crumpled heap, the bishop shakes his
head and tells the people, 'It was a wicked, foolish lie, Mankind
will never fly.' But Brecht's point was not pessimistic: eventually,
mankind would learn to fly.

The radical left suffered violent repression in the Miner's Strike, political desolation in the era of victorious globalisation, and, more recently, abject failure to win a democratic majority, despite public sympathy for left-wing policies and the undeniable failure of the capitalist system. Still, the system is broken, and without an organised response, the future is a wasteland of climate refugees, broken democracies and economic decline. For all the tut-tutting bishops, the radical left will eventually have to reassemble its broken wings and jump again, because the alternative is unimaginably bleak.

Notes

Introduction

1 Peter Mair, *Ruling the Void: The Hollowing of Western Democracy* (London: Verso, 2013).

2 Editorial, 'The Guardian View on Scotland and Brexit – Nicola Sturgeon Speaks for Britain', *Guardian*, 28 June 2016.

3 Libby Brooks, ' "A special day": How a Glasgow Community Halted Immigration Raid', *Guardian*, 14 May 2021.

4 For example, Jeremy Gilbert has commented on the *Politics Theory Other* podcast that the Scottish government represents 'not radical socialism, but at least a cosmopolitan social democracy [that] is so much the normative common sense'. He adds that the nation is 'a case study on our own doorstep of an entire political culture being shifted to the left' and that 'you can accuse your opponents of being anti-Scottish . . . because they're neoliberal'.

5 BBC, 'Health of Children in Scotland "Among Worst in Europe" ', 26 January 2017, at bbc.co.uk; Scottish Trades Union Congress, 'Broken Promises and Offshored Jobs: STUC Report on Employment in the Low-Carbon and Renewable Energy Economy', 2019 – pdf at stuc.org.uk.

6 Lamiat Sabin, 'Scotland Drug Deaths Still Worst in Europe as Number Rises to Record High', *Independent*, 30 July 2021.

7 Tom Nairn, 'Union on the Rocks', *New Left Review* II: 43 (January–February 2007).

8 Richard Marsh, 'Which Scottish Currency?' *Sceptical Scot* (blog), 18 October 2020, at sceptical.scot; Laurie Macfarlane, 'The SNP Must Rethink Its

Economic Model for an Independent Scotland', *openDemocracy*, 27 October 2020; Jim Cuthbert, 'Naively Neo-Liberal', *Scottish Left Review* 106 (July 2018).

9 James Connelly, 'Socialism and Nationalism', 1897, available at marxists.org.

10 Ulrich Beck, 'The Cosmopolitan Perspective: Sociology of the Second Age of Modernity', *British Journal of Sociology* 51 (21 August 2008), p. 85.

11 Within the broadly defined liberal, anti-Brexit cultural sphere, there are exceptions, such as the republican Anthony Barnett. See A. Barnett, *The Lure of Greatness* (London: Unbound Publishing, 2017).

1. 2016 and All That

1 John Kampfner, *Why the Germans Do It Better* (London: Atlantic, 2020), p. 10.

2 David Broder, *First They Took Rome: How the Populist Right Conquered Italy* (London: Verso, 2020), p. 1.

3 For example, Paris Gourtsoyannis, 'Scottish Independence Vote Should Have Sounded Alarm on Russia', *Scotsman*, 21 July 2020.

4 For example, Douglas Brinkley, 'Dean Acheson and the "Special Relationship": The West Point Speech of December 1962', *Historical Journal* 33, no. 3 (1990): 599–608.

5 Davie Kirkwood, *My Life of Revolt* (London: George G. Harrap, 1935), pp. 201–2.

6 Peter Mandelson, *The Third Man: Life at the Heart of New Labour* (London: Harper, 2010).

7 Tariq Ali, 'Starmer's War', *New Left Review: Sidecar*, 16 December 2020, at newleftreview.org.

8 For example, Perry Anderson, *The Indian Ideology* (London: Verso, 2012).

9 Ben Fine, 'Financialisation and Social Policy', in Peter Utting, Shahra Razavi and Rebecca Varghese Buchholz, eds, *Global Crisis and Transformative Social Change* (London: Palgrave Macmillan, 2012), pp. 103–22.

10 Steve Keen, 'The Ten Graphs which Show How Britain Became a Wholly Owned Subsidiary of the City of London (and What We Can Do about It)', *openDemocracy*, 24 April 2017, at neweconomics.opendemocracy.net.

11 Danny Dorling, 'Peak Inequality', *New Statesman*, 4 July 2018.

12 Ibid.

13 Luke Raikes, *The Devolution Parliament: Devolving Power to England's Regions, Towns and Cities*, IPPR, February 2020, p. 10.

14 *Financial Times*, 'Full Text: Gordon Brown's Speech to the CBI', 28 November 2005.

15 Iain Withers and Lawrence White, 'Britain's Labour Says It Would Halt RBS Privatisation', *Reuters*, 6 February 2019.

16 Ibid.

17 *Novara Media*, 8 May 2019.

18 Chris Giles, 'Why London Deserves a Thank-you Note from the Rest of Britain', *Financial Times*, 8 June 2017.

19 Doreen Massey, *Global City* (Cambridge: Polity, 2007).

20 Ben Wray, 'The City of London Extracts Wealth from the UK's Regions, Inquiry Submission Finds', *Source*, 19 August 2019.

21 Bhaskar Sunkara, 'The Exercise of Power', *Jacobin*, 25 February 2019, at jacobinmag.com.

22 See Philip Cunliffe, *Cosmopolitan Dystopia* (Manchester: Manchester University Press, 2020).

23 Kimiko de Freytas-Tamura, 'Tony Blair Says Iraq War Helped Give Rise to ISIS', *New York Times*, 25 October 2015.

24 Mark Curtis, *Secret Affairs: Britain's Collusion with Radical Islam*, updated edn (London: Serpent's Tail, 2018 [2010]), p. 2.

25 David Leigh and John Hooper, 'Britain's Dirty Secret', *Guardian*, 6 March 2003.

26 See Chapter 6, below.

27 See, for example, Christopher Bickerton, *European Integration: From Nation-States to Member States* (Oxford: OUP, 2012); Philip Cunliffe, *The New Twenty Years Crisis* (Montreal: McGill-Queen's University Press, 2020).

28 Susan Watkins, 'Britain's Decade of Crisis', *New Left Review* II/121 (January–February 2020).

29 See Neil Davidson, Patricia McCafferty and David Miller, eds, *Neoliberal Scotland* (Cambridge: Cambridge Scholars, 2010).

30 Ali, 'Starmer's War'.

31 SpectatorTV, 'Andrew Neil Clashes with Scottish Nationalist over Independence Claims', YouTube, 18 December 2020.

2: Nationalism, Internationalism and Independence

1 For example, the *Economist*, 'Britain: Back to Being the Sick Man of Europe?', 19 July 2017.

2 See, for example, Chantal Mouffe, *For a Left Populism* (London: Verso, 2018).

3 Sivamohan Valluvan, *The Clamour of Nationalism: Race and Nation in Twenty-First Century Britain* (Manchester: Manchester University Press, 2019).

4 See Chapter 3, below.

5 Karl Marx and Friedrich Engels, *The Communist Manifest* (London: Vintage, 2018), p. 39.

6 Solomon Bloom, *The World of Nations: A Study of the National Implications in the World of Marx* (New York: Columbia University Press, 1941). Sourced from Mike Davis, *Old Gods, New Enigmas: Marx's Lost Theory* (London: Verso, 2018), p. 167.

7 Leon Trotsky, 'On the National Question', May 1923, at marxists.org.

8 E. J. Hobsbawm, *Nations and Nationalism since 1780: Programme, Myth, Reality* (Cambridge: CUP, 1992 [1990]), p. 34.

9 Karl Marx, 'Letter from Marx to Engels in Manchester', London, 10 December 1869, at wikirouge.net

10 Karl Marx, 'The British Rule in India', *New York Herald Tribune*, 10 June 1853, at marxists.org.

11 Karl Marx, 'Karl Marx on India', *New International*, July 1842, at marxists.org.

12 Erica Benner, *Really Existing Nationalisms* (London: Verso, 1995), p. 52.

13 V. I. Lenin, 'The Right of Nations to Self-Determination, Chapter 1: What Is Meant by the Self-Determination of Nations?', 1914, at marxists.org.

14 J. E. Murkins, 'Preliminary Issues', in Jo Erik Murkens with Peter Jones and Michael Keating, *Scottish Independence: A Practical Guide* (Edinburgh: Edinburgh University Press, 2002), p. 12.

15 Ibid, p. 13.

16 Michael Keating, 'Independence in an Interdependent World', in Jo Erik Murkens et al., *Scottish Independence*.

17 *Scotsman*, 'Salmond: Scots Nationalism "Not Violent Due to No Oppression" ', 27 March 2017.

18 Miroslav Hroch, *European Nations: Explaining Their Formation* (London: Verso, 2015).

19 For a deeper exploration of the relationship between nationalism, national identity and the nation-state, see Neil Davidson, *Nation-States: Consciousness and Competition* (London: Haymarket, 2017).

20 BBC, 'Cameron Speaks Out on Patriotism', 27 January 2006, at bbc.co.uk.

21 James Meek, 'James Meek on Brexit and the Myth of St George', Verso blog, 5 March 2019, at versobooks.com; Fintan O'Toole, 'Unionism Traps Itself in a 1950s Sci-Fi B-Movie', *Irish Times*, 3 March 2018.

22 Jamie Grierson and Pamela Duncan, 'Britons Most Positive in Europe on the Benefits of Immigration', *Guardian*, 2 May 2019.

23 Steve Boggan, 'Election '97: Patriotic Blair Sets Out Global Vision', *Independent*, 22 April 1997.

24 For a deeper exploration of 'Anglobalisation', see James Foley and Pete Ramand, *Yes: The Radical Case for Scottish Independence* (London: Pluto, 2014), Chapter 1.

25 Linda Colley, *Britons: Forging the Nation 1707–1837* (New Haven, CT: Yale University Press, 2005).

26 For more on this, see Cédric Hugrée, Etienne Penissat and Alexis Spire, *Social Class in Europe: New Equalities in the Old World* (London: Verso, 2020).

27 Tom Nairn, *The Break-up of Britain: Crisis and Neo-Nationalism* (London: Verso, 2021 [1977]).

28 See Chapter 5, below.

29 BBC, 'Nicola Sturgeon Would Change SNP Name', 18 September 2017, bbc.co.uk.

30 Antonio Gramsci, *Selections from the Prison Notebooks of Antonio Gramsci*,

ed. Quintin Hoare and Geoffrey Nowell-Smith (London: Lawrence & Wishart, 1971), p. 176.

31 David Miller, 'Who Rules Scotland? Neoliberalism, the Scottish Ruling Class and Its Intellectuals', in Neil Davidson, Patricia McCafferty and David Miller, eds, *Neoliberal Scotland* (Cambridge: Cambridge Scholars, 2010).

3. The Emergence of a Movement for Scottish Independence, 2012–14

1   James Mitchell, 'The Referendum Campaign', in Aileen McHarg, Tom Mullen, Alan Page and Neil Walker, eds, *The Scottish Independence Referendum: Constitutional and Political Implications* (Oxford: OUP, 2016), p. 75.

2   David Torrance, *'We in Scotland': Thatcherism in a Cold Climate* (Edinburgh: Birlinn, 2009), pp. 190–1.

3   BBC, 'Rally Calls for Independence Vote', 30 June 2009, at bbc.co.uk.

4   David McCrone and Lindsay Paterson, 'The Conundrum of Scottish Independence', *Scottish Affairs* 40 (2002), pp. 56–7.

5   William Miller, 'The Death of Unionism?', in Thomas M. Devine, ed., *Scotland and the Union: 1707–2007* (Edinburgh: Edinburgh University Press, 2008), p. 179.

6   Scottish Centre for Social Research, 'SNP Victory Not Based on Increased Support for Independence', Press Release, 30 October 2007.

7   McCrone and Patterson, 'Conundrum of Scottish Independence', pp. 56–61.

8   Richard M. Worcester and Roger Mortimore, *Explaining Labour's Landslide: How Tony Blair Swept to Victory* (London, Politico, 1999), p. 178.

9   Ibid., p. 228.

10 McCrone and Patterson, 'Conundrum of Scottish Independence', pp. 69–70, 73–4.

11 Lesley Riddoch, 'Scottish People Would Have Voted for "Devo Max". That's Why It's Not an Option', *Guardian*, 15 October 2012.

12 Pauline Bryan and Tommy Kane, eds, *Class, Nation and Socialism: The Red Paper on Scotland 2014* (Glasgow: Glasgow Caledonian University Archives, 2013), p. 193.

13 See below, 'Project Fear and the Ruling Class Offensive' (this chapter).

14 Hugh Bochel, David Denver, James Mitchell and Charles Pattie, *Scotland Decides: The Devolution Issue and the Scottish Referendum* (London: Routledge, 2000), pp. 116–19.

15 Paul Hutcheon, 'The Growth of the Yes Movement', *Sunday Herald*, 21 September 2014.

16 Willie Sullivan, *The Missing Scotland: Why Over a Million Scots Choose Not to Vote and What It Means for Our Democracy* (Edinburgh: Luath, 2014), pp. 19–20.

17 This episode is one of the few collectively positive experiences recounted in Darren McGarvey's necessarily bleak memoir and polemic, *Poverty Safari: Understanding the Anger of Britain's Underclass* (Edinburgh: Luath, 2017), pp. 70–8, 221–2.

18 Suki Sangha and David Jamieson, 'The Radical Independence Campaign', *RS21* 2 (2014), p. 29.

19 Lesley Riddoch, 'Radical and Unexpected in Scots has Taken Place . . . People Power has Triumphed', *Sunday Herald*, 14 September 2014.

20 See, for example, Jonathan Freedland, 'If Britain Loses Scotland It Will Feel Like an Amputation', *Guardian*, 5 September 2014.

21 Mitchell, 'Referendum Campaign', pp. 90–1.

22 Colin Barker, 'Empowerment and Resistance: "Collective Effervescence" and Other Accounts', in Paul Bagguley and Jeff Hearn, eds, *Transforming Politics: Power and Resistance* (London: Palgrave Macmillan, 1999), pp. 25–6.

23 George Kerevan, 'Vote's Biggest Loser is Scottish Labour', *Scotsman*, 20 September 2014.

24 Peter Geoghegan, *The People's Referendum: Why Scotland Will Never Be the Same Again* (Edinburgh: Luath, 2015), p. 9.

25 Colin Kidd, 'Reflections on the Independence Referendum', *London Review of Books*, 11 September 2014, p. 14.

26 Tom Gordon, 'One Year On: Will Better Together Change Their Tactics?', *Sunday Herald*, 23 June 2013.

27 Scottish Labour Party, 'Ambition for Scotland', 2001, p. 11.

28 Seumas Milne, 'Salmond's Scotland Won't Be an Escape from Britain', *Guardian*, 11 September 2014.

29 Ben Jackson, 'The Break-Up of Britain: The Left and Scottish Nationalism', *Renewal* 22 (2014), pp. 20–1.

30 Comments made by George Galloway, ' "Just Say Naw . . .": An Evening with George Galloway', Respect Party, 2014.

31 John Robertson, 'Fairness in the First Year? BBC and ITV Coverage of the Scottish Independence Campaign from September 2012 to September 2013', Creative Futures, University of the West of Scotland, 2013.

32 Participant-observation by the authors.

33 Will Hutton, 'We Have 10 Days to Find a Settlement to Save the Union', *Observer*, 7 September 2014; Jason Cowley, 'A Shattered Union', *New Statesman*, 13 September 2014; Martin Kettle, 'Don't Let Alex Salmond Blind You to the Yes Campaign's Dark Side', *Guardian*, 17 September 2014; Philip Stephens, 'The World is Saying No to Scottish Separation', *Financial Times*, 11 September 2014; Polly Toynbee, 'Share Values Matter More than Where the Border Lies', *Guardian*, 19 August 2014. For a definitive refutation of the 'ethnic campaign' myth, see James Foley and Pete Ramand, *Yes: The Radical Case for Scottish Independence* (London: Pluto, 2014), pp. 38–40.

34 Tim Shipman and Jason Allardyce, 'Yes Leads in Scots Poll Shock', *Sunday*

Times, 7 September 2014; Sarah Neville and Clive Cookson, 'Ruling Elite Aghast as Union Wobbles', *Financial Times*, 12 September 2014.

35 Severin Carrell, 'Scottish Independence: TNS Poll Finds Single Point Separates Yes and No', *Guardian*, 8 September 2014.

36 Kiran Stacey, George Parker, Mure Dickie and Beth Rigby, 'Scottish Referendum: How Complacency Nearly Lost a United Kingdom', *Financial Times*, 19 September 2014.

37 Judith Duffy, 'An Explosive Breach of the Rules: Salmond Blasts Treasury as Its BBC Email Is Exposed', *Sunday Herald*, 14 September 2014.

38 Joe Pike, *Project Fear: How an Unlikely Alliance Left a Kingdom United but a Country Divided* (London: Biteback, 2015), pp. 138–9.

39 Fred Dews, 'Lord George Robertson: "Forces of Darkness Would Love Scottish Split from United Kingdom"', *Brookings Institute*, 7 April 2014.

40 Peter Hennessy, *The Kingdom to Come: Thoughts on the Union Before and After the Scottish Referendum* (London: Haus, 2015), p. 97.

41 See, for example, Simon Johnson, 'Britain's Enemies Will "Exploit Scottish Independence to Cut UK Power"', *Telegraph*, 17 October 2012.

42 Philip Stephens, 'The World is Saying No to Scottish Separation', *Financial Times*, 12 September 2014.

43 'UK RIP?', *Economist*, 13 September 2014.

44 'Rise of the Ayes', *Economist*, 13 September 2014, p. 30.

45 Magnus Gardham, 'Brown's Plea: Vote No for the Sake of Our Children', *Herald*, 18 September 2014; Nicholas Watt, 'A Scottish Plea and Scottish Play as Brown Takes to Stage', *Guardian*, 18 September 2014.

46 George Monbiot, 'A Yes Vote in Scotland Would Unleash the Most Dangerous Thing of All – Hope', *Guardian*, 9 September 2014.

47 Allan Massie, 'In Truth, the SNP Were Lamentable', *Scotsman*, 20 September 2014; Andrew Whitaker, 'Labour's Big Beasts "Hauled No Camp Back from Brink"'.

48 Comparable figures for Yes voters were: disaffection with Westminster politics (74 per cent), the NHS (54 per cent), tax and public spending (33 per cent) and oil (20 per cent).

49 Sam Wetherell, 'Exit Stage Right: The Case Against Scottish Independence', *Jacobin*, 15 September 2014, at jacobinmag.com.

50 Eric J. Hobsbawm in conversation with Antonio Polito, *The New Century* (London: Abacus, 2000), p. 115. For a detailed discussion of 'majority disengagement', see Peter Mair, *Ruling the Void: The Hollowing of Western Democracy* (London: Verso, 2013), pp. 17–44.

51 Mitchell, 'Referendum Campaign', p. 90.

52 Michael Ashcroft, 'How Scotland Voted, and Why', Lord Ashcroft Polls, 19 September 2014, at lordashcroftpolls.com; YouGov, 'Yougov Survey Results', 18 September 2014.

53 Jessica Elgot, 'Why Are So Many Scots from Ethnic Minorities Voting Yes?', *Huffington Post*, 14 June 2014.

54 John Mellon, 'Class Divisions and the Scottish Referendum', *British Election Study*, 17 June 2014.

55 Andrew Gilligan, 'Small Firms Making Big Claims for Scottish Independence', *Telegraph*, 31 August 2014.

56 It is also worth noting that Labour-supporting commentators fawned over leading capitalists – particularly Wood, who criticised the Yes campaign. See, for a particularly egregious example of this type of grovelling, Catherine McLeod, 'There Is Only One Real Team Scotland', *Herald*, 10 September, 2014.

57 Geoghegan, *People's Referendum*, pp. 158–9.

58 Ben Wray, 'Want Less Tories in Scotland? Build Social Housing', *Source*, 9 September 2017.

59 Personal communication, RM to Davidson, 9 October 2014.

60 Mark Diffley and Christopher McLean, '35 Years of Scottish Attitudes towards Independence', *Times*, 15 March 2012.

61 Robert Worcester and Mark Diffley, 'Why It Is Hard to See Much Hope for Salmond and His Political Dream', *The Times*, 9 May 2013.

62 Colin Kidd, 'After the Referendum', *London Review of Books* 36, 19 (9 October 2014): 20.

63 Mick Brown, 'After Scotland Votes No, the Kingdom Is Still United, but Uneasily So', *Sunday Telegraph*, 20 September 2014.

64 Kevin McKenna, 'How Can You Console a Heartbroken and Angry Daughter? You Can't', *Observer*, 21 September 2014.

4. The Collapse of Scotland's Red Wall

1 Robert Waller and Bryon Criddle, *The Almanac of British Politics*, 7th edn (London: Routledge, 2002), p. 350.

2 Brown, *My Life, Our Times* (London: Random House, 2017).

3 Chris Bickerton, 'Labour's Lost Working-Class Voters Have Gone for Good', *Guardian*, 19 December 2019.

4 Jon Stone, 'Mhairi Black Speech: SNP MP Puts Finger on Problem with Labour Party', *Independent*, 14 July 2015.

5 Gerry Hassan and Eric Shaw, *The Strange Death of Labour Scotland* (Edinburgh: Edinburgh University Press, 2012), p. 3.

6 Christopher Harvie, *Floating Commonwealth* (Oxford: OUP, 2008), p. 148.

7 Alastair McIntosh Gray, *A History of Scotland: Modern Times* (Oxford: OUP, 1989), p. 71.

8 Alan Murie, 'Scottish Housing: The Context', in D., Sim, ed., *Housing and Public Policy in Post-Devolution Scotland* (Coventry: Chartered Institute of Housing, 2004), p. 24.

9 Douglas Robertson and Regina Serpa, 'Social Housing in Scotland', in

Kathleen Scanlon, Christine Whitehead and Melissa Fernández Arrigoitia, eds, *Social Housing in Europe* (Oxford: Wiley-Blackwell, 2014), p. 43.

10 Scottish Government, *Housing Statistics for Scotland 2018*, Scottish Government, 25 September 2018, p. 8.

11 Hassan and Shaw, *Strange Death of Labour Scotland*, p. 3.

12 Ibid., p. 407.

13 Richard J. Finlay, 'Patriotism, Paternalism and Pragmatism: Scottish Toryism, Union and Empire, 1912–65', in David Torrance, ed., *Whatever Happened to Tory Scotland?* (Edinburgh: Edinburgh University Press, 2012).

14 David McCrone, *The New Sociology of Scotland* (London: Sage, 2017), p. 153–4.

15 David Torrance, *'We in Scotland': Thatcherism in a Cold Climate* (Edinburgh: Birlinn, 2009).

16 See, for example, Corey Robin, *The Reactionary Mind: Conservatism from Edmund Burke to Sarah Palin* (Oxford: OUP, 2011).

17 Scottish Executive, *The Way Forward: Framework for Economic Development in Scotland*, June 2000, p. 7.

18 Gordon Brown and Douglas Alexander, *New Scotland, New Britain* (London: Smith Institute, 1999), p. 11.

19 Iain Dale, 'From the Archives: In Conversation with Alex Salmond', originally published on *Total Politics*, July 2008, access at iaindale.com.

20 Brown and Alexander, *New Scotland, New Britain*, p. 7.

21 Wendy Alexander, *Chasing the Tartan Tiger: Lessons from a Celtic Cousin?* (London: Smith Institute, 2003), p. 6.

22 Fintan O'Toole, *Ship of Fools: How Stupidity and Corruption Sank the Celtic Tiger* (London: Faber & Faber, 2009), p. 10.

23 *Scotsman*, 'Guess Who Jack Has Had Round for Dinner?', 3 February 2005.

24 Scottish Executive, *Scottish Economic Report*, 2006, p. 18.

25 Ian Fraser, 'Salmond's Silence on Banking Is "Elephant in Room" for Scottish Independence' (blog), 17 June 2011, at ianfraser.org.

26 Alison O'Connor, *A Guide to Gross Value Added (GVA) in Scotland*, Scottish Parliament, 2016, p. 24.

27 Darren McGarvey, *Poverty Safari: Understanding the Anger of Britain's Underclass* (Edinburgh: Luath, 2017).

28 Deborah Mattinson, *Talking to a Brick Wall: How New Labour Stopped Listening to the Voters and Why We Need a New Politics* (London: Biteback, 2010).

29 Robin Cook, *The Point of Departure* (London: Simon & Schuster, 2003), p. 353.

5. The Fault Line of SNP Hegemony

1 Dani Garavelli, 'Inside the Alex Salmond Trial', *Scotsman*, 23 March 2020.

2 Tom Gordon, 'New Poll Puts SNP on Course for Record Holyrood Win Despite Salmond Fall-Out', *Herald*, 29 March 2020.

3 David Edgerton, *The Rise and Fall of the British Nation* (London: Allen Lane, 2018).

4 Stephen Maxwell, 'The '79 Group Papers: The Case for Left-Wing Nationalism', in *The Case for Left-Wing Nationalism* (Edinburgh: Luath, 2013).

5 Tom Nairn, *The Break-up of Britain: Crisis and Neo-Nationalism* (London: Verso, 2021 [1977]), p. 117.

6 Gordon Brown, 'Introduction', in *The Red Paper on Scotland*, EUPSB, 1975, p. 8.

7 Jimmy Reid. 'Alienation: Rectorial Address', University of Glasgow, 28 April 1972, pdf at gla.ac.uk.

8 Ibid. p. 13.

9 John McGrath, *The Cheviot, the Stag and the Black, Black Oil* (London: Bloomsbury, 2015 (1974)), p. 162.

10 Quoted in David Torrance, *Salmond: Against the Odds* (Edinburgh: Birlinn, 2012).

11 Ibid.

12 Stephen Boyd, George Kerevan and Katherine Trebeck, *Tackling Timorous Economics: How Scotland's Economy Could Work Better for Us All* (Edinburgh: Luath, 2017).

13 Gerry Hassan, 'Alex Salmond, Rupert Murdoch, and the Pitfalls of Crony Capitalism' (blog), 26 April 2012, at gerryhassan.com.

14 For more on devo max, see Chapter 3, above.

15 Ian Jack, 'The Triumph of Nicola Sturgeon', *Guardian*, 23 April 2015.

16 Chris Bickerton and Carlo Invernizzi Accetti, *Technopopulism: The New Logic of Democratic Politics* (Oxford: OUP, 2021).

17 David Torrance, *Nicola Sturgeon* (Edinburgh: Birlinn, 2014).

18 Ibid.

19 See Chapter 3, above.

20 See Chapter 2, above.

21 James Foley, 'Against "Salmond Derangement Syndrome"', Conter (blog), 4 April 2021, at conter.scot.

22 BBC, 'Poll "Backs" Section 28', 31 May 2000, at news.bbc.co.uk.

23 Andrew Learmonth, 'SNP MP Alyn Smith "Scapegoating People with Disabilities" in NEC Row', *National*, 14 August 2020.

24 Iain MacWhirter, 'Divisions Set to Go Nuclear if SNP Ditches Unilateral Stance', *Herald*, 25 November 2020.

25 Stewart McDonald, 'Why I'm Backing the SNP's New Pro-Israel, Pro-Palestine Group', STV, 12 October 2016, at archive.news.stv.tv.

26 Michael Keating and Paul Cairney, 'Scotland Has Its Own Political Class – Just like Westminster', *Herald*, 20 January 2020.

27 Chris Green, 'Satisfaction with Scotland's Public Services Sinks to Record Low', iNews, 4 November 2018.

28 David McCrone, 'Are Scots European?', Centre on Constitutional Change (blog), 21 June 2016, at centreonconstitutionalchange.ac.uk.

29 Ibid.

30 Neil Davidson, Minna Liinpaa, Maureen McBride and Satnam Virdee, *No Problem Here* (Edinburgh: Luath, 2018).

6. Progressive Neoliberalism Confronts the Pandemic

1 Ferdinand Mount, 'Superman Falls to Earth', *London Review of Books*, 2 June 2020.

2 Mure Dickie and John Burn-Murdoch, 'Scotland's Coronavirus Record Flattered by Contrasts with South', *Financial Times*, 2 June 2020.

3 Neil Kempe, 'A Predictable Crisis', *Common Weal*, 20 May 2020, p. 5.

4 Allyson Pollock and Colin Leys, *NHS PLC: The Privatisation of Our Healthcare* (London: Verso, 2004), p. 169.

5 Competition and Markets Authority, 'Care Home Market Study: Final Report', UK Government, 30 November 2017.

6 Gill Plimmer, 'Private Equity and Britain's Care Home Crisis', *Financial Times*, 8 February 2020.

7 Vivek Kotecha, *Plugging the Leaks in the Care Home Industry*, Centre for Health and the Public Interest, 7 November 2019, at chpi.org.uk.

8 International Long-Term Care Policy Network, 'Mortality Associated with COVID-19 in Care Homes: International Evidence', 14 October 2020, p. 23, pdf at ltccovid.org.

9 GMB, 'GMB Scotland Open Letter to First Minister Nicola Sturgeon', 8 April 2020, at gmbscotland.org.uk.

10 Darren McGarvey, 'Hate Crime Bill Will Not Help the Poor, Homeless or the Addicted', *Daily Record*, 30 October 2020.

11 Rebecca McQuillan, 'Coronavirus: Black Health and Social Care Staff "More Fearful" of Infection', *Herald*, 30 June 2020.

12 For a vivid account of this dispute, see Chris Bambery, *A People's History of Scotland* (London: Verso, 2018).

13 Conor Darcy and Torsten Bell, *The £1 Trillion Pie: How Wealth Is Shared across Scotland*, Resolution Foundation, June 2018, at resolutionfoundation.org.

14 Chris Green, 'Nicola Sturgeon Hits the Road as Poll Suggests Scots Are Losing Faith in SNP's Handling of Public Services', iNews, 5 December 2019.

15 Neil Mackay, 'The Big Read: SNP Target 2026 in "Roadmap for Independence" from Party's Top Strategist Andrew Wilson', *Herald*, 18 October 2020.

16 Andrew Wilson, 'Recovering Towards Enlightenment', Charlotte Street Partners (blog), 31 March 2020, at charlottestpartners.co.uk.

17 Sean Bell, '"Fred Goodwin Absolutely Loved It": Ian Fraser on How an Andrew Wilson RBS "Factsheet" Shows Why He Was the Wrong Person to Write the Growth Commission"', *Source*, 16 May 2019.

18 Benoit Van Overstraeten, 'Stop! French Philosopher Latour Urges No Return to Pre-Lockdown Normal', *Reuters*, 8 May 2020.

Conclusion

1 Daniel Bensaïd, 'Leaps, Leaps, Leaps: Lenin and Politics', July 2002, at daniel-bensaid.org.

2 Hal Draper, *Two Souls of Socialism* (1986), at marxists.org.

3 Andreas Malm, *How to Blow Up a Pipeline* (London: Verso, 2021).

4 Tom Gordon, 'Key Sturgeon Advisor Urges "Softest Possible Form of Independence"', *Herald*, 14 February 2019.

5 BBC, 'Labour Candidate Lisa Nandy Criticised for Catalonia Remarks', 16 January 2020.

6 Ben Wray, 'The Scotland Papers', Bella Caledonia (blog), 22 November 2019, at bellacaledonia.org.uk.

7 Dan Hind, *The Magic Kingdom: Property, Monarchy and the Maximum Republic* (London: Zero, 2014), p. 16.

8 Ibid., p. 86.

9 Ibid., p. 90.

10 Abbé Sieyès, *What Is the Third Estate?* (Praeger: 1789 [1964]).

11 Dominick Caddie and Alfie Stirling, 'Half of UK Families Are £110 Worse Off a Year Since 2019 General Election', New Economics Foundation (blog), December 2021, at neweconomics.org.

12 Laurie Macfarlane, 'Shooting for the Moon: Why We Need a New Mission for a Zero-Carbon Future', *openDemocracy*, 1 August 2017, at neweconomics.opendemocracy.net.

13 Cinzia Arruzza, Tithi Bhattacharya and Nancy Fraser, *Feminism for the 99%: A Manifesto* (London: Verso, 2019).

14 Matthew Smith, 'Labour Economic Policies Are Popular, So Why Aren't Labour?', YouGov, 12 November 2019, at yougov.co.uk.

15 British Social Attitudes Survey, 'Social Inequality in England and Scotland', October 2020, pdf at bsa.natcen.ac.uk.

16 New Economics Foundation, 'Framing the Economy: How to Win the Case for a Better System . . ', 2018, pdf at neweconomics.org.

17 Far from finger-pointing, this is intended as a partial self-criticism. All three authors were at least partially involved in setting up the RISE project.

18 David Broder, 'A Party Fighting for Socialism Has to Put Workers Front and Center: Interview with Raoul Hedebouw', *Jacobin*, 12 December 2021, at jacobinmag.com; Mímir Kristjánsson, 'A New Working-Class Party Is on the Rise in Norway', *Jacobin*, 27 September 2021, at jacobinmag.com; Ben Wray, 'Scotland's Communities: Divided by Money', *Source*, 16 September 2020, at sourcenews.scot.